JAY D. ADKISSON

The Charging Orders Practice Guide

Understanding Judgment Creditor Rights Against LLC Members

AMERICAN BAR ASSOCIATION
Business Law Section

LLCS, PARTNERSHIPS AND UNINCORPORATED ENTITIES COMMITTEE

Cover design by Catherine Zaccarine/ABA Publishing.

Page layout by Quadrum Solutions.

Printed in the United States of America.

22 21 20 19 18   5 4 3 2 1

ISBN: 978-1-64105-264-1

Discounts are available for books ordered in bulk. Special consideration is given to state bars, CLE programs, and other bar related organizations. Inquire at Book Publishing, ABA Publishing, American Bar Association, 321 N. Clark Street, Chicago, Illinois 60654-7598.

www.ShopABA.org

Table of Contents

Introduction

If one looks at the totality of statutory partnership and LLC law as a radar screen, the charging order is barely a blip, mentioned with any gravity only in section 504 of the Uniform Partnership Act, section 703 of the Uniform Limited Partnership Act, and section 503 of the Uniform Limited Liability Company Act (collectively as the "Uniform Acts"). Even those sections do little more than describe the ultimate effect of a charging order, without illuminating the slightest on seemingly basic issues such as how an order might be obtained or what it should look like.

Every day, hundreds of thousands of partnerships and LLCs conduct business without the slightest regard to charging orders. The managers and owners of these entities are much more concerned with issues of immediate importance, such as distributions, fiduciary duties, associating and disassociating members, tax issues, and the like, all in addition to actually operating the business. Day to day, the very concept of a charging order for those involved with such businesses seem about as relevant as the current temperature on the dark side of the moon.

Nonetheless, when business planners discuss choice of entity with their clients, the charging order seems to invariably become an important piece of the conversation, if not to dominate it entirely. The reason for this is that the charging order, or, more accurately, the *exclusivity* of a creditor's remedy to a charging order, offers the prospect for some degree of asset protection for the value of the owner's investment therein. This sort of protection is not found for other forms of investments, whether stock investments into a corporation or buying a bond—those things are immediately and easily available to creditors of the owner.

Thus, the charging order has become extremely useful in the marketing of partnerships and LLCs. Some states have modified their own charging order laws in an attempt to make those laws even more creditor-unfriendly than the Uniform Acts, and entity formation promoters in those states will often discuss charging order first, and everything else as if almost an afterthought. All of this creates a situation where the charging order has an outsized prominence in the discussion of partnership and LLC law relative to the many other issues of arguably much greater importance; I liken it to somebody going to the Super Bowl and focusing on the quality of the hot dogs.

The problem is, as mentioned, the Uniform Acts tell us about the effects of a charging order but little else. When creditor-debtor litigation arises that involves charging orders, the litigants and the courts must fill in the rest of the procedure *ad hoc* based on such legal precedent as may exist in a given jurisdiction. Only

California has adopted anything like a procedural statute to give guidance to that which is substantively mandated by the Uniform Acts, and even California's guidance is little more than a few dozen (though extremely helpful) words. It is as if the Uniform Acts painted a small red dot in the middle of a large canvass, and litigants and judges have start with that dot and paint something akin to da Vinci's *The Last Supper*; that the final product often ends up looking like some tortured combination of a Rothko and a Pollock should be of little surprise.

Even in California, the state which has more statutory and opinion law guidance than any other, the remedy of a charging order is little known and less understood. As late as 2010, I appeared at oral argument on a motion for charging order in a substantial case, *Bay Guardian Company vs. New Times LLC*, the latter being the then-owner of the $200 million Village Voice chain of newspapers. The judgment of my client (Bay Guardian) at that time exceeded $20 million, and the parties had filed extensive briefs prior to the hearing. Nonetheless, the hearing began with the judge's words uttered in the utmost seriousness: "*Mr. Adkisson, what is a charging order?*"

Ultimately, the court granted the charging order, but to add context, this took place in the Remedies Department of the San Francisco Superior Court, being a court that routinely hears judgment enforcement matters, i.e., if any court should know something about charging orders, this would be the one. But this very competent and respected judge, who had been on the bench for many years, had simply never come across a charging order before. His response was anything but atypical; rare is the bench officer to whom I have not had to explain the rudiments of what a charging order is and what it does.

That there is *de minimis* statutory guidance on charging orders has similarly lead to a recent avalanche of appellate litigation and opinions about charging orders, meaning that at least one party in the case believed that the trial court got the issue egregiously wrong. Here also, charging order litigation has consumed a quantity of judicial resources grossly disproportional to the charging order's relative importance to other partnership and LLC issues, although mitigated somewhat by the fact that many ordinary partnership and LLC disputes are between members and thus likely to end up in unreported arbitration proceedings, whereas charging order disputes are solely about the use of a judicial remedy and thus all of them end before somebody in a black robe.

The absence of any meaningful statutory guidance about charging orders, and the struggles of the courts to fill in the gaps as best they can, provided the impetus for this book. Whether it gets close to that mark is a question that only readers will be able to answer.

This project is the result of the very substantial assistance given by more than 65 persons, nearly all of whom are members of the LLCs, Partnerships and Unincorporated Entities Committee (LPUE) of the Business Law Section of the American Bar Association, who volunteered their valuable professional time to assist with every aspect. It would thus be an error to say that this is "my" book, but rather it was intended to be, and is, the end result of literally years of labor by the LPUE Committee members and a few others regarding the topic of charging orders generally, as embodied in numerous programs and articles on the subject, and more specifically those persons' direct assistance with this work.

Special thanks go to Professors Carter Bishop and Dan Kleinberger for their initial conceptualizing about this project, and more specifically to Carter Bishop for literally years of intense discussions about the bankruptcy issues and to Dan Kleinberger for similar discussions on just about everything.

The informal Executive Committee for this project consisted of Louis Conti, Allan Donn, Harry Haynsworth, Lisa Jacobs, Garth Jacobsen, Robert Keatinge, Steven Leitess, Scott Ludwig, Johnny Lyle and Tom Rutledge, all of who put in very substantial work in editing, commenting, and assisting with administrative issues. Tom Rutledge here must be additionally applauded for his efforts in moving this project through the ABA publication process, and for drafting the difficult chapter on tax issues.

Many more folks substantially contributed to this project and offered their assistance, including Andy Anderson, Samuel Beavers, Matthew Berlin, James Borchers, Brad Borden, Joseph Boucher, David Campbell, Sherri Marie Carr, Kenneth Clingen, Jim D'Esposito, Ike Devji, Diana Espanola, Tyler Ferguson, George Flint, III, Henry Geha, Robert Guinness, Brent Herrin, Maurice Holloway, Kristie Iatrou, David Johnson, Michael Johnson, Frank Johnstone, Carl Kanowski, Ken Kettering, David Lacki, Kyung Lee, Mark Liepold, John Meyer, Kenneth Michaels Jr., Suzanne Odom, Tom Orrick, Chris Pitet, Tom Rafferty, Chris Riser, Alberto Rodriguez, Ryan Scarcella, Dale Schedler, Mark Sharpe, Craig Shepard, Dave Slenn, Edwin Smith, Allen Sparkman, Jonathan Stemerman, Matt Stewart, Josep Suchyta, Gregory Taggart, T. Rankin Terry, Sean Trice, Michael Ushkow, Jeff Verdon, Marc Ward, Spencer Weisbroth, Tim Werner, Jim Wheaton, and John Williams. If I have left somebody out, such was not my intent and I deeply apologize.

The credit for this work that I absolutely refuse to share with others are for any errors and omissions found herein, which are mine and mine alone.

Jay D. Adkisson
Las Vegas, Nevada, 2018

About the Author

Jay D. Adkisson was graduated from the University of Oklahoma (B.A. 1986, J.D. 1988, with honors), where he was a member of the Oklahoma Law Review. He practices in the area of creditor-debtor law and captive insurance in the southwestern United States and has his offices in Las Vegas and Newport Beach, being admitted to practice law in Arizona, California, Nevada, Oklahoma, and Texas. Jay's participation in the American Bar Association includes Chair of the Committee on Captive Insurance, Business Law Section, 2011–2014; Chair of the Insurance and Financial Services Committee, Real Property Trusts & Estates Section, 2015–2016; and ABA Section Advisor to the following drafting committees of the Uniform Laws Commission: Uniform Voidable Transactions Act of 2014; Uniform Protected Series Act of 2017; Uniform Anti-SLAPP Act (in drafting); and Uniform Registration of Canadian Money Judgments Act (in drafting). His books include *Asset Protection: Concepts & Strategies*, with co-author Chris Riser (McGraw-Hill, 2004), and *Adkisson's Captive Insurance Companies* (iUniverse, 2007), and he writes the "Wealth Conservation" column for Forbes.com. Jay has also twice been an expert witness to the U.S. Senate Finance Committee.

CHAPTER 1

Introduction

A charging order is a statutory remedy that allows a creditor to place a lien on the economic rights to distributions of a member of a limited liability company, or of a partner of a general or limited partnership, so that those distributions are diverted from the debtor, where they would normally have gone, and instead cause them to be paid to a judgment creditor.

Charging orders do not exist at common law; rather, they are authorized by state laws concerning partnerships and LLCs, almost all of which derive from versions of the Uniform Partnership Act (UPA), the Uniform Limited Partnership Act (ULPA), and the Uniform Limited Liability Company Act (ULLCA). Each of these uniform acts was created by the Uniform Law Commission (ULC), which is a body comprised of typically governor-appointed state commissioners who lobby for their enactment. Together, the UPA, ULPA, and ULLCA are known as the "Harmonized Acts" because the ULC revised them concurrently in 2013, making the language used for their key aspects nearly alike. States generally have respected the harmonization process and its uniformity goal. Some states, however, have substantially tinkered with both the language and substantive effect of the Harmonized Acts as they relate to charging orders. For example, some states have eliminated the ability of a creditor to foreclose on a charging order, which creates both benefits and problems in those states.

Here, our analysis will address charging orders under the legal framework of the Harmonized Acts, which may have been modified or changed by particular states. Practitioners should cautiously scrutinize applicable law, which may vary. For instance, only California has coordinated its post-judgment procedure with the Harmonized Acts. In all other states, courts have enacted their own ad hoc procedures to implement the charging order provisions of the Harmonized Acts. As a result, nothing here should be taken as legal advice or opinion or be presumed to apply as law in any given state.

The charging order is an anachronism in law, dating back to the English Partnership Act of 1890, which has been unfittingly imported into American remedy law since 1914.[1] At their root, English and American remedy law

1. *See* UPA § 28 (1914).

fundamentally diverge; whereas English remedy law requires a "charging order" to tie up the debtor's property, American remedy law normally allows a creditor to place a lien on that property. Therefore, the charging order of the English Partnership Act is problematic within the framework of American remedy law. The resulting challenges have been compounded as the charging order provision of the English Partnership Act was transcribed into the original Uniform Partnership Act of 1914 and copied into subsequent revisions of that act, as well as the ULPA and ULLCA.

In concept, creditors should simply be able to provide a copy of their judgment to the entity or file a copy of the judgment with the appropriate secretary of state, automatically creating a lien on the debtor's interest. Unfortunately, the Harmonized Acts do not produce this result. Instead, the law of charging orders has taken on a life of its own, mostly spurred as a misuse for asset protection purposes, and so persists as an anomaly, a "peculiar mechanism,"[2] or an oddity of American law.[3]

2. 91st St. Joint Venture v. Goldstein, 114 Md. App. 561, 582, 691 A.2d 272, 283 (1997).

3. Jay David Adkisson, Charging Orders: The Peculiar Mechanism (Dec. 1, 2016), *available at* https://ssrn.com/abstract=2928487.

CHAPTER 2

History of the "Peculiar Mechanism"[1]

The charging order appears rarely in opinions predating World War I to address odd situations in garnishment law, but now is almost exclusively found in the law of partnerships and, more recently, limited liability companies (LLCs). In those realms, the charging order has taken on a life of its own, with some states racing each other to have the "best" charging order provisions to foster entity formation and registered agents' business within those states. Creditors, although describing the "race" in less-than-flattering terms, have been developing their own strategies for defeating or circumventing the much-ballyhooed "exclusivity" of the charging order remedy. To understand why this unique remedy even exists, and why it has graced or cursed the area of partnership and LLC law, we must retrace the history of Anglo-American law to where a fork in the road developed in how each country would handle security interests that were created by creditor claims.

The lien was not a part of the English common law; instead, it was first suggested in 1791 to be a "mechanic's lien" by Thomas Jefferson as a means to further the construction of the District of Columbia. After adoption by the Maryland legislature that same year, the concept quickly spread to other states.[2] The concept was not a particularly new one; the Romans had developed the concept of the *obligare rem*, by which a creditor took an interest in a *pignus* (the object of a security interest) to secure a debt.[3] The Roman security interest had survived into the civil law of the continental European states, of which the Francophile attorney Jefferson was likely aware.

1. *See Goldstein*, 691 A.2d at 283 (contrasting "standard execution procedures rather than the peculiar mechanism of the charging order which is subject both to the broad discretion of the trial court and to redemption by the debtor").

2. *See generally* Chas E. Davidson, The Mechanics Lien Law of Illinois: A Lawyer's Brief Upon the Topic 6 (1922).

3. *See, e.g.*, Rudolph Sohm, The Institutes: A Textbook of the History and System of Roman Private Law 300 (Trans. James Crawford Lidlie) (3d ed. 1970).

Now we have materialman's liens, tax liens, mortgage liens, attorney's liens, mineral liens, maritime liens, warehouser's liens, HOA liens, municipal liens, U.C.C. liens, judgment liens (of which the charging order lien is but one), and the list goes on and on. Thanks to our third president, America has become the land of the free, the brave, and the lien.

While America went the way of the lien, the United Kingdom adopted the notion of the charging order to the same effect. That a debtor's interest in shares of stock could be "charged" was formalized in the first two acts of Queen Victoria.

Judgments Act of 1838

> XIV. Stock and shares in public funds and public companies belonging to the debtor, and standing in his own name, to be charged by order of a judge.
>
> And be it enacted, that if any person against whom any judgment shall have been entered up in any of her Majesty's Superior Courts at Westminster shall have any government stock, funds, or annuities, or any stock or shares of or in any public Company in England (whether incorporated or not), standing in his name in his own right, or in the name of any person in trust for him, it shall be lawful for a judge of one of the Superior Courts, on the application of any judgment creditor, to order that such stock, funds, annuities, or shares, or such of them or such part thereof respectively as he shall think fit, shall stand charged with the payment of the amount for which judgment shall have been so recovered, and interest thereon, and such order shall entitle the judgment creditor to all such remedies as he would have been entitled to if such charge had been made in his favour by the judgment debtor; provided that no proceedings shall be taken to have the benefit of such charge until after the expiration of six calendar months from the date of such order.[4]

Thus, under U.K. law, the method for a judgment creditor to create and maintain a legal interest on the debtor's property was through the vehicle of the charging order. When the United Kingdom codified its partnership law in 1890, the charging order was thus the natural and accepted method of achieving that end.

4. Judgments Act, 1838, 1 & 2 Vict., c. 110, § 23 (Eng.).

Partnership Act of 1890 c. 39 (Regnal. 53 & 54 Victoria)

> 23. Procedure against partnership property for a partner's separate judgment debt.
>
> (1) After the commencement of this Act a writ of execution shall not issue against any partnership property except on a judgment against the firm.
>
> (2) The High Court, or a judge thereof, or the Chancery Court of the county palatine of Lancaster, or a county court, may, on the application by summons of any judgment creditor of a partner, make an order charging that partner's interest in the partnership property and profits with payment of the amount of the judgment debt and interest thereon, and may by the same or a subsequent order appoint a receiver of that partner's share of profits (whether already declared or accruing), and of any other money which may be coming to him in respect of the partnership, and direct all accounts and inquiries, and give all other orders and directions which might have been directed or given if the charge had been made in favour of the judgment creditor by the partner, or which the circumstances of the case may require.
>
> (3) The other partner or partners shall be at liberty at any time to redeem the interest charged, or in case of a sale being directed, to purchase the same.
>
> (4) This section shall apply in the case of a cost-book company as if the company were a partnership within the meaning of this Act.
>
> (5) This section shall not apply to Scotland.[5]

It would be incorrect to pretend that America had totally ignored the concept of the charging order. *Cross v. Brown*[6] and *Hunter v. Strider's*[7] are a pair of opinions in which charging orders were used to enforce writs of garnishment. By and large, however, the procedure was an oddity that was employed in unusual circumstances where no clear remedy existed, and in such a rare case, to borrow

5. Partnership Act, 1890, 53 & 54 Vict., c. 39, § 23 (Eng.). For those curious as to why Scotland was excluded, we find further up in the Partnership Act of 1890 at § 4 that:

> (2) In Scotland, a firm is a legal person distinct from the partners of whom it is composed, but an individual partner may be charged on a decree or diligence directed against the firm, and on payment of the debts is entitled to relief pro ratâ from the firm and its other members.

6. 33 A. 147 (R.I. 1895).
7. 23 S.E. 567 (W. Va. 1895).

the concept of the charging order from the east side of the Atlantic seemed as good an idea as any other.

The point is that the charging order was not wholly alien to American law when it came time for the United States to codify its own partnership laws.[8] The ULC, which at that time had a slavish adoration for the Law Commission in England that bordered on the embarrassing, borrowed heavily from the Partnership Act of 1890, including the concept of the charging order, even though the rest of American law had largely chosen and had already been following, for just short of a century, the different path of the lien beginning in 1791.[9]

Ultimately, we adopted the English charging order to accomplish what should have been done directly and simply through an American lien. The unexplained rumblings heard by the drafters of the Uniform Partnership Act (UPA) of 1914 was Jefferson rolling in his grave.

Uniform Partnership Act of 1914

> § 28. Partner's Interest Subject to Charging Order.
>
> (1) On due application to a competent court by any judgment creditor of a partner, the court which entered the judgment, order, or decree, or any other court, may charge the interest of the debtor partner with payment of the unsatisfied amount of such judgment debt with interest thereon; and may then or later appoint a receiver of his share of the profits, and of any other money due or to fall due to him in respect of the partnership, and make all other orders, directions, accounts and inquiries which the debtor partner might have made, or which the circumstances of the case may require.
>
> (2) The interest charged may be redeemed at any time before foreclosure, or in case of a sale being directed by the court may be purchased without thereby causing a dissolution:
>
> > (a) With separate property, by any one or more of the partners, or
> >
> > (b) With partnership property, by any one or more of the partners with the consent of all the partners whose interests are not so charged or sold.

8. *But see Goldstein*, 691 A.2d at 277 ("In the United States . . . the 'charging order' procedure was a complete innovation . . . .").

9. *See* City of Arkansas City v. Anderson, 752 P.2d 673, 682 (Kan. 1988) ("[T]he charging order came into being as a part of the English Partnership Act of 1890 [that] was the model for section 28 of the Uniform Partnership Act, which is quite comparable to the original English version.").

> (3) Nothing in this act shall be held to deprive a partner of his right, if any, under the exemption laws, as regards his interest in the partnership.[10]

By contrast, the limited partnership was first introduced into American law by New York's Limited Partnership Act of 1822, which was itself based on the French *société en commandite*.[11] Predictably, given that the charging order was an English invention, New York's innovation had no charging order provision.[12] Although the limited partnership was alien to the English partnership law upon which the UPA of 1914 was based, when the ULC adopted the ULPA in 1916, section 22, which provided for the English remedy of the charging order, was included.

We then waited some 14 years after the 1914 adoption of the UPA before an appellate court finally was presented with a case involving a charging order arising under the UPA: *Rader v. Goldoff*.[13] There, the creditor of a partner had obtained an injunction that compelled a bank to freeze partnership assets until they could be executed upon by the creditor.[14] The injunction was vacated, with the court blandly reciting that the charging order provision of New York's UPA must be followed and awarding the debtor $10 in costs.[15]

Soon thereafter, the California Court of Appeals took up the challenge in *Sherwood v. Jackson*,[16] where one partner sued and obtained a personal injury judgment against the other partner and then tried to dissolve the partnership to enforce the judgment against the debtor-partner's share of the assets.[17] The California panel nixed this attempt, holding (based upon the New York holding in *Rader*) that the creditor-partner's exclusive remedy was the charging order procedure.[18]

The California experience is important to us, for in 1946 it brings us *Hensley v. Popkin*,[19] which appears to be the first opinion to address the effect of a charging order as creating not only a lien on the debtor-partners' interest, but

---

10. Unif. P'ship Act § 28, 6 U.L.A. 244 (Unif. Law Comm'n 1914).

11. J.J. Henning, The Cape and Natal Special Partnerships Limited Liability Act: A Statutory History, 21 Fundamina No. 2, 251 at 260 (Unisa Press, 2015).

12. The author has been unable to identify how creditors of "special partners" (as limited partners were then referred to under the New York LPA and its progeny) were treated prior to the adoption of the ULPA in 1916.

13. 228 N.Y.S. 453 (N.Y. App. Div. 1928).

14. *Id.* at 456.

15. *Id.* at 456–57.

16. 8 P.2d 943 (Cal. Ct. App. 1932).

17. *Id.* at 943.

18. *Id.* at 944.

19. 171 P.2d 916 (Cal. Dist. Ct. App. 1946).

a lien that was subject to priority as to any other lien.[20] It also brings us *Ribero v. Callaway*,[21] which recognized the right of the nondebtor partners to appeal a charging order to assert their defense that the debtor whose interest was charged was never actually a partner.[22]

For nearly 50 years following the New York decision in *Rader*, New York and California case law, often playing off each other's opinions, dominated the area of charging orders, with those two states producing nearly as many opinions on the topic as the rest of the states combined.

Tropical Interlude

In the South Pacific, in the vast, peaceful ocean between Hawaii and New Zealand, lies the Cook Islands. First named the Hervy Islands by the famed British explorer who would chance upon them in 1773, and then renamed the Cooks in his honor by an obscure Russian cartographer in 1820, the 15 sparsely populated islands would appear to be a most unlikely candidate for the massive tremor that it was to ultimately generate in the American law of charging orders. Even less likely, the tremor would be initiated by a Denver lawyer who was then about as well known as the Russian cartographer.

The Cook Islands follow English law, given that they are a protectorate of New Zealand, which itself is a Commonwealth country, with its highest court of appeals being the Privy Council in London. Looking for sources of revenue other than the occasional *National Geographic* reader, the Cook Islands enacted their International Trust Law (ITL) in 1984 by which they sought trust business from around the globe. There were few takers.

Then, in 1989, Denver lawyer Barry S. Engel persuaded the Cook Islands' parliament, because it was in a territory having less than 40,000 inhabitants, to amend the ITL to include certain provisions that were (charitably) unfriendly to creditors. The settlor-beneficiary of a self-settled trust was given protection as to his or her beneficial interest, a concept that had been anathema on public-policy grounds throughout Anglo-American jurisprudence since at least the reign of Elizabeth I. Other features were built into the ITA to deter creditors from even attempting to challenge a trust formed in the Cook Islands and to make even the mere attempt at a challenge horrendously expensive.

Thus, the fledgling industry known today as "asset protection planning" was born, and a few, and then many, U.S. tax and estate planning practitioners jumped on the concept as a way of increasing practice revenues. In 1989, there was not a single practitioner nationwide who was listed in Martindale-Hubbel as practicing in the area of asset protection. Today, lawyers naming that as one of

20. *Id.* at 917–18.
21. 196 P.2d 109 (Cal. Dist. Ct. App. 1948).
22. *Id.* at 111–12 (note the partners lost on the merits of the case).

their practice areas number in the tens of thousands. Thus, Barry Engel forever cemented his legacy as the true "father of asset protection," though not just a few hucksters would later take the title for themselves to try to impress their unfortunate clients.

The effect on American trust law has been similarly dramatic, with Alaska passing the first "domestic asset protection legislation" in 1997, followed closely by Delaware later that same year. As of this writing, there are now 15 states that provide some level of protection to the settlor-beneficiary of self-settled trusts.[23] The drama would not be confined to trusts.

One of the first beneficiaries (or victim, some might lament) of the asset protection craze was the little-known charging order. Ignoring that the purpose of the charging order was to protect the nondebtor partners from being forced into an involuntary partnership with somebody's creditor under the most exalted and all holy[24] "pick-your-partner principle" that has characterized partnership law since the adoption of the UPA in 1914, asset protection planners quickly realized that these provisions could also be used (or misused, depending on one's point of view) by the debtor-partner to prevent creditors from accessing the debtor-partner's assets that had been contributed to the partnership.[25]

Thus, the massive tremor spawned in the Cook Islands now hit partnership law as well. Partnerships would henceforth be formed not just to facilitate commercial enterprises, but as the family piggy bank, and thus the "family limited partnership," originally conceived as an estate planning tax shelter to take advantage of limited partnership interest discounts, gained its asset protection teeth. Meanwhile, back in the more mundane area of ordinary business planning, other changes were taking place that would bring partnership law to its current footing.

---

23. *See generally* David G. Shaftel et al., The American College of Trust & Estate Counsel, ACTEC Comparison of the Domestic Asset Protection Trust Statutes (2015), http://www.actec.org/assets/1/6/Shaftel-Comparison-of-the-Domestic-Asset-Protection-Trust-Statutes.pdf (discussing the 15 states with settlor-beneficiary of self-settled trusts).

24. As if nobody was getting together to do deals before the UPA was adopted in 1914.

25. An alternative view is that the charging order does not have as its basis *in personam delicti*, but rather the asset segregation function. If a creditor were able to seize the judgment-debtor's interest in the partnership, the judgment-creditor would be a mere assignee of that interest and "pick-your-partner" would not be violated. Rather, the charging order goes to the asset segregation aspect of the partnership pursuant to which, although assets were held, under the Uniform Partnership Act, as tenants in partnership, a partner could not cause the application of those assets to satisfy the partner's individual debts. *See* Thomas E. Rutledge, *I May Be Lost But I'm Making Great Time: The Failure of* Olmstead *to Correctly Recognize the Sine Qua Non of the Charging Order*, 13 J. Passthrough Entities 65 (Nov./Dec. 2010)

Kaiser William Invades Wyoming

If the Cook Islands were an unlikely place for a sea change in trust law, then Wyoming was just as unlikely a candidate for a dramatic change in partnership or corporate law. Long known as the state one must pass through to reach Yellowstone, Wyoming's Devil's Tower briefly became popular for the final scenes in Steven Spielberg's 1977 film, *Close Encounters of the Third Kind*.[26] That year something else was happening in Wyoming that also had its genesis in the reign of Victoria.

Just as America borrowed heavily from the English Partnership Act of 1890, so did the fledgling German Empire of Kaiser William II.[27] He borrowed heavily from his cousin Queen Victoria's Companies Act of 1862 to create the limited liability company known as the *Gesellschaft mit beschränkter Haftung*, or more popularly and more pronounceable, "GmbH," which became, and remains, quite popular, as any owner of an automobile manufactured by BMW GmbH might attest.

Although the United States had long before adopted limited partnership (LP) legislation, that "statutory bastard"[28] suffered from the necessity of having general partners that were generally liable for the debts of the partnership. Further, LPs carried various and sometimes undesirable baggage from their partnership heritage.

In 1977, Wyoming took the plunge and adopted the first LLC act[29]—and then watched the new entity languish because nobody really knew how it might be treated for tax purposes.[30] It was only in 1988 that guidance from the Internal Revenue Service (IRS) proclaimed that the LLC would be taxed as a partnership for tax purposes if the "four factors" test was satisfied.[31] Then, on December 18,

---

26. Close Encounters of the Third Kind (Columbia/EMI 1977).

27. Father of the ill-fated Wilhelm who would lead Germany to defeat and financial ruin in the Great War.

28. Green v. Bellerive Condos. Ltd. P'ship., 763 A.2d 252, 256 (Md. Ct. Spec. App. 2000) ("[W] e have characterized a charging order against a limited partnership interest as 'nothing more than a legislative means of providing a creditor some means of getting at a debtor's ill-defined interest in a statutory bastard, surnamed "partnership," but corporately protecting participants by limiting their liability as are corporate shareholders.'").

29. An interesting history of the origins of the limited liability company is found at S. Pace, *The Origins Behind the Limited Liability Company*, 59 Ohio. State L.J. 1459 (1998)

30. *See generally*, Robert R. Keatinge et al., *The Limited Liability Company: A Study of the Emerging Company*, 47 Bus. Law. 375 (1992); *see also* Thomas Earl Geu, *Understanding the Limited Liability Company: A Basic Comparative Primer (Part One)*, 37 S.D. L. Rev. 44 (1991–92); *Understanding the Limited Liability Company: A Basic Comparative Primer (Part Two)*, 37 S.D.L. Rev. 467 (1991–92); Thomas E. Rutledge & Lady E. Booth, *The Limited Liability Company Act: Understanding Kentucky's New Organizational Option*, 83 Ky. L.J. 1 (1994–95).

31. *See* Rev. Rule 88-76, Comm'r of Internal Revenue v. Culbertson, 337 U.S. 733, 737–48 (1949).

1996, the IRS issued its simplified "check-the-box" regulations effective January 1, 1997.[32] With the check-the-box regulations, practitioners (and their clients) were relieved of troublesome Kintner classification regulations and, with respect to multiple-member LLCs, were able to structure the inter-se management of the LLC as they saw fit without the risk of inadvertently triggering classification of the LLC as an association taxable as a corporation.

It could not have come at a better time because the asset protection industry that started in the Cook Islands was beginning to break into the mainstream, and Family Limited Partnerships (FLPs) had already become a popular estate planning tool. Now we had an entity that could be taxed as either a partnership or corporation, did not require a general partner that was generally liable, did not drag along most of the baggage of partnership law, and was (in theory) easy to manage—with charging order protection too.

The Check-The-Box regulations paved the way for the success of the LLC, and, indeed, the ULC had been working on a new ULLCA, which was adopted in 1996, in anticipation of those regulations. The ULLCA was revised a decade later to give us the Revised Uniform Limited Liability Company Act (RULLCA) that we know today. Meanwhile, the Task Force of the Committee on Partnerships and Unincorporated Business Organizations of the American Bar Association's Section of Business Law[33] had drafted the Prototype LLC Act, it being the model for many of the early adoptions.[34] In turn, the 1992 Prototype LLC Act was revised as the Revised Prototype LLC Act.[35]

> SECTION 503. CHARGING ORDER.
>
> (a) On application by a judgment creditor of a member or transferee, a court may enter a charging order against the transferable interest of the judgment debtor for the unsatisfied amount of the judgment. A charging order constitutes a lien on a judgment debtor's transferable interest and requires the limited liability company to pay over to the person to which the charging order was issued any distribution that would otherwise be paid to the judgment debtor.
>
> (b) To the extent necessary to effectuate the collection of distributions pursuant to a charging order in effect under subsection (a), the court may:

---

32. 26 C.F.R. §§ 301.7701-2(e), 301.7701-3(c)(iii) (2015).

33. Now named the Committee on LLCs, Partnerships, and Unincorporated Entities.

34. The 1992 Prototype LLC Act is reproduced at 3 LARRY E. RIBSTEIN & ROBERT R. KEATINGE, RIBSTEIN & KEATINGE ON LIMITED LIABILITY COMPANIES, Appendix C.

35. REVISED PROTOTYPE LIMITED LIABILITY COMPANY ACT, 67 BUS. LAW. 117 (Nov. 2011).

> (1) appoint a receiver of the distributions subject to the charging order, with the power to make all inquiries the judgment debtor might have made; and
>
> (2) make all other orders necessary to give effect to the charging order.
>
> (c) Upon a showing that distributions under a charging order will not pay the judgment debt within a reasonable time, the court may foreclose the lien and order the sale of the transferable interest. The purchaser at the foreclosure sale obtains only the transferable interest, does not thereby become a member, and is subject to Section 502.
>
> (d) At any time before foreclosure under subsection (c), the member or transferee whose transferable interest is subject to a charging order under subsection (a) may extinguish the charging order by satisfying the judgment and filing a certified copy of the satisfaction with the court that issued the charging order.
>
> (e) At any time before foreclosure under subsection (c), a limited liability company or one or more members whose transferable interests are not subject to the charging order may pay to the judgment creditor the full amount due under the judgment and thereby succeed to the rights of the judgment creditor, including the charging order.
>
> (f) This [act] does not deprive any member or transferee of the benefit of any exemption laws applicable to the member's or transferee's transferable interest.
>
> (g) This section provides the exclusive remedy by which a person seeking to enforce a judgment against a member or transferee may, in the capacity of judgment creditor, satisfy the judgment from the judgment debtor's transferable interest.[36]

The prefatory note to RULLCA pays appropriate homage to its roots:

> Charging Orders: The charging order mechanism: (i) dates back to the 1914 Uniform Partnership Act and the English Partnership Act of 1890, and (ii) is an essential part of the "pick your partner" approach[37] that is fundamental to the law of unincorporated businesses. The new Act continues the charging order mechanism, but modernizes the statutory

---

36. Rev. Unif. Ltd. Liab. Co. Act § 503, 6B U.L.A. 145–46 (Unif. Law Comm'n 2006 & Supp. 2015).

37. *But see* Thomas E. Rutledge, *supra* note Ch. 2, fn. 25.

> language so that the language (and its protections against outside interference in an LLC's activities) can be readily understood.[38]

For reasons largely having to do with perception from a competitive viewpoint, i.e., "We had better make our charging order provisions more attractive than those of other states, or else we might lose formation business at home," various states have (often irrationally) enacted their own, unique charging order provisions. Thus, the sleepy and unusual charging order, for which historically there has been little use or controversy, has recently—with the rise of asset protection planning as a popular area—taken on an energetic life of its own.

38. 6B U.L.A. 58, Prefatory Note.

CHAPTER 3

Nature of the Charging Order

To understand the charging order, we must first understand what happens when a creditor obtains a judgment against a corporate shareholder. A creditor who wins a judgment against the shareholder of a corporation can enforce it by levying the stock. This means that the local sheriff goes to the shareholder and makes the shareholder turn over the physical share certificates to that sheriff. Alternatively, if the shareholder refuses to cough up the shares or they have never actually been issued, the corporation can be forced to issue new shares to the sheriff. The shares are then auctioned off by the sheriff to whoever bids for them.

If no good cash bid has been made by a third-party buyer, the creditor will sometimes acquire the shares itself at the auction by bidding part of the creditor's judgment against the shares, also known as "credit bidding." If the shares are publicly traded, the creditor can then sell the shares at the market trading price. If the shares are privately held and the creditor acquires a majority share, the creditor can vote to wind up the company and thus access the debtor's share of the company's value.

The benefit of corporations is that they typically have three levels of control that separate the investors from the day-to-day management of the business. First, the shareholders have a vote, and their vote can make major changes to the articles and bylaws of the corporation, as well as elect the directors. Second, the directors have a vote, and they can make significant decisions on behalf of the corporation and elect the officers. Third, the officers are empowered to run the corporation on a daily basis and make significant decisions subject to the ratification or approval of the directors.

Importantly, the shareholders are divorced from day-to-day decisions. A change in the composition of shareholders may not immediately affect the operations of the business. The shareholders must wait until they meet to elect new directors, and only if new directors are elected are the officers likely to change. If the new creditor-shareholder holds less than a majority stake, then the business may not change at all. If, for instance, a creditor levies upon the debtor's one-hundred shares in Microsoft Corporation, which at the time of this writing had a paltry 8.26 billion issued and outstanding shares, it is unlikely that there will be many long faces in Redmond, Washington.

Contrast this with a partnership or LLC, where the owners of the business are usually active in the business.[1] The partners have agreed among themselves that they—and only they—will run the business, and their partnership agreement prohibits new partners without unanimous consent.[2] A change of a partner could have a dramatic and negative effect upon the chemistry of the partnership. If Microsoft were a partnership, even a partner holding a 0.01-percent interest could presumably come into its offices and start tinkering with its operating system.

Thus, partnerships are treated differently than corporations for judgment collection purposes. The purchaser of corporate shares at a judicial sale will not immediately be able to jump into the management of the company and disrupt its operations. Not so with a partnership, which lacks the legal separation of ownership and management.

A creditor who holds a judgment against a partner in a partnership (or a member in an LLC) is not normally allowed to take the debtor's interest. Instead, the creditor is allowed to take a lien against the debtor's interest so that any profit distributions that would have been made to the debtor will instead be made to the creditor. It is here that we should realize that a partner's or member's "interest" is really a bundle of several different rights and privileges within the partnership or LLC, of which the right to distributions is but one.[3]

The legal vehicle by which the lien is placed on the debtor's distributive rights is the charging order, which exists primarily to prevent a creditor's enforcement action from disrupting the business of the partnership. The explanation given by the court in *Taylor v. S & M Lamp Co.*[4] is most helpful:

---

1. *See* Green v. Bellerive Condos. Ltd. P'ship, 763 A.2d 252, 256 (Md. Ct. Spec. App. 2000) (stating that charging orders "are purely statutory tools that judgment creditors use to reach partnership interests of indebted partners .... [W]e have characterized a charging order against a limited partnership interest as 'nothing more than a legislative means of providing a creditor some means of getting at a debtor's ill-defined interest in a statutory bastard, surnamed "partnership," but corporately protecting participants by limiting their liability as are corporate shareholders.'" (*quoting* Bank of Bethesda v. Koch, 408 A.2d 767, 770 (Md. Ct. Spec. App. 1979)).

2. *See, e.g.*, UPA § 402(b)(3); ULPA §§ 301(b)(3) & 401(b)(3); ULLCA § 401(c)(3).

3. Hellman v. Anderson, 284 Cal. Rptr. 830, 834 (Cal. Ct. App. 1991) ("[A] partner's right in specific partnership property is different from his interest in the partnership. The property rights of a partner are (1) his rights in specific partnership property, (2) *his interest in the partnership*, and (3) his right to participate in the management. A partner's interest in the partnership is his share of the profits and surplus, and the same is personal property."); Madison Hills Ltd. P'ship II v. Madison Hills, Inc., 644 A.2d 363, 366 (Conn. App. Ct. 1994) ("The partner's interest in the partnership is one of three property rights the partner possesses; the others are the partner's rights in specific partnership property and the right to participate in partnership management.").

4. 12 Cal. Rptr. 323 (Cal. Dist. Ct. App. 1961).

> Lord Justice Lindley gave the following reason for the English rule forbidding execution sale of a partner's interest in the partnership to satisfy his nonpartnership debt:
>
> When a creditor obtained a judgment against one partner and he wanted to obtain the benefit of that judgment against the share of that partner in the firm, the first thing was to issue a [fiery facias], and the sheriff went down to the partnership place of business, seized everything, stopped the business, drove the solvent partners wild, and caused the execution creditor to bring an action in Chancery in order to get an injunction to take an account and pay over that which was due the execution debtor. A more clumsy method of proceeding could hardly have grown up.
>
> It was to prevent such "hold up" of the partnership business and the consequent injustice done the other partners resulting from execution against partnership property that the [California Charging Order] code sections and their counterparts in the Uniform Partnership Act and the English Partnership Act of 1890 were adopted. As we view those code sections they are not intended to protect a debtor partner against claims of his judgment creditors where no legitimate interest of the partnership, or of the remaining or former partners is to be served.[5]

The purpose of the charging order remedy and its exclusivity as a remedy under RULLCA section 503(g) and the other partnership acts is to prevent disruption of the partnership's business.[6] This can be done by keeping the creditor from otherwise enforcing the judgment directly against the debtor-partner's share

---

5. *Id.* at 328 (citations omitted). In *91st Street Joint Venture v. Goldstein*, the Maryland Court of Special Appeals declared:

> A charging order is the statutory means by which a judgment creditor may reach the partnership interest of a judgment debtor. Prior to its availability, the courts would resort to common law procedures for collection that were ill-suited for reaching partnership interests. Typically, despite the fact that individual partners do not have title in partnership property, partnership property would be seized under writs of execution; the debtor partner's interest in the partnership would be sold, often to the judgment creditor, subject to the payment of partnership debts and prior claims of the partnership against the debtor partner; and the sale of the debtor partner's interest would result in compulsory dissolution and winding up of the partnership. . . . The charging order [is a] solution to this procedural nightmare . . . .

691 A.2d 272, 275 (Md. Ct. Spec. App. 1997) (citations omitted).

6. Baybank v. Catamount Constr., 693 A.2d 1163, 1165 (N.H. 1997) ("The statutory remedy of a charging order was designed to prevent the personal creditors of a limited partner from disrupting the partnership business by seizing partnership assets on execution."); Lauer Constr. Inc. v. Schrift, 716 A.2d 1096, 1098 (Md. Ct. Spec. App. 1998) ("The purpose of [a charging order]

of the assets and to prevent a forced "business divorce."[7] It is not meant to protect the debtor-partner's interests,[8] but rather protects the nondebtor partners[9] from being forced into what amounts to an involuntary partnership with somebody's creditor.[10]

The Effect of the Charging Order

Under U.K. law, the charging order was the end in itself—the debtor's interest in the partnership was "charged" with the payment of distributions to the creditor until the debt was satisfied. In the United States, the method is different, even if the ultimate result is nearly the same. Under American law, the issuance of a charging order has the effect of involuntarily creating a non-U.C.C. security interest in favor of the creditor by a lien on the debtor's right to distributions that

---

is to protect the partnership business and prevent the disruption that would result if creditors of a partner executed directly on partnership assets.").

7. *91st St. Joint Venture*, 691 A.2d at 282 (stating that purpose of charging order is not to permit court to facilitate or force upon a debtor a "business divorce"). *See e.g., Baybank*, 693 A.2d at 1167 ("Such an application of partnership property to pay the personal debts of a partner, however, is precisely what the charging order provisions of the ULPA and the UPA are intended to prevent."); Windom Nat'l Bank v. Klein, 254 N.W. 602, 604 (Minn. 1934) ("Plain is the purpose that all partnership property is to be kept intact for partnership purposes and creditors."); Keeler v. Acad. of Am. Franciscan Hist., Inc., 943 A.2d 630, 633 (Md. Ct. Spec. App. 2008) ("The purpose of the charging order is 'to protect the partnership business and prevent the disruption that would result if creditors of a partner executed directly on partnership assets.'").

8. *Hellman*, 233 Cal. App. 3d at 845–46 (charging order remedy exists to prevent interference in partnership business or with partnership assets to detriment of nondebtor partners but is not meant to protect interest of debtor partner).

9. Union Colony Bank v. United Bank of Greeley Nat'l Ass'n, 832 P.2d 1112, 1116 (Colo. App. 1992) (stating that the charging order "remedy arose in response to the unique issues which confront partnerships, specifically the need to protect the interests of the non-debtor partners."); Christensen v. Oedekoven, 888 P.2d 228, 232 (Wyo. 1995) ("The charging order procedure protects the interests of the nondebtor partners by giving the judge wide latitude to control the creditor's actions against the partnership.").

10. Brant v. Krilich, 835 N.E.2d 582, 592 n.20 (Ind. Ct. App. 2005). The Court of Appeals for Indiana ruled:

> [U]nless the operating agreement provides otherwise, an assignee only becomes a member of an LLC if the other members unanimously consent. There is no reason why our courts should disregard the intent of the General Assembly to protect the close-knit structure of a LLC and violate the other members' interests and rights by declaring that they must accept a judgment creditor of a member into full membership with all the rights appurtenant thereto when the judgment debtor could not transfer those rights himself.

Id.

requires the LLC to make all future distributions to the creditor[11] until the judgment is satisfied.[12]

One might think of a charging order as an aerosol can that sprays the lien upon the debtor-member's interest, much in the manner that a child might spray paint his or her bicycle a different color. In the end, it is the paint (the lien) that is important and lasting, and the charging order itself is of as little consequence as the empty can once it has accomplished its task—with one critically important exception.

The exception does not relate to the lien, but rather to ancillary provisions in the charging order that help to make it truly effective. The typical charging order will not just place the lien, but will also command that the debtor-member may not take any loans, salary, fees, etc., or any other actions that would get money out of the LLC through the backdoor, thus defeating the charging order.[13]

As a matter of procedure, a creditor is not required to throw in these other provisions, but instead could bring a separate motion for an order in aid of execution or the like. However, it is so much easier to simply bundle these

---

11. Arkansas City v. Anderson, 752 P.2d 673, 684 (Kan. 1988) ("[W]e hold that the issuance and service of a proper charging order is sufficient to require the partnership to pay the judgment debtor's share of distributable partnership profits to the judgment creditor or to the court to await further orders of the court."); Beach Park Assoc. v. Heron, No. H023320, 2003 WL 22000591, at *1 (Cal. Ct. App. Aug. 25, 2003). The California Court of Appeals declared:

> [C]harging orders required each partnership to pay to appellant "any and all income, revenues, distributions, compensation, fees, repayment of debt, or personal property, tangible or intangible, or [sic] whatever sort or nature, that have, at any time from the date of service of the notice of motion herein on the respective partnerships or thereafter, become due, payable, or distributable to any one or more of the judgment debtors, or as to which any one or more of the judgment debtors has become entitled . . . ."

Id.

12. *Beach Park Assoc.*, 2003 WL 22000591, at *23 (finding amounts collected from charged partnership interests are credited against the underlying judgment, and in no case would holder of charging order be permitted to collect more than underlying judgment, plus interest, etc.); *Anderson*, 752 P.2d at 684 ("[T]he extent of [payments made pursuant to a charging order are] limited to any amounts due on the unsatisfied judgment.").

13. Gerry Niesar has pointed out to the author that because a charging order only applies to transferrable interests, it does not (in the absence of ancillary provisions) reach the salary or wages of the debtor-member, and the creditor would instead be required to employ the remedy of garnishment as to such compensation. The author is unaware of any case that addressed this ingenious and possibly novel argument but cannot presently conceive of an argument as to why it might be incorrect. On the other hand, Tom Rutledge pointed out in his editing of the draft of this book that "there may be different outcomes under different acts. Under harmonized RULLCA, a compensatory payment to a member is not a distribution. In contrast, under most other acts, compensatory payments, even if accounted for as guaranteed payments, are still distributions made to the member. Which of course gets us back into our debate as to whether garnishment limits apply to compensatory distributions."

provisions into the charging order. This is the (possibly sole) benefit to the creditor of the charging order procedure.

California's enforcement of judgments law specifically addresses charging orders.[14] There, the filing of a motion for charging order and service upon the LLC or its members creates a temporary lien on the debtor-member's interest. The lien then becomes permanent until the judgment is paid once the motion is granted.[15] In all other states, a creditor must file a motion for temporary restraining order or preliminary injunction, etc. to attempt to tie up the debtor-member's distributions pending the hearing on the motion for charging order. The lien created by the charging order must be accorded priority like any other judgment lien.[16]

The fact that the creditor who has successfully obtained a charging order ends up with a lien and only a lien (although there may be some ancillary provisions to effectuate the lien in the text of the charging order) has certain ramifications, the most important of which is that like any other ordinary[17] lienholder, the creditor does not gain any management rights within the LLC.[18]

---

14. Consistency between general remedies law and the charging order is rare. The charging order typically is ignored in remedies law. This treatment is at least in part consequent to the fact that the charging order, a substantive remedy, is addressed in business organization law rather than in a traditional remedies code.

15. *See* CAL. CIV. PROC. CODE § 708.320 (West 2015).

16. *Anderson*, 752 P.2d at 684 ("[A] valid charging order does create a lien upon the debtor partner's distributive share of present and future profits as of the time of service upon the partnership. The lien or charge thus established has priority over other security interests which are not perfected prior to the date of service of the charging order."); Union Colony Bank v. United Bank of Greeley Nat'l Assoc., 832 P.2d 1112, 1115 (Colo. App. 1992) ("[L]ien [created by the charging order] attaches at the time the order is served upon the partnership. And, upon attachment, the charging order has priority, for full satisfaction of the creditor's judgment, over any other charging order subsequently served upon the partnership, regardless of the order in which the judgments were entered and the previous efforts, if any, made by the creditor to satisfy the judgment by other means.").

17. Green v. Bellerive Condos. Ltd. P'ship, 763 A.2d 252, 260 n.8 (Md. Ct. Spec. App. 2000) ("Of course, we recognize that a partnership agreement may 'otherwise provide' for assignment of such management rights.").

18. Cadle Co. v. Ginsburg, No. CV950076811S, 2002 WL 725500, at *2 (Conn. Super. Ct. Mar. 3, 2002) ("[A] charging order merely gives the judgment creditor the rights of an assignee of the member's interest in the limited liability company and does not entitle the assignee to participate in the management and affairs of the limited liability company or to become or exercise any rights of a member."); *Green*, 763 A.2d at 262 ("In the context of a proposal to purchase partnership debt, the right to consent is essentially a right to participate in the decision regarding whether the partnership should commit its resources to pursue the partnership opportunity. Like the right to information about partnership opportunities, a partner's right to consent to another partner's pursuit of a partnership opportunity is a management right of a partner that remains

Some decisions have likewise held that the lien created by the charging order does not independently create any right of a creditor to demand information about the LLC's operations and affairs, although a wily creditor may be able to figure out some other method to ferret out this information.[19]

As for our poor, downtrodden debtor-member, he retains in an unfettered fashion whatever management rights that he had before the charging order was entered, including his own rights as a member to information about the LLC's activity (and this information is usually fair game for a creditor in post-judgment examination proceedings).[20]

Case Study: *Inman*[21]

Husband and Wife divorced in Florida with Husband to make $1 million in alimony payments to Wife over some years. By agreement, these payments were to be secured by liens on certain assets, including on Husband's interests in three Colorado entities that were apparently investing in real estate there.

Husband, however, did not fulfill his promise to secure the liens on the Colorado entities. Wife then obtained a Florida judgment on the divorce agreement, which she domesticated in Colorado. The Colorado court issued charging orders against Husband's interests in all three Colorado entities.

Back in Florida, Husband filed for Chapter 11 bankruptcy, and Wife timely filed her proof of claim to which she attached the Florida judgment and the Colorado charging orders.

---

with the indebted partner after his right to receive distributions in the limited partnership has been transferred via a charging order.").

19. Lumbermens Mut. Cas. Co. v. Luciano Enters., LLC, No. A01-309 CV JWS, 2005 WL 2340709, at *3 (D. Ala. Sept. 21, 2005) ("Neither the federal discovery rules nor the Alaska discovery rules contemplate regular, monthly disclosure such as plaintiff requests. Plaintiff is not entitled to have a regular, financial disclosure requirement included in the charging order."); *Green*, 763 A.2d at 261 ("Because the receiver had only the rights of an assignee, and such rights do not include the right to demand or receive information regarding partnership opportunities, the trial court was legally correct in ruling that the receiver was not entitled to separate notice of the opportunity to purchase the Note.").

20. *Green*, 763 A.2d at 264 ("[A] charging order does not prevent indebted partners from participating in partnership affairs, at least to the extent an applicable partnership agreement allows. Nor does it prohibit the indebted partner from keeping the charging creditor informed about partnership affairs."); Madison Hills Ltd. P'ship II v. Madison Hills, Inc., 644 A.2d 363, 367 (Conn. App. Ct. 1994) ("Under the UPA, however, a charging creditor is entitled to more than just the rights of an assignee. The UPA provides that the charging creditor is entitled to the distributions to which the partner is entitled *plus* the benefit of all other orders, directions, accounts and inquiries that the partner could make. Assignees under the UPA are denied the latter benefit.") (internal citations omitted).

21. *In re* Inman, 2012 WL 2374419 (Bankr. S.D. Fla., 2012).

In the ensuing adversary action, Husband attempted to challenge the Colorado charging orders, arguing that those charging orders should not be given full faith and credit by the federal bankruptcy court sitting in Florida. The court disagreed:

> The Charging Liens each satisfy the finality element. In Colorado, "[a] final judgment is defined as one which ends the particular action in which it is entered, leaving nothing further for the court pronouncing it to do in order to completely determine the rights of the parties involved in the proceeding." . . . Such a final judgment must be entered on the merits of the case by a court of competent jurisdiction. . . . The Colorado Court is a court of competent jurisdiction. It is clear from the face of the Charging Liens, which were not stayed, appealed or otherwise challenged, that they ended the action and left nothing for the Colorado Court to determine with regard to the rights of the Plaintiff and the Defendant. Each Charging Lien contains findings showing that it was entered on the merits of the case. [Internal citations omitted.]

Case Study: *Weddell*[22]

Two longtime business partners started a venture to develop geothermal energy and formed several companies, including two limited liability companies. One of the partners, the debtor, alone became embroiled in an unrelated lawsuit that was to eventually mature into a judgment against the debtor for over $6 million.

A year before this judgment was entered, the other partner used his 60-percent majority interest to remove the debtor from management of the two companies. Soon after the $6 million judgment was entered against the debtor, the creditor in that lawsuit obtained a charging order against the debtor's interests in the two companies. The other (nondebtor) partner then bought out the debtor's interest in one of the companies, as allowed by its operating agreement, for $100.

Although the debtor's interests were charged by his creditor, the debtor sued the other (nondebtor) partner to determine his rights in the partnership—in other words, whether his removal from management and the $100 buyout were appropriate.

The Nevada district court held that the charging order divested the debtor of both his membership and management rights in the two LLCs, and thus concluded that the other (nondebtor) partner was the sole manager of those companies. Importantly, the district court also held that these business activities were

22. Weddell v. H2O, Inc., 128 Nev. Adv. Op. #9 (Mar. 1, 2012).

"simply strategic" and not meant to defraud the creditor (which was not a party to this litigation).

On appeal, the Nevada Supreme Court held that:

> [U]nder Nevada law, judgment creditors have no right to participate in the management of the limited-liability company and only obtain the rights of an assignee of the member's interest—receiving only a share of the economic interests in a limited-liability company, including profits, losses, and distributions of assets. By limiting a creditor's right to exercise the debtor member's management rights, we ensure that creditors of a limited-liability company cannot disrupt and interfere with the management rights of other members. This conclusion rests on the uncontested right of a member to choose his or her associates and to encourage investing by enabling limited members to invest money and to share profits, but without risking more than the amount they contributed.

The opinion discussed the history of Nevada's limited liability company statute, as well as the historical basis for charging orders:

> Charging orders were formed by the English Partnership Act of 1890 as a result of an artificial and clumsy procedure whereby the town sheriff went down to the partnership's place of business, seized partnership assets, closed the partnership, infuriated the solvent partners, and caused the judgment creditor to bring an action for an injunction.

The remedy of the charging order was thus specifically crafted to prohibit a creditor from either taking the assets of the LLC itself or taking over management of the company:

> Consequently, the judgment creditor does not unequivocally step into the shoes of a limited-liability member. The limited access of a judgment creditor includes only the rights of an assignee of the member's interest. . . . A judgment creditor, or assignee, is only entitled to the judgment debtor's share of the profit and distributions, takes no interest in the LLC's assets, and is not entitled to participate in the management or administration of the business. . . . After the entry of a charging order, the debtor member no longer has the right to future LLC distributions to the extent of the charging order, but retains all other rights that it had before the execution of the charging order, including managerial interests.

Having determined that the charging order did not affect the debtor's management rights, the court remanded the case back to the district court to determine whether the debtor was properly bought out of his membership interest under the companies' operating agreements.

CHAPTER 4

Using the Charging Order

Creditors employ charging orders primarily for two reasons. The first is straightforward: to capture the revenues from the debtor's economic interest to satisfy the judgment. Once the charging order is properly in place, distributions as made will be routed to the creditor instead of the debtor until the judgment has been satisfied in full from this and other sources of collection.

Whether the creditor can derive any substantial revenues from a charging order depends, of course, on the extent of the debtor's interest and the nature of the LLC.

Consider a debtor's interest in a "family LLC" holding undeveloped real estate. In such a case, the LLC was probably not making much in the way of distributions before the charging order was entered, and distributions will likely be small and fleeting afterwards, too. Contrast this with an LLC organized as a large hedge fund that regularly throws off sizeable distributions to it members. There, the creditor might derive substantial payments made to the charging order.

Even in the case of the family LLC, however, the creditor has a chance of obtaining sizeable distributions. This is because the charging order not only picks up interim distributions, i.e., distributions that are made while the LLC continues in business, but also liquidating distributions that are made to members when the LLC is wound up.

Although anecdotally it seems that most LLCs elect a perpetual or long-term duration when organized, in reality most LLCs serve their purposes for a number of years and then are wound up. Although the debtor might not want the LLC wound up and the consequent diversion of liquidating distributions to the judgment-creditor, the other members might want their money more immediately. Given that most states allow judgments to be renewed (if they expire at all) *ad perpetuam*, a patient creditor might simply sit on the charging order for years or even decades to see if anything significant is distributed—the creditor, after all, has nothing to lose by waiting the debtor out if the judgment is not otherwise satisfied.

This brings us to the second primary use of a charging order, which is a part of a larger strategy to deprive the debtor of cash and thus financially strangle the debtor.[1] Creditors, particularly sophisticated creditors, often take a larger view of the debtor's situation whereby actually collecting money through judgment enforcement efforts is secondary to causing financial pain to the debtor and forcing a settlement. This is arguably the most common use of the charging order by many creditors. For these creditors, cutting off the debtor's cash flow is the cake, and any distributions that the creditor might receive in the meantime is the icing.

The charging order accomplishes this by disrupting the cash flow that the debtor was receiving from the LLC, instead redirecting that cash flow to the creditor. Even if, as occurs with many closely held LLCs, the debtor is able to persuade the other members to forgo distributions for the time being, the debtor itself is still deprived of the cash flow from those distributions.

This method seems to work particularly well where the creditor has a judgment against a parent company that has dropped its most valuable assets down to subsidiary LLCs. In such situations, the revenue of the entities is irregular, i.e., subsidiaries A, C, and E are profitable, but subsidiaries B, D, and F are not. In such a case, obtaining a charging order against all the entities prevents the debtor parent from shuffling money among the entities such that A, C, and F can assist B, D, and F with their immediate cash-flow needs.

The strategy also works well with individual debtors. Individuals usually have established lifestyles, and litigation is costly. Depriving such debtors of the ability to fund their lifestyles and even to fund much of a defense to judgment enforcement actions can pay a creditor healthy dividends.

Case Study: *Detroit Memorial Partners*[2]

Angelo Alleca started a series of investment funds and allegedly used the money from the newer funds to cover investment losses in the older funds while concealing all losses from investors.

The fraud culminated in a promissory note scheme, whereby investors bought promissory notes from a company known as Detroit Memorial Partners, LLC (DMP), the name for which derives from an attempt by the company to purchase distressed cemeteries. DMP was founded by Mark Morrow, who was enlisted to sell interests in DMP's promissory notes.

The SEC eventually got wind of all this and brought an enforcement action on May 30, 2013, and had a receiver for DMP appointed on September 24, 2013.

1. This strategy is sometimes known as the "Anaconda Plan," in reference to a strategy developed by General Winfield Scott during the first year of the U.S. Civil War, by which the Union would blockade the South and financially strangle it, and which ultimately led to the financial collapse of the Confederacy in the last year of that war.

2. SEC v. Detroit Memorial Partners, LLC, 2016 WL 6595942 (N.D. Ga. Nov. 8, 2016).

The SEC had earlier filed an enforcement action and obtained a freeze against Alleca.

It is true that in litigation there is often the quick and the dead. Here, we find the quick being one of the jilted investors, Leonard J. Walter, who sued DMP for breach of contract for failing to pay on some of the promissory notes in which he had invested. Walter sued DMP on April 12, 2013; obtained a default judgment on June 21, 2013, for $200,000 plus another $4,875 in unpaid interest; and was granted a charging order September 11, 2013, against one of DMP's assets—Midwest Memorial Group, LLC (MMG).

Note that Walter obtained his charging order for DMP's interest in MMG just 13 days before the SEC had a receiver appointed for DMP.

Skip forward to 2016, when DMP's receiver asked the court to approve a plan of distribution of DMP, which would include DMP's interest in MMG—the interest against which Walter had his charging order. Walter objected to the plan of distribution on the grounds that, because of his charging order, he was a secured creditor as to the MMG interest and thus held a priority interest, putting him first in line before either the receiver or any other creditors of DMP.

For his part, DMP's receiver filed a response stating that the receiver was an "equity receivership" arising from an SEC enforcement action, and the court has wide discretion to effectively re-prioritize a creditor's security interest (here, meaning Walter's) to benefit all victims of an investment scheme equally.

All this led to the opinion of the U.S. District Court for the Northern District of Georgia. The court addressed the equity receivership argument, basically stating that the argument would work if the receiver were appointed before Walter obtained a lien against MMG's interest because the appointment of a receiver, equity or otherwise, could not defeat an existing security lien. Thus, the salient question was whether Walter's charging order gave him a valid lien against the MMG interest.

Apparently, it was agreed among all the parties that Michigan law would apply, although quite likely the result the court ultimately reached would be about the same under the laws of any other state.

The court found that under Michigan law, a charging order creates a lien on the membership interest of the debtor-member. The court noted that the lien created by the charging order is "a distinctive or limited lien" because it only gives the creditor the right to receive any distributions that might be made to the debtor-member in the future and does not allow the creditor to otherwise assert rights against the assets of the LLC itself or attempt to exercise any management control.

Moreover, the charging order does not make the creditor a lienholder of the LLC itself, but only of the debtor-member. Essentially, the charging order makes the creditor an "involuntary assignee" of the debtor's interest until the judgment is paid in full.

In the meantime, DMP's receiver had taken over $7.8 million as DMP's "distributive share" of a settlement MMG received from a lawsuit against Smith Barney. Given that Walter had a priority lien by way of the charging order against DMP's interest in MMG, the court held that Walter was entitled to $200,000 of this money, plus accrued interest.

This is a sound opinion that illustrates both (1) the charging order as a vehicle to create a lien, and (2) the lien created by a charging order entitled to priority like any other lien.

Note that as "just a lien," the charging order is an efficient judgment enforcement remedy. Here, Walter didn't attempt to foreclose on his lien, but simply let it (and, ultimately, the receiver) do its work, and eventually he was paid in full on his judgment.

There is another lesson here, however, which goes back to the "quick and the dead." Walter was smart and quick, and the 13-day difference between his charging order being issued and the SEC getting its receiver was the difference between Walter being paid in full or receiving only a proportionate share along with other jilted investors. Walter was quick, and ultimately that made all the difference.

CHAPTER 5

Charging Order Procedure

To the surprise of most practitioners who do not regularly practice in the area of creditor-debtor law, most post-judgment enforcement procedures do not implicate the court directly, but instead work through the clerk (acting in an almost perfunctory role) and the sheriff. For instance, most post-judgment writs, such as writs of execution, writs of attachment, writs of garnishment, etc., are normally issued by the clerk upon the request of the creditor, and often with only the slightest review to ensure that all the paperwork is in good order.[1] Thereafter, the sheriff simply follows the instructions of whatever writ the sheriff must deal with that day, and takes possession of property, holds judicial sales, etc. Probably the vast bulk of garden-variety collection cases never require a judge to make anything approaching an actual decision.

The placing of a lien on the debtor's property is even easier. For real property, the creditor files an abstract of judgment with the local county title clerk or recorder or equivalent office, and—voila!—the lien is thereby instantly created upon the debtor's real property. Similarly, liens on personal property can be established variously by filing forms with the local secretary of state, similar to a UCC-1, or by the service upon the debtor of certain writs. To create a lien on most personal property, the creditor can literally "mail it in."

The same is not true of the charging order, which requires that the creditor file a motion for charging order with the court (regarding *which* court we will get to presently), serve the debtor and often either the LLC or all its members, and then have a hearing before the court whereby the merits of the charging order are considered. It is a time-consuming and arguably needless procedure in most cases. Given that rare is the case where the debtor will have anything like a viable defense to a charging order, by and large, the hearing on the motion only provides the debtor with an opportunity to show up and annoy everybody with nonsensical arguments while whining about how unfair it all is.

1. *See generally* A. Schonviesner & P. Young, How to Collect When You Win a Lawsuit in California (2016 ed.), *available at* https://goo.gl/hBhJTU.

When granted, the charging order by its terms "charges" (i.e., creates a lien[2] upon) the transferrable interest of the debtor-member, i.e., the right to distributions.[3] The effect is to divert to the creditor the payments that would otherwise have been made to the debtor[4] and to create a liability of the LLC to make those payments.[5]

The charging order is similar in many respects to what would be a garnishment proceeding against the debtor-member's right to distributions, but a charging order is not a garnishment and is, in many ways, a more flexible remedy.[6] The charging order is also quite similar to an assignment order, which is often used to assign to creditors the interests in royalties and other income streams, and to an attachment order, which places an involuntary lien on the

---

2. *Madison Hills Ltd. P'ship II*, 644 A.2d at 366 ("The UPA permits a judgment creditor of a partner to place a type of lien known as a charging order on the partner's interest in the partnership."); Union Colony Bank v. United Bank of Greeley Nat'l Assoc., 832 P.2d 1112, 1115 (Colo. App. 1992) ("[C]harging order creates a lien upon a debtor partner's interest in the partnership, to wit, his distributive share of partnership's profits and surplus.")

3. *See* Cadle Co. v. Bourgeois, 821 A.2d 1001, 1009 (N.H. 2003); Brant v. Krilich, 835 N.E.2d 582, 592 (Ind. Ct. App. 2005) (Charged "interest is limited to economic interests and nothing more."); *Green*, 763 A.2d at 257 ("Unless otherwise provided in the partnership agreement, an assignment entitles the assignee to receive, to the extent assigned, only the distributions to which the assignor would be entitled.").

4. *Madison Hills Ltd. P'ship II*, 644 A.2d at 366 ("The charging order leaves the partnership intact but diverts to the judgment creditor the debtor partner's share of the profits."); MacDonald v. MacDonald, 1986 WL 5480, at *4 (Del. Ch. May 9, 1986) (pointing out that Delaware's charging order statute "provides a form of execution permitting a judgment creditor to divert a flow of payments from the judgment debtor to the party obtaining the charging order."); 91st St. Joint Venture v. Goldstein, 691 A.2d 272, 278 (Md. Ct. Spec. App. 1997) ("Among the cases we have found that discuss the charging order procedure in any detail, there seems to be at least implicit agreement with Professor Gose's observation that the charging order statute provides two basic collection methods: (1) the diversion of the debtor partner's profits to the judgment creditor; and (2) the ultimate transfer of the debtor partner's interest should the first collection method prove unsatisfactory.").

5. *See* Keeler v. Acad. of Am. Franciscan Hist., Inc., 943 A.2d 630, 635 (Md. Ct. Spec. App. 2002) (prepetition charging order was a liability of the partnership and not the debtor, and was not discharged in bankruptcy).

6. Beach Park Assoc. v. Heron, No. H023320, 2003 WL 22000591, at *21 (Cal. Ct. App. Aug. 25, 2003) (charging order "is akin to garnishment"); Banc One Cap. Partners v. Russell, No. 74086, 1999 WL 435787, at *4 (Ohio Ct. App. June 24, 1999) ("[A] judgment creditor who has obtained a charging order against a member's interest in a limited liability company garnishes the financial rights that attach to the interest."); Christensen v. Oedekoven, 888 P.2d 228, 232 (Wyo. 1995) ("[C]harging orders are remedies different in character from writs of garnishment").

debtor's interest in some asset.[7] A charging order is not, however, any of these alternative collection devices. It is indeed a "peculiar mechanism."[8]

As previously mentioned, the form of the charging order will routinely contain detailed ancillary provisions to keep the debtor-member from benefitting from the LLC by other by distributions, i.e., taking money out the back door. These provisions typically include prohibiting the LLC from making loans to the debtor-member, paying the personal debts of the debtor-member, or paying wages or salary (if they were not paid before) to the debtor-member. Even in the absence of such ancillary provisions, however, the creditor may still have avenues for relief in such cases.[9] Failure of the LLC to abide by these provisions may subject the LLC to contempt.[10]

The RULLCA and the partnership acts only vaguely set out the availability, basic application, and exclusivity of the charging order. Only California has adopted a conforming procedure for charging orders, which is found in the California Code of Civil Procedure:

> (a) A lien on a judgment debtor's interest in a partnership or limited liability company is created by service of a notice of motion for a charging order on the judgment debtor and on either of the following:
>
> (1) All partners or the partnership.
>
> (2) All members or the limited liability company.
>
> (b) If a charging order is issued, the lien created pursuant to subdivision (a) continues under the terms of the order. If issuance of the charging order is denied, the lien is extinguished.[11]

---

7. An argument can be made that a charging order is simply a species of the remedy of attachment that is unique to LLCs and partnerships.

8. *Green*, 763 A.2d at 256 ("A charging order is a unique tool. Although it has some characteristics of both an assignment and an attachment, it is neither."); Deutsch v. Wolff, 7 S.W.3d 460, 463 (Mo. Ct. App. 1999) ("[A] charging order is not an assignment or attachment of a partnership interest."); Nigri v. Lotz, 453 S.E.2d 780, 782 (Ga. Ct. App. 1995) ("A charging order . . . is not an assignment of the limited partner's interest to the creditor, nor does it confer upon the creditor the status of a substituted limited partner.").

9. PB Real Estate, Inc. v. DEM II Props., 719 A.2d 73, 74 (Conn. App. Ct. 1998) (turnover order against LLC would be granted where LLC had made payments disguised as "legal staff" expenses to debtors in violation of charging order.).

10. Joshlin Bros. Irrigation v. Sunbelt Rental, Inc., No. CV-13-397, 2014 WL 248104, at *2 (Ark. Ct. App. Jan. 22, 2014).

11. Cal. Civ. Proc Code § 708.320 (West 2003).

Other states are not so lucky, however, causing the courts in those states when faced with a motion for charging order to deal with the "peculiar mechanism" in an ad hoc fashion.[12]

Case Study: *Textron Financial*[13]

Textron Financial Corporation sued New Mexico resident Michael S. Gallegos in the U.S. District Court for Rhode Island for a loan made on a hotel deal gone bad. Textron was awarded a nearly $22 million verdict, but apparently was only able to collect a little more than $10,000.

Textron then assigned the judgments to SPE LO Holdings, which did some snooping around for Gallegos' assets, eventually obtaining documents from the California Secretary of State's office that indicated Gallegos was at least the manager (it was unclear whether he was also a member) of two California entities: Pacific Pearls Hotel LLC and Pacific Pearl Management LLC.

SPE then filed a motion for charging order in the U.S. District Court for the Central District of California against any interest Gallegos had in the two LLCs. The court gave a nice, short summary of a charging order as follows:

> When there's a money judgment against an LLC member personally, but not against the LLC, the member's interest may be reached by a charging order. . . . A charging order is a lien on the member's distributional interest. . . . It only allows the judgment creditor to receive distributions to which the member would otherwise be entitled; it doesn't entitle the creditor to participate in the LLC's management or exercise the rights of a member. . . . It thereby protects other members of an LLC from being forced to involuntarily share governance responsibilities with someone they did not choose, or from being forced to accept a creditor of another member as a co-manager. [Internal citations and quotations omitted.]

Here, SPE did not hire a process server to deliver a copy of the motion to the two LLCs, but instead simply dropped a copy in the mail.

---

12. 91st St. Joint Venture v. Goldstein, 691 A.2d 272, 280 (Md. Ct. Spec. App. 1997):

> [Section] 28 of the UPA is drafted in the most general terms and provides courts with very little guidance regarding particular procedures that should be used to further the goals of the charging order. The generality of its terms could be read to sanction the fashioning of charging order procedures on a case-by case basis and without regard to collection procedures already in place with respect to judgment debtors generally. . . . [W]e view it as just an unfortunate circumstance that § 28 was adopted in Maryland and most other jurisdictions without any additional elaboration of procedure.

Id.

13. Textron Fin. Corp. v. Gallegos, C.D. Cal. Case No. 15cv1678 (Oct. 7, 2015).

For his part, Gallegos (but not the companies) opposed the motion for charging order, asserting basically three arguments:

(1) the California Secretary of State documents were not admissible;
(2) personal service by a process server of the motion for charging order was not made on the LLCs; therefore, they were not a party to the motion; and
(3) there is no proof that Gallegos was a member of the LLCs such that he had an interest that could be charged.

Or, as the court put it: "He doesn't contend that the Secretary of State records are inaccurate. Nor does he deny that he's a member of the LLCs. He just argues that SPE LO hasn't proved it."

Gallegos lost on his first argument, that the California Secretary of State documents were not admissible, largely because no witness from the Secretary of State's office authenticated them (i.e., they were "hearsay"). The court rejected this argument because as public records, the court can and did take judicial notice of the documents.

Gallegos also lost on his second argument, which is that the notice of the motion given to the two LLCs by mail was insufficient. The court noted that personal service by a process server is not required, but notice by mail of the motion was adequate to satisfy the requirements of California law. It was also wholly unnecessary to make the LLCs a party to the motion for charging order.

This brings us to Gallegos last argument, which is that there was no proof that he was a member of the two LLCs. On this point, the court noted that prior California state court opinions require that a creditor present "substantial evidence" that the debtor has an interest in the LLC (or partnership) to be charged. However, given that the California Secretary of State documents only showed that Gallegos was a "manager" without also clearly showing that he was a "member," SPE failed on its burden of proof, and its motion would therefore be denied.

However, "[t]o avoid the possibility that Gallegos has avoided entry of a charging order by playing coy," the court would allow SPE to conduct discovery on the issue and resubmit the motion if it found that Gallegos also had a membership interest in the two LLCs in addition to being a manager.

CHAPTER 6

Parties to a Charging Order Proceeding

A charging order procedure is fundamentally a post-judgment enforcement action between the creditor and the debtor. As the moving party, the creditor is obviously a party to the proceeding.

The debtor is also a party to the proceeding so that the debtor may protect his or her own rights, such as where he or she might claim that a part of the distributions made from the LLC are exempt under state or federal law.

The real questions are whether the LLC is properly a party to a charging order proceeding, and whether it may appear and assert its own defenses. The answer to both is a qualified "maybe" that leans toward "no" in most cases.[1]

Take the case where a charging order is entered for the debtor's interest in an LLC, but the debtor no longer has (or perhaps never had) an interest in the LLC. Presumably, the LLC could intervene and defend against the entry of the charging order on the basis that there is nothing to be charged.

Why the LLC would want to do this, however, is the real question. Given that a charging order only places a lien on the debtor's interest, if the debtor has no interest, then the lien attaches to nothing but thin air. The LLC should be circumspect about spending legal fees and voluntarily inserting itself into a proceeding in which it has no interest.

However, many courts will make a finding in the charging order (or such a finding is implicit) that the debtor in fact has an interest, which might not be true. The question then becomes whether the LLC should appear and contest such an allegation in the motion, or ignore it. Both courses of action carry perils.

If the LLC doesn't appear and contest the order, it risks a finding that the debtor in fact owns an interest in the LLC when the debtor doesn't. On the other hand, because the LLC was not a party to the proceeding, this finding might

1. Certain states have included provisions in their LLC acts to the effect that the company in which the judgment-creditor holds an interest is not a necessary party to the issuance of the charging order. *See, e.g.*, Ky. Rev. Stat. Ann. § 275.260(6) ("the [LLC] is not a necessary party to an application for a charging order.").

later be challenged on due process grounds. However, contesting the finding later might prove to be substantially more expensive to the LLC than if it addressed the problem up front.

Conversely, if the LLC does appear and contest the order, it becomes a party—at least for purposes of the order ultimately issued—and the order will bind the LLC whichever way it goes. If the court finds that the LLC holds an interest, that finding will be binding upon the LLC, which then might not have a good avenue to appeal.

This dilemma typically arises in situations where the debtor once held an interest in the LLC but was subsequently divested of the interest. In that instance, the records the creditor will find will relate to the time when the debtor had an interest, and will assume that the debtor still holds the interest. This occurs often in post-judgment enforcement proceedings. It is therefore important that, where a member has been dissociated, careful contemporaneous records be kept. This is particularly true where there has been a "late disassociation" of a member, i.e., the member cashed out of the LLC shortly before the charging order proceedings began, or the LLC involuntarily disassociated the member because the member has failed to meet his or her obligations to the LLC.

In addition, the LLC records should clearly state that all of the member's LLC interest, and not just the economic interest, has been terminated or transferred.

CHAPTER 7

Jurisdiction

Jurisdiction over the Debtor

Once the forum court establishes personal jurisdiction and enters judgment against the debtor, that jurisdiction continues into post-judgment enforcement proceedings. The debtor remains before the court that entered the judgment whether the debtor continues to reside (if he or she ever did) in the state or not.

The forum court entering the judgment retains jurisdiction over the debtor for purposes of entering and enforcing a charging order. No cases have challenged a charging order issued by the forum court for lack of continuing personal jurisdiction over the debtor.

Jurisdiction Over the Nondebtor Members

Because a charging order requires compliance by only the LLC and not the nondebtor members, it is not necessary for the court that issues the charging order to have personal jurisdiction over the nondebtor members. The LLC Act does not suggest it, and no court opinion has required it.

Jurisdiction Over the LLC

Forum courts have encountered many more complications dealing with their personal jurisdiction over the LLC. The complications result from the particular LLC Act, the advocacy of the parties, and the particular facts of the case.

Of course, if the LLC is domiciled in the forum state, there is no issue of personal jurisdiction over the LLC. The efficient creditor will first seek charging orders against a judgment debtor's transferrable interest in a domestic LLC.

Difficulties can arise when the LLC is domiciled in another state and the creditor attempts to obtain a charging order from the forum court against the debtor's interest in a foreign LLC. The preliminary problem is the plain language found in the charging order statute that, perhaps unintentionally, limits charging orders to domestic LLCs. The underlying problem is that a court order, including a charging order, cannot compel a foreign LLC's compliance if the court has no personal jurisdiction over the foreign LLC unless the creditor takes steps to domesticate the charging order in the foreign jurisdiction.

The efficient creditor seeking to collect against the distributions made by a debtor or by a foreign LLC is not out of luck, but he or she must take the additional steps of registering the judgment and charging order, or in that jurisdiction seeking a charging order in the state where the LLC is domiciled, and enforce the charging order there.

Case Study: *Wells Fargo*[1]

Sabrina Barber, a Florida resident, was in deep financial distress because of large loans owed to Wells Fargo Bank and Regions Bank.

In 2009, Barber received $1 million from the sale of her Florida home. She deposited the proceeds into a "homestead" account with American Momentum Bank. Later that year, Barber used the funds and accrued interest to purchase a certificate of deposit from the same bank and designated the CD as "homestead" proceeds.

Barker transferred the CD funds to an AIG account in 2010, also designating that account as "homestead" proceeds. Later that year, Barber withdrew $227,026 from the AIG account to purchase a home in Florida.

In 2011 Barber formed Blaker Enterprises LLC. Barber transferred $641,350 from her AIG account, combined it with $228,650 from another AIG account, and opened a managed account for Blaker Enterprises LLC at TD Ameritrade with the $870,000. Later in 2011, Barber transferred $275,000 from the TDA account back to the AIG account, purportedly to avoid management fees on the latter.

In early 2012, Barber transferred $220,000 out of the AIG account, but later claimed not to know where the money went. Soon thereafter, Blaker Enterprises LLC set up a second TDA account, this one self-directed, into which $110,000 was transferred from the existing TDA account. Eventually, all of Blaker Enterprises LLC's funds were in the self-directed TDA account.

Barber testified that she intended to transfer the money in the second TDA account to an investment advisor in Mauritius. By the time that Wells Fargo and Regions sued Barber and Blaker Enterprises LLC, the accounts had been substantially depleted.

In 2013, a Florida state court entered a $62 million deficiency judgment against Barber and Blaker Enterprises LLC in favor of the banks. In 2014, the banks filed a complaint in the U.S. District Court for the Middle District of Florida and included a claim to foreclose on Barber's membership interest in Blaker Enterprises LLC, or at least for a charging order against Barber's interest. The defendants moved to dismiss the banks' attempt to foreclose on Barber's membership interest in Blaker Enterprises LLC, or for a charging order against that interest.

1. Wells Fargo Bank v. Barber, 2015 WL 470589 (M.D. Fla. Feb. 4, 2015).

The Florida debtor analogized its foreign LLC case to that of an earlier Florida state court's dealing with foreign corporations *Sargeant v. Al-Saleh*,[2] in which the Florida Fourth District Court of Appeals held that a Florida creditor could not compel a Florida debtor to turn over the stock certificates of an offshore corporation located outside of Florida. Instead, the creditor must seek relief in the foreign jurisdiction.

The federal court noted that Florida LLC law (like the law of all states) permits a judgment creditor to obtain a charging order against a debtor's interest in a domestic Florida LLC for the unpaid judgment plus post-judgment interest. The charging order establishes a lien against the debtor-member's interest in the LLC, channeling the distributions made by the LLC to the creditor instead of to the debtor-member.

A charging order lien is analogous to a security interest in a debtor's personal property under U.C.C. Article 9. If a person buys a car with a secured loan, the lender takes a lien against the car title to secure repayment of the note one has given the bank. If one fails to pay on the note, the creditor can foreclose on its lien, i.e., cause the car to be seized by the sheriff (or, more likely, a repo man) and sold at auction. Similarly, a charging order establishes for the creditor a lien in a debtor's interest in an LLC. In most states, the creditor can then foreclose on the lien under appropriate statutory circumstances (just like foreclosing the lien on one's car), meaning that the debtor's economic interest can be put up for auction.

The *only* property right against which a creditor gets a lien through the charging order process is the debtor-member's right to distributions. The creditor's charging order does not control the entire LLC interest (as is the case when a creditor levies on and sells stock), but has only the rights to distributions made by the LLC until the judgment is paid or expires.

If the judgment creditor forecloses and the LLC interest is sold at auction, the buyer gets only those distribution rights in perpetuity. The purchaser is not thereby a member or otherwise vested with the power to participate in the LLC's management. After foreclosure, however, the right to distribution is no longer limited to the duration of the judgment, but will survive the expiration of the judgment.

The difference between the perpetual loss of distribution consequent to foreclosure and a temporary loss of distributions, along with some misunderstandings about the purpose of a charging order, has bothered the bars of some states enough to convince their legislatures to amend their LLC laws to prevent a creditor from foreclosing the lien created by a charging order.

2. 137 So. 3d 432, 434 (Fla. 4th DCA 2014), *reh'g denied* (May 5, 2014), *review denied,* SC14-1120, 2014 WL 6460179 (Fla. 2014).

Still, most states allow creditors to foreclose on charging orders, Florida has unique formula. For charging order foreclosure purposes, Florida differentiates between single-member LLCs and multimember LLCs. Foreclosure is allowed in the case of a debtor-member's interest in a single-member LLC, but not in a multimember LLC. One might look at the law as effectively saying, "Florida debtors can't shield assets from creditors in a single-member LLC." Florida's position makes sense because historically the purpose of a charging order is to protect the nondebtor members from being forced into an involuntary partnership with another member's creditor, and not to create a protected piggy bank for some individual.

Case Study: *Barber*

Barber and Blaker Enterprises LLC presented the court with a twisty plot: Blaker Enterprises LLC is a Nevis LLC. Nevis is a small Caribbean island and part of the two-island Federation of St. Kitts and Nevis. It is a popular off-shore jurisdiction for business entity formation because it has an LLC ordinance that closely mirrors typical U.S. LLC law, but is domesticated far, far away on a resort island.

Barber and Blaker Enterprises LLC argued that the federal court for Florida lacked personal jurisdiction over the LLC so that the absence of such personal jurisdiction precluded the banks' foreclosure on the Florida resident's interest in Blaker Enterprises LLC. Blaker relied heavily on the Florida appellate court's ruling in *Sergeant* that lack of jurisdiction over the foreign share certificates precluded a Florida sale. Barber and Blaker Enterprises LLC argued that the banks could foreclose on the LLC organized in Nevis, only in Nevis.

The court disagreed. It reasoned that *Sergeant* involved certificated shares of a stock corporation while *Barber* involved an uncertificated interest in an LLC, which is "intangible personal property" having a situs where its owner resides. Given that Barber resided in Florida, her interests in Blaker Enterprises LLC were in Florida and subject to *in rem* jurisdiction in Florida.

Barber and Blaker Enterprises LLC next argued that Nevis law controlled both the charging order process and foreclosure of the charging order. Both Florida law and Nevis law allow for a charging order against the debtor-member's interest in an LLC; however, Florida law allows foreclosure with a single-member LLC, but Nevis law does not. Similarly, Nevis law allows the LLC to redeem the debtor-member's interest made subject to a charging order, but Florida law does not have such a provision. Given that the court was a federal court sitting in diversity jurisdiction, it applied the choice-of-law rules as if it were a state court sitting in that same district. Thus, Florida choice-of-law rules applied.

The base legal issue is whether the debtor-member's property interest in an LLC can be used to satisfy a judgment. If that interest is personal property, in particular an uncertificated interest in an LLC, the property is deemed to be located where the debtor resides. In *Barber*, the debtor resided in Florida, so the court properly applied Florida law, not Nevis law. Harmonizing this result and rationale with the definition of a limited liability company as a domestic LLC in the Florida charging order statute is challenging.

Finally, under Florida law, the court analyzed whether foreclosure was necessary, or whether the distributions from the LLC to the charged interest were likely to pay off the judgment in a reasonable time.

By way of example, if a creditor with a $10,000 judgment holds a charging order against a debtor's interest in an investment LLC paying $2,000 per month in distributions, the creditor will see the judgment paid off in five months, so there is no need to allow the creditor to foreclose.

In contrast, Barber owed the Banks over $62 million, and it was nearly impossible that distributions from Blakely Enterprises LLC would ever come close to satisfying that debt or even the interest on the judgment debt. Therefore, the court ruled that foreclosure on LLC interests is a possible remedy under a charging order and denied Barber's and Blakey Enterprises LLC's motion to dismiss on this point.

Case Study: *Mahalo Investments*[3]

First Citizens Bank & Trust Company, Inc. (FCB) won a judgment of over $3 million against Mark Epstein, Andrew Kelly, and their company, Mahalo Investments III, LLC, in the State Court for Cobb County, Georgia.

During the post-judgment discovery of the debtors' assets, FCB learned that Epstein and Kelly owned interests in several additional LLCs. FCB then filed, in that same case and with the same case number, an application for charging order against the debtors' interests in the LLCs. The application was granted, and the charging order was issued.

The debtors appealed the decision to the Georgia Court of Appeals, arguing that it was improper for the state court that had issued the judgment to also issue the charging order, and instead (they argued) FCB should have brought a separate action against the LLCs in whatever states those LLCs had been formed. The opinion doesn't identify these states, and as we shall see, it really doesn't matter in Georgia.

As to limited liability companies, Georgia law provides:

> On application to a court of competent jurisdiction by any judgment creditor of a member or of any assignee of a member, the court may charge the limited liability company interest of the member or such

3. Mahalo Inv. III, LLC v. First Citizens Bank & Trust Co., Inc., 2015 WL 687922 (Ga. App. Feb. 19, 2015).

> assignee with payment of the unsatisfied amount of the judgment with interest . . . .[4]

In an earlier RULPA case before the Georgia Supreme Court, *Prodigy Centers/Atlanta v. T-C Assoc., Ltd.*,[5] the Peach State's highest court commented upon the charging order provisions found in both the LLC and limited partnership statutes there:

> [E]ach statute provides a means by which a judgment creditor or a partner may cause the diversion of monetary payments the partner expects to receive from the partnership to the partner's judgment creditor. Under both statutory schemes, the judgment creditor must initiate a collateral proceeding in which the creditor seeks a court order charging the debtor partner's partnership interest with payment of the unsatisfied amount of the judgment, or serves process of garnishment on the partnership. . . . A judgment creditor must initiate the identical collateral proceedings in order to attach a lien to a chose in action.

So what is a "collateral proceeding"? The debtors argued that it meant that FCB was required to bring a new lawsuit against the LLCs whose membership interests were to be charged.

"No," said the Georgia Court of Appeals. That language means only that the creditor must bring a "proceeding" in the sense of an application for charging order in the state court. There is utterly no need to initiate a new case involving the same parties; instead, the same court can issue the charging order after a hearing on the application.

Appellants next argued that the Georgia State Court was not "a court of competent jurisdiction" because it did not have personal jurisdiction over the LLCs whose interests were charged. This argument presumed that the LLCs whose interests were to be charged were required to be made parties to the application proceeding. The debtors argued that the LLCs were affected, directly or indirectly, by the charging order and for that reason needed to be named as party defendants.

The charging order provisions found in Georgia law (which largely track the RULLPA and ULLCA) are silent on the issue, i.e., they do not say whether an LLC (or LP) whose interests are charged must be made a party to the lawsuit.

The court then noted that the holder of a charging order does not gain any management rights in an LLC or partnership, but only the right to distributions as they are made to the debtor's/member's interest. Thus, the most important part of the opinion reads:

---

4. OCGA § 14-11-504(c).
5. 269 Ga. 522, 501 S.E.2d 209 (1998) (internal citations omitted).

> We glean from these provisions that the charging order is a mechanism by which a judgment creditor can attach a member's limited liability company interest to satisfy an unpaid judgment, but that the charging order does not permit the judgment creditor to replace the member or otherwise interfere in the governance of the limited liability company. Moreover, it is the judgment debtor's right to possession of distributions in the future that is essentially being levied or charged. Thus, from the limited liability company's standpoint, it is business as usual except that any distributions to the member subject to the charging order are diverted to the judgment creditor. Because the limited liability company has no right or direct interest that is affected by the charging order, we see no reason why it must be added as a party to the proceeding to obtain the charging order. See Bank of America, N.A. v. Freed, 983 N.E.2d 509, 520–521 (Ill. App. Ct. 2012) (rejecting contention that a court must obtain jurisdiction over a limited liability company or partnership in order to charge a judgment debtor's distributional interest in those entities under similar charging order statutes). Thus, we hold that under Georgia's limited liability company act, it is only necessary for a court to have jurisdiction over the judgment debtor to have the authority to enter charging orders against the judgment debtor's interest.

Thus, the state court's issuance of the charging order against Epstein's and Kelly's interests in the LLCs was quite appropriate, even if the Georgia courts did not have personal jurisdiction over those entities, and the charging order was affirmed.

No subsequent reported case history explores whether the Georgia charging order can be enforced against the foreign LLC as a judicial order against an entity subject to the limited specific personal jurisdiction of Georgia or only as a contractual matter asserting the Georgia debtor's contract rights against the foreign LLC. The distinction would matter in addressing a dispute about the amount of the distributions owed the Georgia debtor and the power of the Georgia court to adjudicate that dispute.

Case Study: *Rockstone Capital*[6]

Edwards entered into a stipulated judgment with the creditor and agreed to pay the creditor certain monthly payments; however, Edwards did not make the scheduled payments, and the creditor sought to enforce the judgment against Edwards in Connecticut Superior Court.

---

6. Rockstone Capital, LLC v. Marketing Horizons, Ltd., 2013 WL 4046597 (Conn. Super. July 17, 2013) (unpublished).

Edwards owned interests in two limited liability companies: Marketing Ventures, LLC and Nonprofit Solutions, LLC. The creditor filed a motion for charging order in Connecticut seeking to charge Edwards's interests in these two companies.

Edwards objected to the motion against Nonprofit Solutions, LLC, claiming *inter alia* that because Nonprofit Solutions, LLC was not a Connecticut company, the court lacked jurisdiction to enter the charging order.

The court first pointed out that Edwards had no standing to assert a claim for lack of personal jurisdiction on behalf of Nonprofit Solutions, LLC:

> Nonprofit Solutions, LLC is not seeking dismissal, nor is it a party. Edwards seeks dismissal on Nonprofit Solutions, LLC's behalf. Edwards has asserted no basis upon which his standing to do so is conferred.

In other words, if Nonprofit Solutions, LLC desired to object to the motion, it needed to appear before the court to do so; Edwards could not raise any objection for it. Nonprofit Solutions, LLC would have to intervene—or as law professor Arthur Miller once put it, "must parachute into the middle of the case"—to assert any objection.

Beyond that, Nonprofit Solutions, LLC was not, and did not need to be, a party to the proceeding because the motion was not directed against Nonprofit Solutions, LLC:

> Nonprofit Solutions, LLC is not a party of record in this action. The court is not exerting jurisdiction over Nonprofit Solutions, LLC. Defendant Edwards offers no authority for his assertion that a court must have jurisdiction over a limited liability company in order to enforce a judgment against an individual who is a member of that entity.
>
> The statute governing the issuance of a charging order against a limited liability company . . . does not require that the limited liability company be made a party to an action seeking such an order. It is not necessary to make a limited liability company a party because a charging order merely gives the judgment creditor the rights of an assignee of the member's interest in the limited liability company . . . [A]n assignment of a limited liability company interest entitles the assignee to receive only the distributions to which the assignor would be entitled . . . An assignment does not dissolve the limited liability company or entitle the assignee to participate in the management and affairs of the limited liability company or to become or exercise any rights of a member . . . An action seeking a charging order does not impact the rights or interests of a limited liability company to the degree necessary to require that it be made a party in order for the action to proceed. . . . The court has jurisdiction over Edwards' interest in the two limited liability com-

> panies, not over the limited liability companies themselves. [Internal quotations and citations omitted.]

With that, the Connecticut trial court entered the charging order against foreign LLCs over Edwards' objections.

Case Study: *Shanghai Real Estate*[7]

Shanghai Real Estate Ltd. obtained a judgment in Connecticut against Mark and Linda Greenberg. To enforce the judgment, Shanghai sought to collect against the personal assets of the Greenbergs, including their investment assets, which seemed to mostly consist of ownership of numerous limited liability company (LLC) interests.

Shanghai asked the court to enter charging orders against 34—yes, 34—limited liability companies in which the Greenbergs had various interests. Twenty-one companies were registered with the Connecticut Secretary of State and were indisputably subject to personal jurisdiction in Connecticut. The interests in these LLCs were owned by Mark Greenberg, and he stipulated to an order charging the interests of these 21 companies.

In addition, Mark Greenberg owned nine more LLCs, and Linda Greenberg owned three more LLCs. All were out-of-state (foreign) LLCs not registered in Connecticut. The couple objected to the Connecticut court issuing charging orders against the interests of these out-of-state LLCs on the basis that the court had no personal jurisdiction over them. The court rejected this argument:

> The proposed order which the plaintiff submitted to the court with its brief does not order the foreign companies to do anything. The proposed order is directed to the defendants only. It orders the defendants to:
>
> (1) provide the plaintiff's attorney with the name and address of each of the managers and managing members of each of the foreign companies;
>
> (2) charge the defendants' interests in the foreign companies to pay all present and future distributions, credits, drawings, or payments due to the defendants to be paid to the plaintiffs until the judgment is satisfied in full, including, interest and costs;
>
> (3) take no loans, directly or indirectly, from the foreign companies until the judgment is satisfied in full, including interest and costs;

---

7. Shanghai Real Estate Ltd. v. Greenberg, 2014 WL 660624 (Conn. Super. Jan. 28, 2014) (unpublished).

> (4) not undertake, enter into or consummate any sale, encumbrance, hypothecation or modification of the defendants' membership interest in any of the foreign companies except in the context of a bona fide sale to an unrelated third party and the defendants shall provide ten business days' notice of any such sale to the plaintiff's attorney.
>
> The language of the order being sought by the plaintiff is unobjectionable. It is directed to the defendants only. The court has jurisdiction over the defendants. So, even if the defendants would have standing to object to an order directed to foreign companies, the plaintiff is not currently seeking such an order. Accordingly, the defendants' objection to the application for a charging order is overruled.

With that, the Connecticut trial court entered the charging order against the dozen out-of-state LLCs that were not registered in Connecticut.

CASE STUDY: *SPATES*[8]

Christopher Spates owed $82,730.64 in child-support obligations to three different mothers, and the Child Support Division of the Texas Office of the Attorney General (OAG) was trying to collect on the three child-support judgments.

Spates was the sole member of Prodigy Services, LLC, which got into a dispute with another business, Eni U.S. Operating Company, and Prodigy sued Eni in Harris County, Texas (where Houston is located).

The OAG got wind of the lawsuit, moved to intervene, and asked the court in the Prodigy lawsuit against Eni to impose charging orders and capture any proceeds that Prodigy might win to satisfy the domestic support judgments. A week later, Prodigy and Eni settled, the terms of which required Eni to pay Prodigy $257,500. Apparently worried about the OAG's liens, Eni asked the trial court to enter an order, which it did, allowing Eni to pay the $257,500 into the court's registry.

The OAG then filed a request for a charging order against Spates's interest in Prodigy Services LLC, and requested that the court disburse $82,730.64 to the OAG to satisfy Spates's child-support judgments. Over Prodigy's objections, the court granted the OAG's request.

Prodigy then filed a writ of mandamus with the Texas Court of Appeals seeking to have that court order the district court to distribute all of the Eni settlement to Prodigy instead. The court of appeals agreed, and the district court then ordered the $257,500 paid to Prodigy.

---

8. Spates v. Office of the Attorney General, 485 S.W.3d 546, 2016 WL 354417 (Tex. App. 14th Dist. Jan. 28, 2016).

The next day, however, the district court entered the charging order requested by the OAG in the amount $94,376.54 (the amount to which Spates's child-support obligation had grown in the interim), and directed that any funds that Prodigy distributed to Spates were to instead go to the OAG and the three mothers until the obligation was paid down.

Spates and Prodigy both appealed the charging order, contending that the district court did not have jurisdiction to enter the charging order (recalling that the case before the district court was the Eni litigation, and Spates personally was not a party to that case). They also contended that the OAG was not entitled to a charging order because it did not serve Spates as the debtor with a notice of the request for charging order.

The procedural sword cuts both ways, however, and given that Spates was not a party to the underlying Eni litigation, he also lacked standing to appeal the district court's order, and his appeal was dismissed on this ground at the outset. Prodigy could still appeal, however, and the court of appeals took up its arguments.

First, the court of appeals had to address whether the charging order was even appealable as a final order, holding ultimately that it was because it did finally resolve the rights of the OAG to Spates's distributions from Prodigy.

Prodigy argued that the district court lacked both personal jurisdiction over Spates, because he was not a party to the lawsuit, and subject matter jurisdiction, because the Eni litigation did not involve the OAG or family-law issues. In other words, Prodigy contended that the OAG should have sought the charging order in the family-law court that was hearing the child-support matter, not in the Eni business litigation.

The court rejected both arguments. The court reasoned that a charging order is the exclusive remedy for creating a lien on the debtor's interest in an LLC, and the OAG is empowered by Texas law to create liens on a debtor's assets to collect on a child-support order. In that context, the court found no Texas law limiting OAG's right to enforce the judgments in any case where the debtor has any right to payment. Thus, it was appropriate that the district court entered the charging order against Spates's interest in Prodigy in the Eni business litigation.

The district court entering the charging order did not need Spates to be a party to the Eni litigation. The court explained:

> [I]t was not necessary that Spates be made a party for the trial court to have jurisdiction to enter the charging order. The Business Organizations Code does not require that the judgment debtor be made a party to an action in which a judgment creditor files an application for a charging order against the debtor's membership interest in the limited liability company. Additionally, the charging order in this case is not directed to Spates and it imposes no obligations on him. Likewise,

> the charging order does not entitle the OAG to reach the proceeds of Prodigy's settlement with Eni or Prodigy's property to satisfy the OAG's three money judgments against Spates.

In other words, the charging order merely created a lien on Spates's distributional interest for an existing judgment, and so it was wholly unnecessary that he be joined as a party in the Eni litigation. This same reasoning also took care of Prodigy's procedural arguments, and the court of appeals thus affirmed the district court, leaving its charging order for Spate's distributions from the LLC in place. The issue was not personal jurisdiction over or the state of organization of the LLC, but the absence in the business lawsuit of personal jurisdiction over the judgment debtor. Observing that Spate had not moved to intervene and that the OAG was merely enforcing three judgments already entered against Spate, the Texas Court of Appeals ruled such personal jurisdiction over the judgment debtor was unnecessary.

CHAPTER 8

Discovery

Prior to bringing a motion for charging order, typically the creditor will often engage in substantial post-judgment investigation and discovery to establish the grounds for the motion—namely, that the debtor currently holds an interest in the LLC and the extent of that interest.

Nonjudicial Discovery

It is easy enough to simply hold an examination of the debtor to find out what assets and interests the debtor holds, but that ignores a practical wisdom that has been learned by creditors since time immemorial: Debtors will often tell half-truths and outright lies to protect their assets, even when those debtors are under oath. In fact, most creditors' rights attorneys will presume as much and instead concentrate on building a record of the debtor's lack of veracity to use at some critical point where the debtor will be asking the court to rely upon his or her word as to some issue.

Concepts of best collection practices therefore require the creditor to investigate the debtor's affairs before formal post-judgment asset discovery commences. This is ordinarily done by the creditor running the debtor's name, address, and Social Security number through one of the several database services to compile a substantial dossier on the debtor. This dossier will include, among other things, a credit report that will disclose financial inquiries, i.e., that the debtor has opened or attempted to open bank or other financial accounts, and has credit cards.

LLCs in which the debtor has an interest are discovered not from governmental information about the LLCs themselves, which often does not reveal the debtor's interest unless the debtor is listed as the registered agent for the entity, but rather from bank and other financial accounts on which the debtor has signatory capacity. Thus, if the debtor has opened an account with a local bank, the creditor can then either attempt to levy on the account and (this is usually done concurrently) issue a subpoena to the bank for information about the account, i.e., bank statements, copies of signature cards, and cancelled checks. If the account is not held in the name of the debtor, but rather in XYZ LLC, then the creditor has grounds to inquire further about the members of XYZ LLC.

Likewise, information about the debtor's credit cards can be an invaluable source of information to find an LLC because often the debtor will use the LLC to pay off balances and the various annual fees for the LLC itself. The same goes for property records and utility payments, which might indicate an asset owned by an LLC controlled by the debtor.

In addition to financial searches for the debtor, the record in the underlying case will provide clues, if not outright admissions by the debtor, as to the debtor's interests in an LLC.

Written Discovery

Some states authorize written discovery to be propounded upon the debtor in the judgment enforcement phase of the proceeding. If so, this can be a cheap, simple, and expedient way to obtain information on the debtor's interest in any LLC and the extent of that interest. Documents may be sought from the debtor relating to the LLC that might be in the debtor's possession, such as the operating agreement and IRS Form K-1.

Debtor Examination

In the majority of cases, information on whether the debtor has any interests in LLCs, and the extent of those interests, will be developed through a post-judgment examination of the debtor.

A debtor's examination is technically a hearing in open court, but it often is conducted away from the courtroom, such as in a free conference room or jury room, the hallway, and the courthouse cafeteria. The procedure is much like a deposition, with the main difference being that the judicial officer is available to immediately resolve objections and throw the debtor in jail if the debtor refuses to answer a legitimate question about applicable assets.

Although a creditor is not usually required to bring his or her own court reporter (they are almost never supplied by the court), it is difficult to imagine the utility of such an examination without making a record of the debtor's responses. The record can also be quite useful if the debtor refuses to answer a question, thus requiring judicial intervention.

Facially, the purpose of a debtor's examination is to learn information about the debtor's assets and finances, but if the creditor has done its investigatory work ahead of time, this often means gaining little more than the debtor's on-the-record confirmation of the assets discovered during that process. Some creditors' rights attorneys would argue that the primary purpose of a debtor's examination is to catch the debtor in lies regarding applicable assets to impeach the debtor's credibility when the creditor seeks more invasive remedies, such as the appointment of a receiver.

Many statutes that provide for debtor examination also authorize the court to enter a turnover order at the conclusion of the examination. The turnover order typically will require the debtor to turn over to the levying officer (usually the local sheriff) those nonexempt assets that were discovered by the creditor during the examination. The turnover order can be useful in regard to the debtor's LLC interests where, for instance, those interests have been certificated, and the only way for the creditor to perfect a security interest in those interests is to have physical possession of the certificates. However, the charging order procedure itself makes no distinction between LLC interests that have been certificated and those that have not; the same procedure is followed in both events.

Third-Party Examination of the LLC or Other Members

Nearly all states allow for some procedure that allows a creditor to conduct an examination of a third party who is believed by the creditor to have information that may be of use in discovering the debtor's assets. Such examinations typically require a court order and a showing as to the information sought. If the court issues such an order, creditors in serving the third party will often include a subpoena *duces tecum* seeking certain documentary evidence; indeed, in a large number of such events, it is only the documents that are sought by the creditor, and the third party is never required to physically appear at the examination.

Third-party examinations of the LLC, through its designated representative or of the other members, may be useful to the creditor in determining whether the debtor still has an interest in the LLC and the extent of the interest.

For the LLC or other member's part, the typical objections to subpoenas may be raised, such as whether the examination will be held within the statutory distance of the court, an overbroad or invasive request for documents or information, etc. The procedure for objecting typically is to file a motion to quash the subpoena, but note that there are often short periods (often mere days within receipt) during which such a motion must be timely filed.

CHAPTER 9

The Motion for Charging Order

Essentials of the Motion

To obtain a charging order, the creditor files a motion for charging order. Typically, this is done by a "noticed motion," i.e., a motion that is set by the court to be heard at a particular date and time, and for which ample notice is given to the debtor and the LLC or its members, although the latter are not necessary parties to the motion (the LLC or its members should be given notice of the pendency of the charging order motion, but the court may enter the charging order even if they don't show up). The giving of notice of the motion for charging order is considered in the following chapter.

Ex Parte Motions

It is possible, however, for a creditor to obtain a charging order ex parte, i.e., without notice (or with short notice) to the debtor, the LLC, or its members. A creditor would attempt to do this when the creditor is concerned that the debtor may attempt to assign his or her interest away prior to the entry of the charging order.

California is the only state to have adopted a procedure for charging orders. It is unnecessary in the Golden State to seek a charging order on an *ex parte* basis because the mere filing of the motion for charging order creates a temporary lien on the debtor's interest.[1] If the motion is granted, the temporary lien becomes permanent until the judgment is paid; if not, the temporary lien simply evaporates.[2]

In other states, it may be possible to accomplish the same result by moving the court to enter either a temporary charging order pending the charging order hearing, or a temporary restraining order (TRO) against the debtor to prohibit the debtor from alienating his or her interest in the meantime. However, motions

1. Calif. Code of Civ. Pro. § 708.320(a).
2. *Id.* § 708.320(b).

of any kind *ex parte* are usually disfavored, and those that are *ex parte* "without notice," i.e., the creditor goes directly to the judge without advising the debtor, the LLC, or its members, are heavily disfavored and may draw the ire of the judge.

Factual Elements of the Motion

A motion for charging order must make certain minimal factual representations to the court. These representations should be supported by evidence and references to the record.

The motion should recite that a valid judgment has been entered against the debtor. A copy of the judgment typically is not attached to the motion, but the motion will refer to the document number and date in the court's files. If the judgment is an older judgment, the motion might need to additionally state that the judgment has not expired or has been renewed.

The motion should also recite that the debtor currently holds an interest in the LLC. The supporting documentary evidence should be attached to the motion because by this stage, the creditor should have already obtained this information through whatever means, including post-judgment discovery.

It is usually not sufficient for a creditor to merely allege that the creditor suspects the debtor has an interest in the LLC. Typically, based upon the information already collected, it will be possible to allege that the debtor holds an interest in the LLC. In other instances, pleading "on information and belief" may be necessary. Such a circumstance might be where the debtor was unclear, in the course of his or her examination, of the exact name of the LLC at issue. As previously discussed, should a charging order be issued with respect to a debtor's interest in an LLC when, in fact, the debtor holds no interest in that LLC, effectively there is a lien against nothing, and no injury is suffered by any third party.

On the other hand, it is probably unnecessary for a creditor to recite the exact amount of the debtor's interest in the LLC. It may be impossible for the creditor to discern its interest in the LLC when the debtor's interest fluctuates. This may occur if other members are admitted or withdraw from the LLC, such as in the case of a hedge fund with many investors.

Legal Elements of the Motion

The motion should state the statutory authority under which the charging order is sought, e.g., "Texas Business Organizations Code § 101.112." In addition, if a state has a procedural statute or rule that governs charging orders, the motion should refer to it.

Accompanying Declaration

The motion should include an attached declaration or affidavit that authenticates the creditor's evidence that the debtor has an interest in the LLC.

This declaration or affidavit is similar to how evidence is authenticated on a motion for summary judgment.

Accompanying Brief

Many courts require that a motion be accompanied by a brief, which in many cases will be redundant to the motion; however, it is a good practice to accompany the motion with a brief, even if not required. The brief gives the court a short background on the case and cites to several of the leading charging order decisions in the jurisdiction. This provides comfort to a judge who might not be familiar with the charging order remedy.

The complexity of a brief will, of course, vary with the complexity of the facts underlying a charging order. In some cases, such as where a charging order is sought against multiple entities, it is helpful to include a chart that shows the court the relationship of the debtor to each entity.

Ancillary Provisions

Creditors often desire that the charging order include various ancillary provisions, such as those intended to prevent "backdoor distributions" made to the debtor by way of loans, "consulting fees," etc. Both the application and brief should set out the provisions that are desired and the evidentiary basis for seeking those provisions. The following case study illustrates why.

Case Study: *Law*[3]

Creditor Robert Law held an Oregon judgment against Debtor Ronald Zemp. Law moved for the entry of a charging order against Zemp's interests in four limited partnerships and a limited liability company (collectively, the companies) in which Zemp was involved as either the general partner of the partnerships or as manager of the LLC.

The form of the charging order proposed by Law contained, in addition to the typical language of such orders which placed liens on Zemp's interests, five additional provisions. These additional provisions were as follows:

1. The companies were to make no loans;
2. The companies were to make no capital acquisitions without the approval of the creditor or the court;
3. The companies were not to sell or modify any interests without the approval of the creditor or the court;

3. Law v. Zemp, 408 P.3d 1045 (Or. 2018).

4. The companies were to provide lots of information to the creditor, including their partnership or operating agreements, federal and state income tax returns, balance sheets, etc.; and
5. The companies were to provide financials to the creditor within 30 days of the close of each accounting period.

None of these limitations expressly authorized by Oregon partnership and LLC law, which merely provides—as nearly all such statutes do—that the court may charge (lien) a debtor's interest in such companies until the judgment has been paid in full, and until that time the creditor is to be considered only a voluntary assignee of the interests who carries almost no other rights than the lien rights.

Zemp didn't defend against Law's motion, but the companies appeared and asserted various objections. First, the companies claimed that Zemp held no interest in the companies. Second, the companies claimed that the five ancillary provisions mentioned above were not authorized by Oregon law and would adversely affect the companies' operations.

Law made various arguments of his own, including that Zemp actually controlled the companies and was operating them as a "class asset protection program" rather than as bona fide commercial enterprises.

The trial court overruled the companies' first objection that Zemp had no interest, and then granted the charging order with four of the ancillary provisions, leaving out only the one that required the companies to provide various information and tax returns to Law.

Making its way up to the Oregon Court of Appeals, the case presented that court with the issue of whether the ancillary provisions allowed by the trial court were proper. The higher court noted that although the ancillary provisions were not provided by Oregon's partnership and LLC laws, there exists a general statute that allows a court to "make all other orders, directions, accounts and inquiries the judgment debtor might have made or that the circumstances of the case might require."

Under this general statute, the court of appeals held as to the four partnerships that the trial court had the power to order the companies to disclose financial information because Zemp himself (as general partner or manager) had that power. However, given that Zemp did not have the unilateral power to make loans, capital acquisitions, or change the interests, those provisions were improper. Even as to the last point, the court of appeals remanded the case back to the trial court to determine whether those provisions were necessary to ensure the companies' compliance with the charging order.

As to the LLC, the court of appeals held that the general statute was not authorized because the Oregon LLC Act did not have a provision that incorporated it by reference (unlike the Oregon Limited Partnership Act). Therefore, all the ancillary provisions were improper as to the LLC.

The court of appeal's ruling satisfied neither Law nor the companies, so everybody appealed the decision to the Oregon Supreme Court.

Oregon's highest court first set out a lengthy review of the history of Oregon's partnership and LLC acts, particularly as they related to charging orders. The court noted that charging orders exist to prevent "an obvious invasion of the rights and interests of nondebtor partners and resulted in disruption of the partnership business and, often, a forced dissolution of the partnership," which would occur if the creditor simply levied on a debtor's interest, as happens with corporate shares.

Against this historical backdrop, the court then looked at the particular issues in this case, starting with the ancillary provisions as directed to Zemp's four partnerships.

The companies argued that ancillary provisions should not be allowed with the partnerships because—their argument distilled to its essence—the general statute allowing courts to make additional provisions to effectuate their orders had been superseded by the specific charging order provisions of the Limited Partnership Act, i.e., they argued the "general rule" which is that "general rules are generally inapplicable."

The court didn't buy the argument that the Oregon legislature intended to cut out the general statute when it enacted Oregon's partnership laws, however. To the contrary, the drafters of Oregon's ULPA anticipated that supporting law could come from other provisions of Oregon law. That the charging order remedy is supposed to be the "exclusive remedy" under Oregon's statute did not change that.

Yet, even the general statute had its limitations, and as applied here it meant that ancillary provisions could be included so long as they did not unduly interfere with the business of the partnerships. The key here is balancing the rights of the creditor, the partnership, and the nondebtor partners. Thus:

> What that standard means, as a practical matter, is that, if a court has reason to believe that the charging order by itself cannot effectively convey to the judgment creditor the debtor-partner's right to distributions and profits—as might happen, for example, if the limited partnership exists only to shelter assets from creditors and has no business that will generate distributions or profits in the ordinary sense of the words, or has been structured in or operated in such a way as to allow money to be transferred to the debtor-partner or his or her agents through a mechanism other than formal distribution or profit sharing—the court may issue ancillary orders that will ensure that the charge on the judgment creditor's share is not evaded. And while the court would be expected to craft its orders, if possible, to avoid interference in the partnership's management, there may be circumstances in which it is not

> possible to effectuate the goal of charging the judgment creditor's share of distributions and profits without some degree of interference in the business. As long as the order effectuates a reasonable balance between the two objectives, it would be authorized.

This brought the court to Zemp's LLC. The court noted the difference identified by the court of appeals, which was that Oregon's partnership law made a reference to the general statute, but the Oregon LLC Act did not. Here, the creditor made the quite rational argument that courts have inherent powers to do certain things so to as to effectuate their orders. The court agreed, noting the necessity of such powers to balance the interests of the creditor, the LLC, and the nondebtor members.

Having recognized the power of the courts to issue ancillary provisions to effectuate a charging order through a long and well-researched discussion, the court then turned to whether the particular ancillary provisions in this case were appropriate.

The court thought not, largely because there was no record evidence that the provisions were necessary—the only proof the creditor offered was that Zemp owned the interests without providing further evidence that these ancillary provisions were necessary:

> The court could not determine, on the basis of that evidence alone, that the ancillary orders were so crucial to the effectiveness of the remedy that the court sought to provide (i.e., access to the debtor-partner's or debtor-member's distributional interest in the partnership or limited liability company) and their effect on the companies' management was so incidental that, on balance, the orders were justified. It follows that none of the challenged ancillary orders were authorized.

Thus, the decision of the court of appeals was reversed and remanded back to the trial court for "further proceedings," presumably to allow the parties to come forward with evidence as to whether the ancillary provisions were justified by the evidence.

CHAPTER 10

Notice of the Motion

A motion for charging order is unique insofar as the parties are required to be given notice of the motion. Both the debtor and the LLC (or, depending on a given statute, its members) must be given notice of the charging order.

Service vs. Simple Notice

Most statutes do not define the type of notice that must be given, and in those jurisdictions, it is usually adequate that notice be given by mail. Some statutes, however, such as California's, require "service of a notice of motion," which means that a process server (or other person authorized to make service) must physically deliver a copy of the notice of motion to the parties.

The best practice is to use a process server in every case to serve the notice of motion of charging order to mitigate the chance of a dispute as to whether the notice was actually received. The debtor has few defenses to begin with, and the LLC has none, such that often the only thing that they can argue to the court is that they did not receive the notice (even if they did).

How Notice Is Given to the LLC

The statutes typically give little or no guidance as to how notice to the LLC is to be given. If the California statute is any guidepost, it provides that service must be made on either the LLC itself or on all of the LLC's members. Giving notice to all the members may not be practical, however, either due to their number or because the creditor often has no way of knowing who they are. The best and often easiest practice is to serve the registered agent for the LLC at the registered agent's listed address.[1]

Note that giving notice to counsel for the LLC usually is insufficient absent a representation by counsel that they are authorized to receive such notice. Counsel often will complain when the LLC is served and accuse the creditor (or creditor's counsel) of improperly communicating with a party known to be represented by counsel. This complaint is meritless because it is the LLC that is required to be

1. Or wherever the registered agent is found, noting that individual registered agents often do a poor job of advising the Secretary of State's office when they move elsewhere. Indeed, a creditor may be required to initiate a "skip trace" investigation to find the registered agent.

provided with notice of the motion for charging order. However, in such a case, it is usually good practice to contact such counsel first and inquire whether they will accept the notice on behalf of their client.

Proof of Notice

Once notice has been given to the debtor and the LLC (directly or through its members), the creditor should file a Proof of Notice of Motion for Charging Order with the court to establish for the record that notice has been given.

CHAPTER 11

Drafting the Proposed Charging Order

The motion for charging order should be accompanied by a proposed charging order, which is often required by a local rule of court to not be filed, but instead be delivered (often electronically) to the court.

Essential Provisions

The proposed charging order shall recite that a motion for charging order has been made and that notice of motion for charging order has been given to the debtor and to the LLC (or its members). The order should then state to the effect that:

> For the reasons set forth in the creditor's Motion for Charging Order, and attachments thereto, the Charging Order will be granted. The debtor's interest in [name of LLC] is hereby charged pursuant to [the statute under which the Charging Order is authorized], until the judgment in favor of ____________________ is paid in full.

Ancillary Provisions

Almost routinely, creditors will include additional provisions in the charging order to give it teeth, i.e., make it more useful in enforcing the judgment. Note, however, that these provisions are typically not authorized by the charging order statute, but must come from some other law. That other law is usually some generic statute or case law to the effect that a court make such other or additional orders to give effect to the judgments and orders of the court. An example is found in California Code of Civil Procedure § 187:

> When jurisdiction is, by the Constitution or this Code, or by any other statute, conferred on a Court or judicial officer, all the means necessary to carry it into effect are also given; and in the exercise of this jurisdiction, if the course of proceeding be not specifically pointed out by this Code or the statute, any suitable process or mode of proceeding

> may be adopted which may appear most conformable to the spirit of this Code.

Many states have similar generic statutes, whereas in others it may be found in case law; however, it is under this general law, and not the charging order authorizing statute, that a creditor will seek to include ancillary provisions.

Note that a creditor must include a request for these ancillary provisions in the motion for charging order and prove up the need for these provisions with admissible evidence.[1]

Prohibiting or Imputing Loans and Other Compensation

To circumvent the effect of a charging order, a debtor may ask the LLC to pass money or other assets to the debtor in a way that is not normally treated as a distribution. These backdoor distributions frequently include the LLC making a loan to the debtor; paying the debtor a salary, consulting fee, or management fee, etc.; paying other debts of the debtor (often paying down credit cards); or doing any or all of the above to some person close to the debtor (an insider), such as the debtor's spouse.

A well-drafted charging order will usually have provisions that either prohibit the LLC from making loans or otherwise compensating the debtor or an insider, or that treat (impute) those loans or other compensation as in the way of a distribution.

Such a provision might read:

> The debtor is hereby prohibited from taking any loans or other compensation or inurement, however described, from the [name of entity], and if any such loans, other compensation or inurement is made to the debtor, then such loans, other compensation or inurement (collectively referred to in this paragraph as "benefits") shall be treated as if a distribution has been made by the [name of entity] in violation of this Charging Order to the debtor. If the debtor receives any such benefits, the debtor shall immediately turn such benefits over to the creditor, not to exceed ten (10) days of the debtor's receipt of the benefits. For purposes of this paragraph, the term "debtor" shall include all persons and entities who are related or subordinate to the debtor.

Note that this provision is also binding upon the debtor as well as the LLC, recalling that charging orders generally also bind both the debtor and the LLC.

---

1. *See* "Case Study: *Law*," *supra*, at pg. 9-3.

Requiring Information from the LLC

A creditor will also frequently attempt to include provisions in the charging order that require the LLC to provide a wealth of information about the LLC to the creditor, such as the profitability of the LLC and how much in distributions are being made to all members. The creditor's rationale for including these provisions is that otherwise the creditor will not be able to monitor the distributions.

The courts almost always reject these provisions for a variety of reasons, not the least of which is that the creditor would be violating the financial privacy of the LLC and its nondebtor members.

This does not mean that the creditor is completely out of luck, however, because the creditor can typically require the debtor in a debtor's exam to bring to court whatever information the debtor has received from the LLC, and possibly also request from the LLC such other information as the creditor requires. A creditor might also have a receiver appointed for the debtor, and the receiver may be able to assert the debtor's rights to obtain information from the LLC.

Unequal Distributions

Normally, a distribution tracks each member's ownership percentage, i.e., if Able, Baker, Charlie, and Donny each own a 25-percent interest in an LLC, then the distribution of $10,000 in profits would be 25 percent to each of them, i.e., $2,500 each.

The LLC's operating agreement may permit, however, the making of "unequal distributions," i.e., allocations that do not match the members' ownership interests. Thus, if Able and Baker have worked particularly hard in a given period, the members may decide to give Able and Baker a larger share of the distribution, say 30 percent each, leaving Charlie and Donny with only a 20-percent allocation.

In the charging order context, the making of unequal distributions has the potential to defeat the rights of the creditors of a member.

In the foregoing example, assume that Donny has become a debtor, and his 25-percent interest has been charged by a charging order. Donny might then say to his fellow members, "Don't make any distributions to my interest because of the charging order, but instead simply make unequal distributions to yourselves for 33.3 percent each until all this blows over. Oh, and feel free to slip me a few bucks every now and then."

Given this potential, some creditors will attempt to craft their charging orders to include provisions that prevent unequal distributions made to the detriment of the creditor while the debtor's interest is charged. Alternatively, language may be included in the charging order that attempts to impute unequal distributions to the debtor, i.e., even if the debtor doesn't actually receive the distribution because of the unequal distribution, the LLC will be treated as having made a normal distribution to the debtor (theoretically rendering the LLC liable to the creditor for the distribution, and possibly in contempt as well).

CHAPTER 12

Defenses to the Charging Order

The LLC's Defenses

The LLC normally has only two potential defenses to a motion for charging order.

First, the LLC can object to the charging order on the basis that it did not receive proper notice of the motion. This defense will arise, for instance, where the creditor gives notice only to the debtor, but not the LLC, and the LLC learns of the motion roundabout from the debtor or otherwise. This is obviously a temporary objection because a creditor faced with a valid objection on this basis would likely cure its deficiency by either giving the LLC appropriate notice prior to the hearing or refiling the motion for charging and giving proper notice to the LLC the second time around. Of course, if the relevant state law does not require that the LLC receive notice of the motion for a charging order, it does not have this defense.

Second, the LLC can object to the charging order on the basis that the debtor is not a member of the LLC. This is probably the only substantive defense the LLC can raise.

The Debtor's Defenses

The debtor has no defense against a charging order in the classic litigation sense. What the debtor may have is the ability to assert a statutory exemption to collection.

Some states also have a "wildcard exemption," which is that the debtor may exempt some small amount of personal assets, say $7,500. If such an exemption exists, it could conceivably be used to protect that amount of the debtor's LLC interest from being subject to the charging order. In these states, it is also possible that the debtor could apply the exemption for that amount of distributions, i.e., the first $7,500 of distributions.

Effect of State Statutory Creditor Exemptions

Section 503(f) of the RULLCA specifically provides that a charging order is subject to any applicable exemptions that might exist for the benefit of the debtor-member.[1] An excellent example of this is found in the *Zavodnick v. Leven*[2] decision, where the court held that distributions from a partnership were "profits due and owing" such that they implicated the 10-percent exemption on execution or other civil process under New Jersey law.[3] The *Zavodnick* court noted that because no exemptions were enumerated in the New Jersey partnership act, it was necessary for the court to look elsewhere for those exemptions, and held:

> Moreover, we perceive no reason why the "exemption laws" that may be invoked in response to an application for a charging order under N.J.S.A. 42:1-28 should exclude the limitation upon executions on "profits" provided by N.J.S.A. 2A:17-56. A partner's periodic receipt of distributions from a partnership engaged in a professional practice plays substantially the same role in the partner's economic life as an employee's wages. The partner typically depends on such distributions to purchase food, shelter, and other necessities for himself and his family. If [debtor] were an associate rather than a partner in the [partnership] law firm, any wage garnishment clearly would be subject to the limitations of N.J.S.A. 2A:17-56. Similarly, if [debtor] were a sole practitioner, the income that he derived from his practice would constitute "earnings" within the intent of N.J.S.A. 2A:17-56. Therefore, we conclude that distributions from the partnership through which [debtor] has chosen to practice his profession are subject to the same limitation on executions under N.J.S.A. 2A:17-56 as an employee's wages or a sole proprietor's earnings.[4]

Importantly, the *Zavodnick* court also held that the charging order was subject to the $10,000 personal property exemption of New Jersey law, thus indicating that a debtor may properly "stack exemptions" with a charging order, which is a quite common practice in American creditor-debtor law as to exemptions generally.[5]

Note that the *Zavodnick* court required the debtor-partner to prove that the distributions received from the partnership were in the nature of wages, and because the partnership was a professional practice, it was not particularly

---

1. Rev. Unif. Ltd. Liab. Co. Act § 503(f), 6B U.L.A. 148 (Unif. Law Comm'n Supp. 2015).
2. 773 A.2d 1170 (N.J. Super. Ct. App. Div. 2001).
3. *Id.* at 1174–75. *See also* MacDonald v. MacDonald, 1986 WL 5480, at *4 (Del. Ch. May 9, 1986) (charging order statute "does not deprive any partner of the benefit of any exemption laws applicable to his partnership interest"); Koh v. Inno-Pacific Holdings, Ltd., 54 P.3d 1270, 1272 (Wash. Ct. App. 2002) (charging order statute "does not deprive any member of the benefit of any exemption laws applicable to the member's limited liability company interest.").
4. Zavodnick v. Leven, 340 N.J. Super. 94, 102, 773 A.2d 1170, 1175 (App. Div. 2001).
5. *Id.* at 1174–75.

difficult for the debtor-partner to do so.[6] In other cases where the role played by the debtor-partner is not so clear, consideration of the issue of whether distributions are in the nature of wages might be more difficult. This can be seen particularly in the case of a largely passive partner who may have a quite difficult time believably arguing that a part of his or her distributions were anything like wages.

Effect of Federal Wage Garnishment Restrictions

One objection that a debtor-member might raise is that the distributions made to the debtor-member are in the nature of wages and thus are protected by the Federal Wage Garnishment Law (FWGL),[7] which protects from garnishment the lesser of: (1) 25 percent of the debtor's "disposable earnings"; or (2) 30 times the federal minimum wage amount.[8]

Section 1672(a) of that law states that the term "earnings" means "compensation paid or payable for personal services, whether denominated as wages, salary, commission, bonus, or otherwise . . . ."[9] This would appear to apply to distributions that were made to the debtor-member for his or her services rendered to the LLC.

Although the act provides protection against "garnishments," that term is defined in section 1672(c) to include "any legal or equitable procedure through which the earnings of any individual are required to be withheld for payment of any debt."[10] The charging order would seem to fit that description.

Planners might consider whether to structure an LLC so that working members are paid some level of salary to better clarify which portion of the members' receipts will be protected by this federal protection (which of course supersedes any contrary state law), and which portion will be pure distributions that will not be so protected and thus subject to the lien, as is specifically contemplated by RULLCA section 405(g).[11]

It is important to note that as of the time of this writing, the issues relating to the application of the FWGL to distributions is substantially unsettled, and there are good but unresolved arguments that creditors and debtors alike might assert.[12]

To illustrate the potential problems in this area, consider the example of five guys who run a neighborhood hamburger joint. Each of the five guys actively

6. *Id.*
7. 15 U.S.C. §§ 1671–1677 (2012).
8. *Id.* § 1673.
9. *Id.* § 1672(a).
10. *Id.* § 1672(c).
11. Rev. Unif. Ltd. Liab. Co. Act § 405(g), 6C U.L.A. 95 (Unif. Law Comm'n 2016).
12. Thomas E. Rutledge, *Garnishment Limits and Charging Orders*, __ J. Passthrough Entities __ (Nov./Dec. 2018) (*forthcoming*)

works in the business cooking and selling hamburgers to patrons. They have also been successful in licensing their franchise rights.

If one of the guys has a creditor, it is possible that a court will view the moneys that debtor earns from his or her own personal services in cooking and selling hamburgers as falling within the ambit of the 20-percent limit on garnishment. It is also possible that the court will view the moneys distributed to the debtor from the franchise rights as not deriving from the personal services of the debtor, and thus being 100 percent exposed to the creditor's charging order lien. In other words, the most likely outcome in any case will involve the court looking behind the formalities of how the debtor's receipts have been characterized, and instead at the substance of whether those moneys were earned due to the personal services of the debtor.

Planners should also take note of at least two possible issues.

First, there is a risk that the debtor may be estopped from arguing that "distributions" were actually earnings if the debtor-member took a contrary position for other reasons, i.e., for federal tax purposes, to avoid or lessen FICA or state taxes, to avoid workers' compensation insurance payments, etc. Where a creditor makes such an argument, the wording of state statutory law and private contractual law (the operating agreement) might or might not help to make a difference one way or another. This issue could come into play in those cases where it is difficult for the court to discern what is earnings and what is profits, and so the court just punts and declares it all profits under the rubric, "you treated it all as profits, so I'm treating it all as profits."

Second, it is likely that a court will look at the long-term relationship between the debtor and the LLC and not merely the most recent pay stub. Thus, a debtor who has been taking distributions for the last eight years, and then when a judgment is entered against him suddenly starts taking a salary and much smaller distributions, might still be determined by the court to have taken distributions notwithstanding the belated recharacterization of his or her income.

Case Study: *Alexander*[13]

The U.S. District Court for the District of Arizona sentenced in 2006 Robert F. Alexander to 96 months for running what is known as a high-yield interest program, a form of Ponzi scheme whereby Alexander promised his investors a rate of return as high as 37 percent.

To reduce his jail time, Alexander agreed to a plea deal under which he was required to make a little over $9.9 million in restitution payments to his victims,

13. U.S. v. Alexander, 2016 WL 2893406 (D. Ariz. May 18, 2016).

commencing with a $300 per month minimum payment that would start upon his release from incarceration. Later, this amount increased to $750 per month.

Upon leaving the pokey, Alexander began doing business through E-Logic, LLC, of which he was the sole employee. E-Logic, LLC wasn't exactly a smashing success, netting Alexander profits of only about $8,100 per year in 2014 and 2015.

Unable to pay the higher $750 per month restitution amount, Alexander soon defaulted on this obligation, and the United States sought to collect by obtaining a charging order against Alexander's 100-percent interest in E-Logic LLC.

Under Arizona law, and pretty much the laws of every other state, a charging order has the effect of putting a lien on the debtor-member's right to distributions and effectively reroutes any distributions made to the creditor. (Notably, and contrary to what is quite wrongly said at about every asset protection seminar, the tax liability stays with the debtor.)

Arizona law also provides, as again does pretty much the laws of every other state, that a charging order is subject to whatever exemptions the creditor might assert against collection. Arizona exemptions effectively track the FWGL, 15 U.S.C. 1671, *et seq.*, which provides that a creditor may only collect against 25 percent of a debtor's net disposable income or, in other words, the debtor may protect 75 percent of his or her earnings after taxes and other withholdings.

The United States contended that the distributions that Alexander received from E-Logic, LLC were in the nature of investment distributions and were not subject to the 25-percent limitation. Alexander responded that the distributions arose from his labors on behalf of E-Logic, LLC and were thus "earnings" even though he received them as distributions and not as wages or salary.

The Court agreed with Alexander:

> The fact that a charging order is entered, however, "does not deprive any member of the benefit of any exemption laws applicable to his interest in the limited liability company." A.R.S. sec. 29-655(B). Arizona law limits garnishment to 25 percent of a garnishee's disposable earnings. A.R.S. sec. 33-1131(B). "Earnings" are defined broadly to include "compensation paid or payable for personal services, whether these payments are called wages, salary, commission, bonus or otherwise." A.R.S. sec. 12-1598(4). "Disposable earnings" is defined as the "amount remaining from the gross earnings for a pay period after the deductions required by state and federal law." A.R.S. sec. 12-1598(3). As the sole member of E-Logic, Defendant receives distributions equivalent to the LLC's annual income. These are provided as compensation for his personal services to E-Logic. These distributions qualify as earnings and are protected by the personal property exemption. The charging

> order therefore cannot deprive Defendant of more than 25 percent of his disposable earnings.

The court therefore entered a charging order in favor of the United States against Alexander's interest in E-Logic, LLC, but limited the amount charged to no more than 25 percent of Alexander's disposable earnings.

Arguably, the court got this decision exactly right. Instead of looking at a wholly superficial distinction of such things as "distribution" or "salary" or "wages," the court looked beyond the superficial legal characterization of "distributions" to find that Alexander's compensation (however defined) arose from the fruits of his labors and were thus earnings for purposes of Arizona's collection exemptions (and, by implication, the FWGL).

To illustrate how all this should logically work, consider three hypotheticals:

(1) Debtor is a member of XYZ LLC and receives $100,000 in distributions that are wholly due to the fruits of his labor. In this case, the 25-percent limitation should apply, as in Alexander's case.

(2) Debtor is a member of XYZ LLC and receives $100,000 in distributions that are not the result of his efforts, but are simply the fruits of a $1 million investment that the debtor made into XYZ LLC some time before. In this case, the 25-percent limitation should not apply, and this result should also be true even if XYZ LLC did not make "distributions" to the debtor, but instead tried to characterize them as "salary" or "wages" or some sort of "fees."

(3) Debtor is a member of XYZ LLC and receives $100,000 in distributions, of which 50 percent are the result of his labors, and 50 percent are the results of profits that are generated by the labors of other members. In this case, the 25-percent limitation would apply to 50 percent of the distribution ($50,000 in earnings), but would not apply to the other 50 percent of distributions (the investment distribution).

The point is, as Judge Campbell tells us, that we must look deeper than the mere characterization of what is being paid, and instead look to what generated those moneys in the first place, i.e., was it the fruits of the debtor's labor (subject to the 25-percent limitation) or simply investment returns (not subject to the 25-percent limitation).

Note that it has become *pro forma* these days for creditors to combine their motion for charging order with a writ of garnishment so that whether the debtor takes "distributions" or "salary" or "wages," the moneys paid to the debtor will be picked up one way or the other. This is in recognition by creditors' rights attorneys that debtors will often seek to game how they are being paid to try to circumvent one or the other remedy. By obtaining both remedies simultaneously, the creditor will catch the moneys whatever they are called by the debtor and the LLC or partnership. Even if the debtor and the LLC or partnership are attempting to play these games, however, that should still not detract from the debtor's statutory entitlement to the 25-percent limitation where the moneys are derived from the fruits of his or her labors.

CHAPTER 13

The Hearing and Notice of the Charging Order

The Hearing on the Charging Order Motion

Whether a court will hold a hearing on a motion for charging order largely depends on whether the matter is pending in federal or state court. Perhaps the majority of federal judges will resolve the motion on only the submissions of the party without the necessity of any hearing. By contrast, state court judges routinely will set a motion for charging order for hearing.

Any litigant seeking a charging order should come to court well-prepared for any eventuality. The debtor will often show up at the hearing, either personally or through counsel, and attempt to assert a last-minute exemption, most commonly arguing that his or her distributions sought to be charged are really in the form of wages and thus subject to the 25-percent limitation on net disposable income of the FWGA.

The debtor may also attempt to argue that a charging order is permissive and not mandatory, and that the entry of the charging order would somehow be unreasonably harsh to the debtor under the circumstances.

The parties opposing the charging order may also attempt to argue that the debtor is not a member of the LLC's interest to be charged. These parties may also attempt to confuse the court as to the debtor's relationship to the LLC. Thus, it is often helpful for the creditor to bring to the hearing a demonstrative exhibit in the form of a simple chart that illustrates for the court the debtor's relationship to the LLC.

The creditor should also have readily at hand evidence that the debtor indeed does have a membership interest in the LLC. If the creditor seeks ancillary provisions in the charging order, i.e., blocking loans made by the LLC to the debtor, the creditor should be prepared to prove up the need for those ancillary provisions as well.

Another argument on a motion for charging order often involves the form of the order itself. The parties opposing the motion will usually attempt to pare down the language of the order to its barest form to create loopholes through which they may seek to get money or other assets to the debtor by some means other than a distribution. This means that the creditor seeking the order must be prepared with authorities from that jurisdiction that support the language of the proposed order tendered by the creditor, which seeks to close these loopholes.

A good strategy for creditors to obtain the language they want is to find a similar form of charging order that has been entered by another court in that jurisdiction. Indeed, a good practice is to have ready copies of several such similar orders to provide to the court at the hearing.

Most courts will not hear a motion for charging order on an *ex parte* basis, and it may be several weeks between the filing of a motion for charging order in the hearing on that motion. To protect against a distribution made to the debtor in the interim, a creditor may seek on an *ex parte* basis the entry of a temporary restraining order that bars making any such distributions.

Is not necessary for a creditor at least in California to seek such a temporary restraining order because under California law, the mere filing of a motion for charging order creates a temporary lien on the debtor's interest.

If the court seems inclined to grant the charging order, but takes the matter under advisement to sort out the language, the creditor should request that the court enter a temporary restraining order barring distributions until the court issues the final order.

Giving Notice of the Issued Charging Order

If the court issues the charging order, then the next step is for the creditor to serve a "notice of entry of charging order" both on the debtor-member and on the LLC (or all its members). As the charging order places a lien on the debtor-member's distributive interest, the giving of the notice of entry of charging order to the LLC has the effect of "perfecting" the lien. From the date of receipt of the notice, the LLC will be potentially liable to the creditor for violating the lien and in danger of being held in contempt for violating the charging order.[1]

Many jurisdictions require that a party must be personally served with an order before that party can be held in contempt for violating that order. Therefore, it is a best practice for the creditor to personally serve, by way of a process server, both the LLC and the debtor with a copy of the charging order.

The reason that the charging order should also be personally served on the debtor is that the debtor is bound by the charging order as well. If the debtor were to receive a distribution in violation of the charging order and not immediately turn it over to the creditor, the debtor risks contempt. Service on the debtor also puts the debtor on notice of any ancillary provisions in the charging order, such as restrictions against taking loans or other forms of compensation.

---

1. *See* Joshlin Bros. Irrigation v. Sunbelt Rental, Inc., 2014 Ark. Ct. App. 65, 2014 WL 248104, at *2–4.

The notice of entry of charging order is a relatively simple document created on a form mirroring the case caption like any other proceeding in the matter, which blandly recites, "You are hereby notified that the attached charging order was entered on X date." A conformed copy (also known as a file-stamped copy) of the charging order should be appended to the notice.

After service of the notice of entry of charging order has been made, the creditor should (where allowed by court rule) file a proof of service of that notice and mail copies of the proof of service to both the LLC and the debtor. This may assist in precluding later attempts by the LLC or the debtor from claiming that they were never served with a copy of the charging order.

CHAPTER 14

Enforcing the Charging Order

Enforcing against the Debtor

As an order entered in the case, a charging order is binding on all the parties—including the debtor. If the debtor receives a distribution in violation of the charging order, then the debtor may be held in contempt if the debtor does not turn over the proceeds of the distribution to the creditor.

The process for holding the debtor in contempt is usually the same as it is to hold the LLC in contempt, which is that the creditor will initiate the contempt process through a motion for an order to show cause to the debtor. The relief sought by the creditor on such a motion is that the debtor will turn over the proceeds of the distribution to the creditor within a few days, or the debtor will face incarceration until the turnover is made.

Whether the underlying judgment may be discharged by the debtor or not, the debtor will probably not be able to discharge a judgment of contempt. Attempting to establish additional monetary liability against the debtor is usually not practical insofar as the debtor is not paying the underlying liability anyway.

Enforcing against the LLC

Contempt

Assume that a charging order has been entered and notice of the charging order has been personally served on the LLC, but the LLC continues to make distributions directly to the debtor-member in defiance of the charging order. In such an event, the creditor's primary remedy against the LLC is to file a motion for an order to show cause as to why the LLC should not be held in contempt for violating the charging order.

A motion to show cause begins the process for a contempt hearing against the LLC, which will be an evidentiary hearing where the creditor must present proof that the LLC was personally served with the charging order but willfully violated it.

Obviously, you can't throw an LLC in jail. However, the court can fashion a contempt remedy to both punish the LLC for its past contempt and ensure that future distributions are made to the creditor benefitting from the charging order, such as a fine against the LLC for the amount of the distribution plus the creditor's attorney's fees incurred in the contempt process, and perhaps an order that creates additional fines against the LLC for failing to heed the charging order.

These fines create a debt against the LLC itself and thus allow the creditor to enforce the fine by levying directly upon the LLC's assets until fully paid.

Where the LLC is in the state and subject to the personal jurisdiction of the forum court, this process is relatively straightforward and like any other contempt proceeding brought against any other business entity, but it becomes more difficult where the LLC is not amenable to the jurisdiction of the forum court.

Where the forum court's jurisdiction over the LLC is lacking, that court has no power to enforce a contempt order against the LLC. In such a case, the creditor must register the underlying judgment against the debtor as a sister-state judgment in the state where the LLC is found (either the state of formation or where it is primarily conducting its business), and then additionally file the charging order as a sister-state order in the case that is created by the registration of the judgment. The creditor can then seek a contempt order in the courts of the state where the LLC is found.

Violation of Lien Rights

A creditor may also be able to bring a damages suit against the LLC for violating the creditor's rights in the lien created by the charging order. This would have the effect of creating direct liability against the LLC for the amount of distribution, thus effectively allowing the creditor to enforce the judgment against the LLC's assets.

As a practical matter, this remedy is unsatisfactory as compared to the contempt remedy because it requires the filing and litigation of a new lawsuit. If a court fails to enter a judgment of contempt against the LLC, or the relief granted by the court is inadequate, then the creditor may decide to try this longer path to direct liability against the LLC.

CASE STUDY: *JOSHLIN BROS.*[1]

Brothers Robert and Kenny Joslin owned an irrigation company together, Joshlin Brothers Irrigation, organized as a partnership (Joshlin Partnership).

Separately, Robert had an outside business unrelated to the Joshlin Partnership. For that other business, Robert borrowed money from Sunbelt Rentals, failed to pay back Sunbelt Rentals, was sued by Sunbelt Rentals, and suffered a default judgment to Sunbelt Rentals.

To collect its judgment, Sunbelt Rentals obtained a charging order against Robert's interest in the Joshlin Partnership. The terms of the charging order, as

1. Joshlin Bros. Irrigation v. Sunbelt Rental, Inc., 2014 WL 248104, 2014 Ark. App. 65 (Ark. App. Jan. 22, 2014) (unpublished).

most do, specifically required the Joshlin Partnership to direct any payments that were due to Robert to Sunbelt Rentals instead.

As a partner of the Joshlin Partnership, and in defiance of the charging order, Robert wrote checks to himself that were drawn on the Joshlin Partnership's bank account. Then, Robert committed suicide.

Sunbelt Rentals moved to hold the Joshlin Partnership in contempt. The Joshlin Partnership (read: surviving brother Kenny) argued that Robert's actions were unauthorized and amounted to fraud by Robert on the Joshlin Partnership, and thus should not be imputed to it.

The trial court disagreed and held the Joshlin Partnership in contempt, and the Joshlin Partnership appealed. On appeal, the higher court held that the Joshlin Partnership didn't raise any of its appellate arguments at the trial court level, and so they were all deemed waived.

Case Study: *McClure*[2]

In July of 2013, Chase Bank won a $20 million judgment against Reginald D. Fowler and an Arizona company called Spiral Broadcasting LLC. Fowler and Spiral owned interests in three Colorado LLCs.

In November of that year, the Arizona court issued charging orders in favor of Chase Bank that created judgment liens on Fowler's interests in the Colorado LLCs. The next month, Chase Bank both served the charging orders on the Colorado LLCs and domesticated its Arizona judgment in Colorado, but not until August 2014 did Chase Bank domesticate the Arizona charging orders in Colorado.

Meanwhile, Fowler and Spiral were also sued by Doug and Nancy McClure, who themselves won a $1.5 million judgment against those two debtors in March 2014.

Instead of having the Arizona court issue the charging orders first and then domesticating those orders in Colorado (as Chase Bank had done), the McClures first domesticated their Arizona judgment in Colorado and then had the Colorado court issue the charging orders against the Colorado LLCs. The McClures then served the Colorado charging orders on the Colorado LLCs, doing so in July 2014, one month before Chase Bank domesticated its Arizona charging orders in Colorado.

A charging order is basically the means by which a court places a judgment lien on an LLC or partnership interest held by the debtor. Think of the charging order as a can of spray paint that coats the debtor's interest with the judgment lien. The lien is said to be "perfected" when it is served on the LLC or partnership.

---

2. McClure v. JP Morgan Chase Bank NA, 395 P.3d 1123 (Colo. App. 2015), *aff'd* 393 P.3d 955 (Colo. 2017).

Once properly placed, a judgment lien is like any other lien and is subject to such things as priority among lienholders. Priority of liens is usually determined on the basis of "first in time is first in right."

The question before the court here was: As between Chase Bank and the McClures, whose charging order lien had priority?

The Colorado lower court held that the McClures' charging order lien, which was perfected in July 2014, had priority over that of Chase Bank, given that the latter's Arizona charging orders were not domesticated in Colorado until August 2014. Chase Bank appealed, thus leading to the following summary of the Colorado Court of Appeals opinion.

The court decided that the key issue was whether the Arizona charging order was enforceable in Colorado. Under the Full Faith & Credit Clause of the U.S. Constitution, Colorado is required to recognize judgments and orders rendered by the courts of other states, but only if those other judgments or orders were "duly rendered."

To domesticate an out-of-state judgment in Colorado, a creditor has the choice of either filing a new lawsuit to recognize the judgment or order, or filing the judgment or order in a Colorado court under the Uniform Enforcement of Judgments Act (Enforcement Act).

If a judgment or order has not been domesticated in Colorado by one of these two means, then it is not enforceable in Colorado. The court then pointed out that although Chase Bank had obtained its charging order in Arizona before the McClures obtained theirs in Colorado, the Chase Bank charging order was not enforceable in Colorado until it was domesticated in that state—after the McClures had already obtained their charging order.

Given that the McClures were the first to obtain their charging order in Colorado, their charging order had priority over that of Chase Bank. This rule, sayeth the court, furthers Colorado's interest in LLCs that are formed in Colorado. Further,

> [o]ur holding will not unfairly burden foreign judgment creditors because Colorado has a simplified procedure for rendering foreign judgments enforceable in Colorado: domestication under the Enforcement Act.... As relevant here, foreign judgment creditors need not anticipate every jurisdiction where their priority might be challenged; but if they seek to establish priority in charging a Colorado LLC, they must follow the [Colorado] procedures. [Internal citations omitted.]

Chase Bank argued that this result would violate the Full Faith and Credit Clause as an impermissible collateral attack on the Arizona charging order, but the court disagreed, noting a U.S. Supreme Court holding that:

> Full faith and credit . . . does not mean that States must adopt the practices of other States regarding the time, manner, and mechanisms

> for enforcing judgments. Enforcement measures do not travel with the sister state judgment as preclusive effects do; such measures remain subject to the evenhanded control of forum law.

This is indeed the law—the judgment enforcement remedies of a state generally stop at its borders, and to enforce a judgment in another state, the creditor must domesticate the judgment there.

With that, the Colorado Court of Appeals affirmed the decision of the lower court, which held that the McClure's charging order had priority over that of Chase Bank.

The Colorado Supreme Court then granted a writ of certiorari to review the case and held that the proper place to obtain a charging order is the place where the LLC were themselves formed, meaning Colorado. Thus, the Arizona charging orders were invalid, and it came down to who obtained a charging order first in Colorado, meaning the McClures. The court placed great weight on the possibility that the debtor might move, and that it was preferable to have a single place where a charging order could be issued. Thus, the Colorado Supreme Court affirmed the decision of the Colorado Court of Appeals.

CHAPTER 15

Complying with the Charging Order

Compliance by the Entity

When served with a charging order, the LLC must take steps to comply with the order. Compliance with the order is often difficult because a financially distressed debtor will often pressure the LLC to circumvent the charging order. The practical rule in this situation is: "Do not make the debtor's problem the LLC's problem." To avoid profitless litigation with the creditor, the LLC should comply not only with the strict language of the charging order, but also its spirit.

Attempting to assist the debtor to circumvent the order exposes the LLC to potential liability to the creditor for violating the lien created by the charging order. Such circumvention includes remunerating the debtor in ways that were nonexistent before the charging order was entered—some examples in lieu of distributions include making loans to the debtor, paying consulting or management fees to the debtor, and paying a salary, among others. Otherwise, compliance with the charging order is relatively simple. Although the charging order is in effect, distributions should be paid to the order of the creditor or as otherwise provided in the order. Some information regarding the payment made to the creditor should be contemporaneously provided to the debtor, who remains a member of the LLC despite the entry of the charging order.

Note that as discussed in Chapter 27, *infra*, the responsibility for paying taxes on distributions remains with the debtor despite being paid to the creditor. Therefore, the LLC must continue to issue the IRS Schedule K-1 to the debtor while the charging order is in effect.

Some states allow the lien created by the charging order to be foreclosed upon, which means that the interest will be sold to the highest bidder at a judicial sale. In such a case, the LLC should treat the purchaser as the new assignee of the debtor's economic rights. This change means that distributions shall continue to be paid to the purchaser even after the debtor resolves the judgment. As of the date of the purchase of the interests, the purchaser shall also receive a Schedule K-1 for distributions received if the LLC is taxed as a partnership.

Other than relating to distributions, the charging order or subsequent foreclosure does not alter the debtor's noneconomic rights in the LLC. The debtor—not the creditor—retains all other rights, including management and voting rights.

Compliance by the Debtor

A debtor generally is not required to act in order to comply with the charging order; however, if the debtor were to receive a distribution subject to the charging order, the debtor must immediately turn it over to the creditor or to the court or risk contempt for violating the order.

Case Study: *Buckeye Retirement*[1]

Anthony Buffa was a private equity investor who got behind on his promissory note to First Third Bank and stipulated to a judgment against him in the amount of $180,000. First Third Bank then sold the judgment to Buckeye Retirement.

Buffa, who admitted to having numerous other creditors including the IRS, conducted his investment activities through an entity called Endeavor, LLC, of which he owned 99 percent and his wife, Nancy Haar, owned the other one percent. Buffa testified that he worked from 54 to 66 hours per week for Endeavor, LLC, which earned him an annual salary of $20,000.

Haar, however, worked only 18 to 32 hours per week for Endeavor LLC, but was given a $120,000 annual salary that had actually paid $75,000 to $100,000 per year. Endeavor LLC also paid for vacations for Buffa and Haar as reflected in its tax returns.

Given that Buckeye Retirement had a charging order lien against Buffa's 99-percent interest in Endeavor LLC, if a distribution had been made, Buckeye Retirement would have received it, but if a big salary had been paid to Buffa, then Buckeye Retirement would have garnished it. Given that Haar was not a debtor, Endeavor LLC could pay money to her instead, and it would avoid creditors.

> When defendant Buffa was asked the reason for this obvious disparity in workload and commensurate pay, defendant Buffa responded that he did not know the rationale behind this, despite being the majority owner by a ratio of ninety-nine to one, and despite being the company's managing member; he testified that it was Haar's decision about how she would be paid.

For his part, Buffa testified that Haar received so much more money than he did to maintain the marital stability of their household, which was probably

1. Buckeye Retirement Co. v. Buffa, 2011 WL 3439022 (D. Conn., Aug. 5, 2011).

right; however, that is not a legal defense to stiffing creditors, and it didn't explain why tax returns prepared by Buffa's brother, a tax attorney, didn't jive with Buffa's testimony as to how the allocation of Endeavor LLC's income should really occur.

After dropping in a footnote that the court was considering the use of the contempt remedy to force correct distributions, the court ordered additional discovery, including the deposition of an officer of Endeavor LLC, and ominously warned Buffa that:

> In light of the significant ramifications of the testimony at this deposition, it goes without saying that it would be highly prudent for defendant to be represented by counsel at this deposition.

Case Study: *Seven Arts Pictures*[2]

The creditor, Jonesfilm, held judgments totaling nearly $1 million against the debtor, Peter Hoffman, and some of his companies, including Seven Arts Pictures Inc., which was apparently traded over-the-counter as a penny stock.

When Jonesfilm learned that Hoffman was using several Louisiana LLCs, Jonesfilm registered its judgment in the U.S. District Court for the Eastern District of Louisiana and began collection efforts there. That court entered charging orders against those LLCs, which included a provision requiring Hoffman and his companies to produce their financial statements, tax returns, and K-1s. Hoffman ignored the charging orders.

A few months later, the court ordered Hoffman's Louisiana companies to garnish any funds that they held on behalf of Hoffman and his other debtor companies. The court then ordered Hoffman's Louisiana companies to answer interrogatories regarding the garnished funds.

One of Hoffman's companies, Leeway, initially responded to the interrogatories by claiming that it held no funds for Hoffman or Seven Arts Pictures. A few months later, however, Leeway admitted that it had actually held nearly $175,000 for Hoffman and Seven Arts Pictures, but transferred those funds away to Hoffman personally, two of Hoffman's debtor companies, and Hoffman's CPAs. Leeway's excuse was remarkable in that Leeway claimed that it had never known that it was holding or had transferred Hoffman's funds, but rather that those funds had been wrongfully transferred without authorization by an employee seeking to cover up her embezzlement scheme. Notably, Leeway's response was signed by the one person who was all of Leeway's VP, secretary, director, bookkeeper, recordkeeper, and manager—Hoffman's wife, Susan.

Justifiably outraged, Jonesfilm moved to hold Hoffman and Seven Arts Pictures in contempt of court for failing to comply with the charging orders

2. Seven Arts Pictures, Inc. v. Jonesfilm, 2013 WL 599661 (5th Cir. Feb. 18, 2013).

(which would have intercepted distributions to Hoffman and Seven Arts Pictures). The court instead immediately ordered Hoffman and Leeway to deliver the $175,000 to the court and referred the contempt issue to a U.S. magistrate judge for further consideration. The U.S. magistrate judge found that Hoffman and Seven Arts Pictures had disobeyed the charging order by failing to cough up the funds or the required financial statements and tax documents.

Acting upon this, the U.S. district court then held Hoffman and Seven Arts Pictures in contempt and ordered them to deliver the $175,000 to Jonesfilm and to provide Jonesfilm with complete financial statements and tax returns and other information. The court also awarded $21,357 in attorney's fees to Jonesfilm. Hoffman and his companies appealed, but were shot down by the Fifth Circuit, which affirmed everything.

Hoffman's appeal was based on his claim that the U.S. district court, sitting in Louisiana, had no personal jurisdiction over him because he resided in California and was therefore void from the outset. He was wrong, mostly from his own doings. As the court noted:

> It was fair to subject Hoffman to suit in Louisiana. He has held himself out as a resident of the state, and the burden on him is minimal seeing as much of his business is done in the state and he owns residences there. Jonesfilm seeks to satisfy its outstanding judgments against Hoffman using his Louisiana property, which gives Louisiana an interest in the outcome of this litigation.

It was thus on these facts quite easy for the Fifth Circuit to pin Louisiana jurisdiction on Hoffman. Strike One.

Next, Hoffman whined about having to produce tax returns, claiming that they should have been protected from discovery to protect his financial privacy and for other reasons. Whether this might have been a good defense against pre-judgment discovery or not, it was a quick loser post-judgment:

> The scope of post-judgment discovery is very broad to permit a judgment creditor to discover assets upon which execution may be made. . . . When a judgment creditor seeks information regarding a judgment debtor's financial position, the relevance of the tax returns to a judgment creditor is virtually presumed. . . . A judgment debtor opposing production of relevant material would be required to show that other sources exist from which the information sought could be obtained.

Given that Hoffman could not prove that the information in the tax returns was otherwise available to Jonesfilm, he wholly failed on his burden of proof on this issue. Strike Two.

Turning to the meat of the controversy, Hoffman and his companies argued first that they could not be held in contempt because the $175,000 had been embezzled by the errant employee. The problem with this excuse was that there was little proof of this other than that Hoffman's companies had filed a police report and sent a letter to their bank about the alleged embezzlement, but there was no other proof that any such thing had actually occurred.

Hoffman next argued that he personally could not be responsible for the failure of Leeway to deliver the $175,000 as ordered by the court because he was not subject to the garnishment order.

Wrong again, as the Fifth Circuit explained:

> Orders granting injunctions bind "the parties' officers, agents, servants, employees, and attorneys" and "other persons who are in active concert" with them or with the parties. Fed R. Civ. P. 65(d)(2).
>
> Hoffman was therefore subject to the garnishment order in two ways. First, he served as director, officer, bank statement recipient, bank signatory, keeper of the books, and manager of Leeway. Second, he acted "in active concert" with Leeway, because he personally, or companies of which he was CEO, or his CPAs, received every penny of the garnished funds from Leeway.
>
> As this court recognized in Waffenschmidt, "[a]n injunction binds not only the parties subject thereto, but also nonparties who act with the enjoined party." In that case, the district court enjoined MacKay, and all persons acting in concert with him, from transferring any funds received from the Waffenschmidts. . . . MacKay was ordered to deposit certain funds with the court, which he was unable to do because he had transferred them to nonparties, in violation of the injunction. . . . The court found two of the nonparties in contempt, and imposed fines in the amounts received, because they were agents or employees of MacKay and acted "in active concert" with him by receiving the funds. . . . We upheld the fines, finding that the court had not clearly erred when it held that they received the money with knowledge of the injunction. [Internal quotations and citations omitted]

Strike Three. Having struck out on the merits, Hoffman's companies attempted to appeal the award of attorney's fees, but lost that, too, with the Fifth Circuit going on to note that:

> It has not escaped our notice that Hoffman, SAP, and Leeway openly defied the district court's order. They appealed it but failed to ask the court to stay the order pending appeal. Adding to their, especially Hoffman's, ongoing demonstration of contempt for the judicial

> process, they failed to "comply promptly with the order pending appeal," as was their obligation absent a stay.[FN15] After nearly a year, the district court held them in contempt again, for disobeying the order. Hoffman, SAP, and Leeway would be wise to fulfill their obligations to the court without delay.

The end of the Fifth Circuit's opinion was footnote 15, within the quoted text above, which stated ominously:

> 15. Maness v. Meyers, 419 U.S. 449, 458–59 (1975) ("Persons who make private determinations of the law and refuse to obey an order generally risk criminal contempt even if the order is ultimately ruled incorrect.").

CHAPTER 16

Receivers to Enforce the Charging Order

Authority for the Receiver

Section 503(b) of ULLCA 2006 provides in paragraph (b) as follows:

> (b) To the extent necessary to effectuate the collection of distributions pursuant to a charging order in effect under subsection (a), the court may:
>
> > (1) appoint a receiver of the distributions subject to the charging order, with the power to make all inquiries the judgment debtor might have made and
> >
> > (2) make all other orders necessary to give effect to the charging order.

Similarly, section 703(a) of ULPA 2001 (as amended in 2013) provides in part that:

> The court may appoint a receiver of the share of the distributions due or to become due to the judgment debtor in respect of the partnership and make all other orders, directions, accounts, and inquiries the judgment debtor might have made or which the circumstances of the case may require to give effect to the charging order.

Finally, section 504 of the Uniform Partnership Act of 1997 (as amended in 2013) provides:

> (b) To the extent necessary to effectuate the collection of distributions pursuant to a charging order in effect under subsection (a), the court may:
>
> > (1) appoint a receiver of the distributions subject to the charging order, with the power to make all inquiries the judgment debtor might have made; and

(2) make all other orders necessary to give effect to the charging order.

Powers of the Receiver

Under the Harmonized Acts, the court may appoint a receiver to basically perform two functions: (1) receive distributions and (2) obtain information from the LLC.

Note that under all the Harmonized Acts, the receiver may only be appointed to take charge of distributions and may not take charge of the LLC itself or the LLC's assets.[1]

Statutes in many states authorize a court to appoint a receiver to aid a judgment creditor.[2] To the extent the Harmonized Acts limit the powers of the receiver, those provisions may limit the more general powers provided under the general execution laws.

Insofar as the receiver's power to receive distributions, a creditor might ask, "What is to be gained by interposing a receiver between the distributions and the creditor, i.e., why wouldn't the creditor simply have the distributions made directly to the creditor"?

In the case of a single creditor, there probably is no reason to appoint a receiver if all the receiver will do is collect distributions. However, a court may be faced with a situation where there is an ongoing dispute among multiple creditors as to who has priority over the distributions. In that case, the receiver can accept the distributions until these priority questions are sorted.

The real power of a receiver is to do something the creditor often cannot do because of case law in certain jurisdictions, which is to request financial information from the LLC.[3] Given that a receiver is presumably both a neutral and an instrument of the court, the receiver can obtain this information and assure the court that distributions are properly being made by the LLC, without the LLC being concerned that the creditor is obtaining financial information about the

1. McClandon v. Dakem & Assoc., LLC, 219 So. 3d 269, 271 (Fla. Ct. App. 2017); RULLCA § 503, cmt.

2. Ala. Code 1975 § 6-6-185; Alaska Stat. Ann. § 09.40.240; Cal. Civ. Proc. Code § 564; Idaho Code Ann. § 8-601; Ky. Rev. Stat. Ann § 275.260(2); Mich. Comp. Laws Ann. § 600.6104; Minn. Stat. Ann. § 575.05; Mont. Code Ann. § 25-14-201; Neb. Rev. Stat. Ann. § 25-1081; Nev. Rev. Stat. Ann. § 32.010; N.J. Stat. Ann. § 2A:17-66; N.Y. C.P.L.R. 5228; N.C. Gen. Stat. Ann. § 1-363; N.D. Cent. Code Ann. § 28-25-12; Ohio Rev. Code Ann. § 2735.01; Okla. Stat. Ann. tit. 12, § 852; S.C. Code Ann. § 15-39-430; Wash. Rev. Code Ann. § 7.60.025; Wis. Stat. Ann. § 816.04.

3. *See* Wells Fargo Bank, Nat. Ass'n v. Continuous Control Sols., Inc., 821 N.W.2d 777 (Iowa Ct. App. 2012).

LLC that it might use for some improper purpose, such as to compete against the LLC.

Note, however, that under the Harmonized Acts, the receiver can only obtain such information that the debtor was able to obtain and is not allowed to go on anything like a broad fishing expedition as to the LLC's affairs and operations generally.

Creditors should be aware that receivers are costly. As of the time of this writing, most court-appointed receivers charge upwards of $250 per hour for their services, and they will have certain immediate expenses, such as the cost of posting a receiver's bond in most jurisdictions. Receivers quite often will require that the creditor advance a certain amount of funds, rarely less than $5,000, to "prime the pump," i.e., fund the receiver's fees and expenses until the receiver is able to take those from collections. Although the fees and expenses of the receiver will ultimately be added to the judgment against the debtor as the costs of collection, in many cases the debtor has no means to pay the judgment in full, which means that the total cost of the receiver will simply reduce the amount ultimately collected by the creditor.

Thus, the decision of a creditor to ask for the appointment of a receiver should not be done without a cost-benefit analysis of whether the receiver will be worth the expense. Indeed, where the receiver will serve no other function than to receive distributions to be held pending the resolution of priority claims of multiple creditors, the more cost-effective procedure might be to simply require that the LLC pay the distributions into the court fund, where allowed, until those competing claims are resolved.

The Receiver as Trojan Horse

The end game of many creditors is to have a general receiver appointed for the debtor. The reason for this is that such a receiver is so invasive of the financial affairs of the debtor—a general receiver can collect and open the debtor's mail, cash checks made to the debtor, sell off prime tickets at sporting events, liquidate real estate and equipment, and in general do about everything that the debtor herself has a legal right to do—that few debtors can withstand having a receiver appointed for them for more than a few weeks. To get rid of the receiver, a debtor will often capitulate very quickly to a cash settlement quite favorable to the creditor.

However, it is precisely because receivers are so invasive of the financial affairs of the debtor that courts are loathe to grant receivers until the creditor has shown the court that it has exhausted every other avenue of collection. The courts in their opinions frequently speak of the receiver being the "collection remedy of last resort." This is a high hill for the debtor to climb.

It has thus developed as a tactic of creditors to ask that a receiver be appointed in regard to the charging order for the limited purpose of collecting distributions and making inquiries to the LLC, and then to later convert the limited-purpose receiver into a general-purpose receiver. This is often done incrementally: The receiver starts out collecting distributions, and the creditor repeatedly moves the court to expand the receiver's powers until the receiver becomes a de facto general-purpose receiver for the debtor.

What practically happens is that the court gets familiar with the receiver, and then ultimately decides that it is easier for the receiver to do the work of collecting from the debtor than the court having to approve and monitor multiple independent remedies. Thus, by this tactic, the creditor is able to use the limited-purpose charging order creditor as effectively a "Trojan horse" that gets inside the debtor's gate, and once inside can take the debtor's fortress by storm.

Justifying the Receiver

To justify the receiver, the creditor must show a compelling reason why it will not be inadequate if the court simply directs that distributions from the LLC be paid to the creditor. This justification most often will be found in the ability of the receiver to make inquiries to the LLC to ensure that distributions are properly being made and are not being withheld by the LLC out of sympathy for, or because the LLC is in cahoots with, the debtor.

Note, however, that the creditor may have to show that the receiver will be more effective at obtaining this information than if the court simply required the debtor to obtain the information and turn it over to the creditor at a debtor's examination. To this end, recalcitrance or an outright refusal by the debtor to obtain this information may by itself be enough to justify the appointment of a receiver for this purpose.

Conversely, a party seeking to block the appointment of a receiver should be prepared to demonstrate to the court that there is nothing to be gained by inserting a receiver into the process.

Appointment of the Receiver

The Harmonized Acts may authorize appointment of a receiver, but those acts say nothing about implementing this remedy. The creditor must look to the normal procedures in a particular jurisdiction to appoint a receiver. Given that the appointment of a receiver is an extraordinary remedy, it should not be used, even when authorized, if another legal or equitable remedy is available. A motion to appoint a receiver is granted only when special reasons appear to justify one. In *Hotel 71 Mezz Lender LLC v. Falor*,[4] the court approved the appointment of a receiver. The court discussed factors other courts have considered to justify the appointment: alternative remedies available to the creditor; the degree to which

4. 926 N.E.2d 1202 (N.Y. 2010).

receivership will increase the likelihood of satisfaction; and the risk of fraud or insolvency if a receiver is not appointed.

Powers of the Receiver

Receivers in general have broad powers and may hire their own counsel to conduct discovery and represent them in court proceedings. These powers, however, are greatly tempered by the restriction that receivers can only undertake those actions that are authorized by the court.

The receiver's powers in the context of a charging order are, as mentioned, limited to seeking distributions for the benefit of the creditor (or creditors) and making inquiries to the LLC.

As to the latter, the receiver's power is further limited by the Harmonized Acts to making only those inquiries to which the debtor was entitled. An operating agreement cannot alter the provisions of section 503(b) to the prejudice of third parties.[5]

Whether the receiver can share information gained from the LLC other than the fact and amount of distributions made is usually an issue for the court to determine under the facts of the particular case, but should not be presumed. If the creditor desires this information, then the creditor should include in the motion to appoint a receiver specific provisions allowing the receiver to share this information with the creditor.

Case Study: *Pajooh*[6]

Debtor Danesh Pajooh owned 99 percent of U.S. Capital Investments LLC (Pajooh's sister owned the other one percent). Pajooh also owned the 99-percent limited partnership interest of County Investment LP, with U.S. Capital Investments LLC being the one-percent general partner (U.S. Capital and County Investments).

Given that both Pajooh and U.S. Capital were debtors, the Texas district court appointed a receiver for those two companies, neither of which appeared to have any assets worth collecting other than their cumulative 100-percent interest in County Investments. The creditor chasing Pajooh also obtained charging orders on Pajooh's membership interests in U.S. Capital and County Investments and on U.S. Capital's general partnership interest in County Investments.

It was in County Investment that Pajooh was hiding his valuable assets, including commercial real estate, Pajooh's Lexus, and antiques, among others. The district court therefore also appointed the same receiver for County Investments. This became the point of contention in the appeal of the receivership order to the Texas Court of Appeals:

---

5. RULLCA section 110(c)(11).
6. Pajooh v. Royal West Inv. LLC, Series E, 2017 WL 1173892 (Tex. App. 2017).

> It is well-established that the purpose of a charging order is to protect not the debtor, but the non-debtor members of a partnership or LLC. The leading cases are, in bankruptcy, *In re Albright*, 291 B.R. 538 (Bk. D. Colo. 2003), and in state law, Olmstead v. FTC, 44 So.3d 76 (Fla. 2010), and they essentially hold that protecting non-debtor members is nonsensical where there are no non-debtor partners to protect, as with County Investments.

The Texas Court of Appeals distinguished *Albright* and *Olmstead* and essentially adopted a strict constructionist interpretation of the Texas statute, which provides that the charging order is the "exclusive remedy" for pursuing a debtor's interest in a partnership or LLC, period, no deep thought or further analysis required.

The Texas Court of Appeals similarly ruled that it was a mistake to appoint a receiver that had the power to take control of U.S. Capital's interest in County Investments because, again, the charging order was the "exclusive remedy" under the Texas statute.

With that, the Texas Court of Appeals reversed the district court's receiver's orders only to the extent that they empowered the receiver to take over County Investments or U.S. Capital interests in County Investments, but otherwise affirmed the receivership order.

CHAPTER 17

Pre-Foreclosure Redemption

Statutory Authority

RULLCA (2006, as amended 2013) provides at sections 503(d) and (e) as follows:

> (d) At any time before foreclosure under subsection (c), the member or transferee whose transferable interest is subject to a charging order under subsection (a) may extinguish the charging order by satisfying the judgment and filing a certified copy of the satisfaction with the court that issued the charging order.
>
> (e) At any time before foreclosure under subsection (c), a limited liability company or one or more members whose transferable interests are not subject to the charging order may pay to the judgment creditor the full amount due under the judgment and thereby succeed to the rights of the judgment creditor, including the charging order.

ULPA (2001, as amended 2013) provides at section 503(c) as follows:

> (d) At any time before foreclosure under subsection (c), the partner or transferee whose transferable interest is subject to a charging order under subsection (a) may extinguish the charging order by satisfying the judgment and filing a certified copy of the satisfaction with the court that issued the charging order.
>
> (e) At any time before foreclosure under subsection (c), a limited partnership or one or more partners whose transferable interests are not subject to the charging order may pay to the judgment creditor the full amount due under the judgment and thereby succeed to the rights of the judgment creditor, including the charging order.

UPA (2001, as amended 2013) provides at sections (d) and (e) as follows:

> (d) At any time before foreclosure under subsection (c), the partner or transferee whose transferable interest is subject to a charging order under subsection (a) may extinguish the charging order by satisfying

> the judgment and filing a certified copy of the satisfaction with the court that issued the charging order.
>
> (e) At any time before foreclosure under subsection (c), a partnership or one or more partners whose transferable interests are not subject to the charging order may pay to the judgment creditor the full amount due under the judgment and thereby succeed to the rights of the judgment creditor, including the charging order.

Operating Agreement Provision

Section 503(d) of the RULLCA provides that before foreclosure, the debtor-member may redeem the liened interest.[1] Section 503(e) provides that the LLC or any other member may redeem the liened interest.[2]

These two paragraphs raise the specter of a situation where the creditor moves to foreclose and simultaneously: (1) the debtor-member attempts to redeem under subsection (d) and offers to pay the creditor; (2) the other members of the LLC vote to have the LLC redeem under subsection (e), and the LLC offers to pay the creditor; and (3) another member of the LLC attempts to redeem under subsection (e) and offers to pay the creditor.

Who wins? Section 503 provides no guidance, and we are thus left with a situation where, possession being nine-tenths of the law, the party whose check is first accepted by the creditor has actually redeemed, and probably wins, an unlikely "race to the creditor."

This is unlikely, however, because of what is required in the way of payment. Most planners would presume that payment would be in some amount tied to the fair market value of the liened interest. Not so, according to the plain text of subsections (d) and (e), which instead require the redeeming party to pay the full amount required to satisfy the judgment.[3]

Nothing prohibits the nondebtor-members from showing up at the judicial sale and bidding on the interest themselves,[4] for which the amount of the winning bid will, in most cases, be much less than the full amount of the debtor's outstanding judgment. Thus, common sense dictates that where the amount of

---

1. Rev. Unif. Ltd. Liab. Co. Act § 503(d), 6C U.L.A. 121 (Unif. Law Comm'n 2016).

2. *Id.* § 503(e); Union Colony Bank v. United Bank of Greeley Nat. Ass'n, 832 P.2d 1112, 1116 (Colo. App. 1992) ("[P]artners may, at any time before foreclosure, redeem or purchase the interest charged or subject to sale.").

3. Rev. Unif. Ltd. Liab. Co. Act § 503(d)-(e), 6B U.L.A. 148 (Unif. Law Comm'n Supp. 2015).

4. Deutsch v. Wolff, 7 S.W.3d 460, 463 (Mo. Ct. App. 1999) ("Where the court directs sale, the interest charged may be purchased by any one or more of the partners without thereby causing a dissolution.").

the outstanding judgment exceeds the fair market value of the interest, the non-debtors would be smarter to bid than to redeem.

Assume that the debtor-member has suffered a $5 million judgment, and the liened interest is worth, on a good day, only $10,000. Probably nobody is going to offer to pay the full amount of the $5 million judgment just to redeem the $10,000 foreclosed interest. This is also why planners should not rely heavily upon redemption to keep the creditor from foreclosing on the interest, not that the creditor will even want to in most cases.

CHAPTER 18

Foreclosure & Redemption

Statutory Authority

Foreclosure of a liened interest means that the creditor can subject the interest to a judicial sale, i.e., the sheriff holds an auction at which the interest is sold to the highest bidder.[1]

The creditor is not required to bid at the auction and, in fact, hopes that some other party will pay a substantial amount for the interest, which the creditor will then cheerfully apply (less the costs of the auction) toward satisfaction of the outstanding judgment.

If the creditor does bid, then the creditor will likely make a "credit bid," whereby the creditor treats as satisfied a portion or all of the judgment in lieu of a cash bid by the creditor. Note that the amount that the creditor applies toward the satisfaction of the outstanding judgment is the amount of the winning bid, not the value of the interest. Assume the appraised fair market value of the interest is $5 million, but nobody shows up at the auction, and the creditor bids only $1 as the winning bid. In that case, the $1 would be applied toward the satisfaction of the judgment even if the creditor soon after sells the interest for $5 million. This scenario is somewhat tempered by the court's mandatory review (as with all judicial sales) of the fairness of the auction, but the point is that the debtor should not blindly presume that he or she will get full credit toward satisfaction of the judgment based on the value of his or her interest which is thereby sold.

Importantly, even if the liened interest is sold at the auction, the only thing the buyer (whether the creditor or somebody else) purchases is the right to distributions. That right becomes a permanent right whereby distributions will be collected after the judgment is satisfied, or even later discharged. That does not mean the buyer obtains any other rights such as management rights in the LLC—that is specifically prohibited by RULLCA section 503(c).[2]

1. 91st Street Joint Venture v. Goldstein, 691 A.2d 272, 280 (Md. Ct. Spec. App. 1997) ("[A]ny transfer of the debtor partner's interest is to take place pursuant to the rules governing judicial sales.").

2. *See* Rev. Unif. Ltd. Liab. Co. Act § 503(c), 6C U.L.A. 121 (Unif. Law Comm'n 2016).

In other words, prior to foreclosure, the creditor has a temporary right to distributions only until the judgment is satisfied. After foreclosure, this right becomes permanent to the buyer regardless of whether the judgment is ever satisfied. In either case, however, the creditor or buyer still does not become anything like a member or manager of the LLC—they have a right only to distributions, nothing more.

Under RULLCA section 503(c) and probably the laws of most states whether they have adopted RULLCA or not, the lien created by the charging order can be foreclosed upon.[3] However, the creditor must first demonstrate to the court that the distributions from the LLC will not satisfy the judgment in some reasonable period of time.[4] This is a call entirely within the court's discretion,[5] and the court may take into account the possible disruption of the LLC and its effect (if any) on the nondebtor members.[6] However, nondebtor members are not required to consent to foreclosure.[7]

---

3. *Id.*

4. Lauer Construction Inc. v. Schrift, 716 A.2d 1096, 1098–99 (Md. Ct. Spec. App. 1998) (judgment creditor has the power to force a sale of the debtor's general partner's interest in a limited partnership); Nigri v. Lotz, 453 S.E.2d 780, 783 (Ga. Ct. App. 1995) ("In general, a charging order is considered the primary method of satisfying the creditor's judgment, but the further step of ordering a sale may be considered appropriate where it is apparent that distributions under the charging order will not pay the judgment debt within a reasonable period of time."); *91st Street Joint Venture*, 691 A.2d at 282 ("[T]he primary means of satisfying a judgment from a partnership interest should be the receipt and distribution of any income or profits due the debtor partner, and that, ordinarily, sale of the interest should not be resorted to unless the judgment could not be satisfied in that manner within a reasonable period of time.").

5. *Nigri*, 453 S.E.2d at 783 ("[T]he trial court has discretion to determine whether or not a judicial sale of the partnership interest is an appropriate means in aid of the charging order."); Stewart v. Lanier Park Med. Office Bldg., Ltd., 578 S.E.2d 572, 574–75 (Ga. Ct. App. 2003) ("The trial court has broad discretion in deciding whether to order a foreclosure and sale of charged interests.").

6. *See, e.g.*, Hellman v. Anderson, 284 Cal. Rptr. 830, 838 (1991):

> We conclude that since the interest acquired by the purchaser of a partnership interest is limited by operation of law to the partner's share of profits and surpluses, with no acquisition of interest in partnership property or management participation, the foreclosure and sale of the partnership interest will not always unduly interfere with the partnership business to the extent of requiring consent of the nondebtor partners. In some cases, foreclosure might cause a partner with essential managerial skills to abandon the partnership. In other cases, foreclosure would appear to have no appreciable effect on the conduct of partnership business. Thus, the effect of foreclosure on the partnership should be evaluated on a case-by-case basis by the trial court in connection with its equitable power to order a foreclosure.

Id.

7. The nondebtor partners must be given prior notice of the foreclosure. Union Colony Bank v. United Bank of Greeley Nat'l Ass'n, 832 P.2d 1112, 1116 (Colo. 1992) (*citing* First Nat'l Bank v. District Court, 652 P.2d 613 (Colo. 1982)). Although their consent to foreclosure is not

To illustrate what this means in practical terms, assume two situations:

(1) The creditor's judgment is for $20,000, and the LLC is a hedge fund that regularly spins off $6,000 per year in distributions to the liened interest. In that case, the judgment will be satisfied in four years, even counting interest on the judgment, and so the court would be unlikely to grant foreclosure.[8]

(2) The creditor's judgment is for $5,000,000, and the LLC is a closely held entity with few assets that irregularly spin off distributions, none of which have exceeded $20,000 in years past, and none at all since the charging order was granted. In that case, it is unlikely that distributions from the liened interest will ever satisfy the judgment, and the court would likely grant foreclosure in such a case.

Note that nothing prevents the creditor from bringing a combined motion for charging order and to foreclose and attempting to do both at the same hearing. The case where such a combined motion might be successful is the second situation above, where it is clear that distributions will never satisfy the judgment, and there is little sense in making the creditor wait for a few months just to tell the court the obvious.

The Monster under the Bed?

The mere thought of foreclosure has caused many planners to freak out and demand that their states' legislature amend its partnership and LLC laws to prohibit a creditor's foreclosure of a liened interest. This is a concern primarily connected with the marketing competitiveness of partnerships and LLCs among states, as it is not a concern borne out by any widespread outbreak of creditors attempting to foreclose on the charged interest. To the contrary, there have been fewer than a dozen reported opinions nationwide over the entire history of partnership and LLC law where a creditor has even attempted to foreclose upon an interest subject to the charging order lien. In other words, creditors are not exactly falling over themselves to foreclose on liened interests, even in the states where such is plainly sanctioned by statute. There are several reasons for this.

First, there is often painfully little for the creditor to gain by foreclosing. The creditor already has a lien on the debtor-member's interest, and if the LLC is making significant distributions, the creditor will quite likely be satisfied to accept those distributions so long as they continue to be made. If not, i.e., the LLC is not

---

required. *Hellman*, 284 Cal. Rptr. at 832 ("consent of nondebtor partners is not an inflexible requirement . . . .").

8. *91st Street Joint Venture*, 691 A.2d at 283 ("Ordinarily, the trial court should consider whether the judgment can be satisfied out of the debtor partner's profits prior to resort to the more drastic method of sale of the debtor partner's interest.").

making distributions to the liened interest, then an auction of the liened interest will not draw any serious bidders, and all the creditor will have done would be to have "thrown good money after bad" through payment of attorney's fees and expenses of the auction.

Second, where the charging order was acquired by the creditor for the strategic purpose of causing financial pain to the debtor by cutting off the debtor's access to funds from the LLC, the lien created by the charging order works just as well as a temporary lien until the judgment is satisfied, as it does if the lien were foreclosed upon and purchased either by the creditor of some third-party buyer.

Third, the creditor has a significant tax incentive to not foreclose and risk acquiring the interest. Prior to foreclosure, the creditor is simply the holder of a lien and as such is not subject to receiving a K-1 from the LLC.[9] However, after foreclosure, the buyer (which might be the creditor who ends up with it) does then become a transferee of the transferrable interest and is potentially liable for its distributive share of the LLC's taxes.

Finally, as discussed more fully below, the creditor has possibly better avenues to explore in attempting to get at the debtor-member's share of the assets of the LLC instead of just seeking a judicial sale of the transferrable interest.

For all these reasons, the threat of foreclosure is the monster under the bed—much more bark than bite. The proof is, again, in the utter paucity of reported opinions where creditors have attempted to foreclose on liened interests.

9. The frequently misinterpreted Revenue Rule 77-137 and IRS General Counsel Memorandum 36960 are not to the contrary. *See* Rev. Rul. 77-137, 1977-1 C.B. 178; I.R.S. Gen. Couns. Mem. 36960 (1977) (on file with author). *See also infra* Chapter 27.

CHAPTER 19

Appealing A Charging Order

Statutory Authority

The Harmonized Acts do not mention an appeal of a charging order. Thus, the authority to appeal a charging order must be found in the other law of the forum jurisdiction for the appeal of post-judgment enforcement orders.

Note that in some jurisdictions, the appeal of a post-judgment enforcement order may only be accomplished by some writ procedure or another, such as a writ of prohibition (if the order is granted) or a writ of mandate (if it is not).

Standing to Appeal

The debtor, being a party to the lawsuit and whose rights are directly affected by a charging order, has standing to appeal; however, the standing of the LLC and the nondebtor members is less certain.

The reason for the confusion is that it is unclear what role the LLC or the nondebtor members play in a motion for charging order, or whether they have even become a party to the proceeding.

The Harmonized Acts, for instance, make no provision for giving even mere notice (much less service of process that would comport with constitutional due process) to the LLC or the nondebtor members of the motion for charging order. At least in California—the only state to have adopted a charging order procedure to attempt to effectuate this remedy—there is an argument to be made the that the LLC or the nondebtor members (depending on who was served) become parties to the charging order proceeding because they are required to be "served with notice." In every other jurisdiction, decisional law must be consulted to resolve this issue (if it can be resolved).

The bottom line is that whether the LLC or the nondebtor members will have standing to press an appeal of a charging order must be tested on a facts-and-circumstances basis and will measure such things as the quality of service and the extent to which the charging order affected their own rights.

Indeed, where the LLC or the nondebtor members were not served with notice of the motion for charging order, but the charging order ultimately issued by the court requires them to take some affirmative action with which they disagree, the LLC or the nondebtor members might be compelled to make a limited appearance before the court that is hearing the matter to challenge that court's jurisdiction and then appeal that decision if it is unfavorable.

Time to Appeal

Orders of the trial court typically may not be appealed until they are a final, appealable order. The granting of a charging order, the principle effect of which is to place a lien on the debtor-member's right to distributions, has the effect of placing this lien on the debtor-member's right to distributions and should ordinarily be immediately appealable at that time.

However, in *Rogers Group, Inc. v. Gilbert*,[1] the Tennessee Court of Appeals held to the effect that a charging order is not immediately appealable upon entry. Instead, that court analogized a charging order to a garnishment and held that the charging order did not constitute a final, appealable judgment until either the LLC had made a payment that was subject to the order, or reported that no payments were owing to the debtor.[2]

1. 2016 WL 2605651 (Tenn. App. May 3, 2016).

2. The *Rogers Group* decision is subject to criticism; *see* Adkisson, J., *Tennessee Charging Order Not an Appealable Final Judgment (Just Yet) In Rogers Group*, Forbes.com (May 31, 2016), *available at* http://goo.gl/QmwWUK.

CHAPTER 20

Conflict-of-Laws Issues

Assume a situation in which the creditor has sued the debtor in State A, the debtor resides in State B, and the debtor has a membership interest in an LLC that has been formed in State C, but that has its principal office in State D. The creditor now brings a motion in federal court in State A (the forum state) for a charging order against the debtor's interest in the LLC. Which state's laws apply?

If the law of states A, B, C, and D are all the same, there is no conflict and thus no issue—what is referred to as a "false conflict."[1] In that case, the law of the forum state (State A) will normally apply. However, assume further a situation in which the laws of those states are disparate. Perhaps State B treats single-member LLC specially; perhaps the creditor's motion also seeks to foreclose on the charged interest, which is subject to strict limitations in State C and is prohibited outright in State D. Such circumstances will require a conflict-of-laws analysis.

The first question in any conflict-of-laws issue is which state's conflict-of-laws rules will be used to work through the conflict. Without going into an extended and somewhat esoteric discussion of why, suffice it to say that the court will almost inevitably use the rules of the forum state (State A).[2]

The next step is to apply those rules to the facts at hand. Given that a charging order is procedural in nature, the laws of the forum state (State A) will normally apply. In the vast majority of cases, this has been the answer: The laws of the forum state apply to charging order disputes. There is an old saw among creditor-rights lawyers that "all collection law is local." Much more often than not, that is the result.

If the conflict is determined to be substantive, however, then the conflict-of-laws analysis becomes more complex. With property, the conflict-of-laws pointer typically goes to the state where the property is located, but where is an LLC interest located, given that it doesn't physically exist anywhere?

---

1. *See, e.g.*, Leonards v. Southern Farm Bureau Cas. Ins. Co., 279 F.3d 611, 612 (8th Cir. 2002) ("We believe, however, that this case presents what has come to be called a false conflict because we conclude that the relevant legal principles are the same in both states with respect to the issue that we find dispositive.").

2. *See generally* Guaranty Trust Co. v. York, 326 U.S. 99 (1945); Restatement (Second) of Conflict of Laws §122 (Am. Law Inst. 1971).

ULLCA section 501[3] provides guidance in that an LLC interest is an interest in personal property. Intangible personal property is said to exist in the jurisdiction of the owner's residence.[4] Therefore, the substantive laws of State B would presumably apply in the hypothetical.

Debtors, or the LLC, often argue that the place for bringing a motion for charging order, and the law applicable to such proceeding, must be only in the state where the LLC was formed. So far, it has been a losing argument whenever attempted.[5]

The first problem is that an LLC interest is personal property.[6] For collection purposes, intangible personal property is "located" either with the debtor, wherever the debtor may be found, or in the debtor's state of domicile.[7] In the vast majority of cases, these are the same because the debtor was originally sued in his or her place of domicile. In either event, however, it is not some distant domicile where the LLC was formed.

The second problem is that for creditor-debtor purposes, an LLC interest may be analogized to a share of stock in a corporation. If a creditor is levying upon a debtor's shares in Microsoft, the creditor does not have to go to Washington state or Delaware to accomplish that result, so why should a charging order be treated much differently? It is, after all, only the debtor's rights that are affected and not those of the LLC (or corporation).

---

3. *Accord* UPA § 501 and ULPA § 701.

4. *See, e.g.*, Wells Fargo Bank v. Barber, 85 F. Supp. 3d 1308, 1314 (M.D. Fla. 2015) ("Unlike stock certificates in a corporation, a membership interest in a limited liability company is intangible personal property, which "accompanies the person of the owner. Therefore, because Barber resides in Florida, Barber's membership interest in [the LLC] is located with her in Florida and is properly subject to *in rem* jurisdiction in this state.") (citations omitted).

5. *See, e.g.*, Montana v. Blixseth (*In re* Blixseth), 484 B.R. 360, 363 (B.A.P. 9th Cir. 2012).

6. *See, e.g.*, Unif. Ltd. Liab. Co. Act § 501 (Unif. Law Comm'n 2006); *see also* Koh v. Inno-Pacific Holdings, Ltd., 54 P.3d 1270, 1271 (Wash. Ct. App. 2002) ("The interest of a member in a limited liability company is personal property."); Deutsch v. Wolff, 7 S.W.3d 460, 463 (Mo. Ct. App. 1999) ("A partnership interest is an economic right to share in the profits and surpluses, most accurately characterized as intangible personal property."); Madison Hills Ltd. P'ship II v. Madison Hills, Inc., 644 A.2d 363, 366 (Conn. App. Ct. 1994) ("The charging order affects only the partner's interest in the partnership, which is personal property.") (citations omitted).

7. *See, e.g.*, Waite v. Waite, 492 P.2d 13 (Cal. 1972):

> An intangible, unlike real or tangible personal property, has no physical characteristics that would serve as a basis for assigning it to a particular locality. The location assigned to it depends on what action is to be taken with reference to it. Thus most cases that place the situs of an intangible asset at the domicile of the owner do so to enable the jurisdiction of the owner's domicile to tax that property or the income derived from it. When, however, the issue, as in this case, involves jurisdiction to compel the obligor to pay one claimant and not a competing claimant, the debt or claim is usually regarded as having a situs in any state in which personal jurisdiction of the debtor can be obtained.

Id. at 17 (citations omitted).

Courts have held in several cases that local law applies to the issuance of a charging order and not the law where the entity is domiciled.[8]

Debtors have attempted to change the forum for the determination of charging orders in at least two cases, *Bay Guardian Co. v. New Times Media, LLC*[9] and *American Institutional Partners, LLC v. Fairstar Resources, Ltd.*[10] In both cases, the debtors filed lawsuits for declaratory judgment in Delaware, where the LLCs were domiciled, seeking injunctions to prevent the creditor from pursuing the charging order remedy in California (*Bay Guardian*) and Utah (*Fairstar Resources*).[11] The creditors in both of those cases successfully thwarted the debtor's attempt by removing the cases to federal court and invoking there the federal Anti-Injunction Act, which prevents a federal court from interfering with an ongoing state proceeding (the charging order motions).

Choice-of-Law Provisions and Internal Affairs

It is standard for operating agreement forms to contain a choice-of-law provision providing that if any dispute arises under the agreement, the dispute will be resolved according to the laws of State X, which is most often the state of formation. Many planners put great faith in these provisions to create certainty as to which law will apply if the LLC or its members wind up in court for whatever reason.

The problem is that a creditor is ordinarily not a party to the operating agreement and therefore is not bound by such a designation. Although these provisions govern disputes between the members, and between the members and the LLC, they cannot bind a nonparty to the agreement.

Some planners place a great deal of reliance upon the "Internal Affairs Doctrine" to determine which law will apply to the resolution of a charging order dispute. This doctrine is codified in ULLCA section 104:

> The law of this state governs:
>
> (1) the internal affairs of a limited liability company; and
>
> (2) the liability of a member as member and a manager as manager for a debt, obligation, or other liability of a limited liability company.[12]

---

8. Am. Institutional Partners, LLC v. Fairstar Res., Ltd., C.A. No. 10-489-LPS., 2011 WL 1230074, at *1–2 (D. Del. Mar. 31, 2011), *vacated on other grounds*; Rockstone Cap., LLC v. Mktg. Horizons, Ltd., No. NNHCV065006818S, 2013 WL 4046597 (Conn. Ct. Super. July 17, 2013).

9. New Times Media, LLC v. Bay Guardian Co., Inc., 2010 WL 1909558 (D. Del. 2010), U.S. Magistrate's Report and Recommendation adopted, 2010 WL 2573957.

10. *Am. Institutional Partners*, 2011 WL 1230074, at *2, 12.

11. *Id.* at *8.

12. Rev. Unif. Ltd. Liab. Co. Act § 104, 6C U.L.A. 25 (Unif. Law Comm'n 2016).

The problem is that the Internal Affairs Doctrine has been consistently held not to apply to outside creditors.[13] "Internal affairs" has been consistently interpreted to mean precisely that, i.e., a dispute between members or a member and the LLC itself.[14] The doctrine does not extend to third-party creditors, [15] even if the effect of the charging order would be to indirectly interfere somehow (that a member would not perform if not getting paid distribution being the most common argument) with the "internal affairs" of the LLC.

CASE STUDY: *EARTHGRAINS*[16]

Earthgrains Baking Companies, Inc. (Earthgrains) sued Sycamore Family Bakery Inc. and Leland Sycamore in the U.S. District Court for the District of Utah over a trademark licensing agreement and other issues. Earthgrains won and ended up with a $2.3 million judgment that grew with statutory penalties, attorney's fees, costs, and interest in excess of $6 million.

To enforce the Utah judgment, Earthgrains obtained a charging order against the Sycamore Family LLC, in which defendant (now debtor) Leland Sycamore had a 48-percent membership interest, and his wife, Jeri Sycamore, likewise had a 48-percent interest. The four Sycamore children each held one-percent interests to round out the ownership. Apparently, the Sycamore Family LLC owns the bulk of the Sycamore family's assets, including a home in Heber, Utah, which was purchased through an $800,000 distribution to Jeri Sycamore.

Earthgrains moved to hold Sycamore Family LLC in contempt for failing to pay over Leland Sycamore's share of the profits and distributions to Earthgrains as required by the charging order.

The LLC defended with the argument that the charging order was improperly issued under Utah law instead of under Nevada law where the LLC had been formed; therefore, there was no valid order, and the Sycamore Family LLC could not be held in contempt. The LLC further argued that this result is mandated by the so-called Internal Affairs Doctrine, which holds that certain disputes involving LLCs can be resolved only under the laws of where the LLC was formed, or such laws as the members agree would be applicable. This argument flopped badly:

---

13. *See, e.g.*, Faulkner. v. Kornman (*In re* The Heritage Org., L.L.C.), 413 B.R. 438, 463 (Bankr. N.D. Tex. 2009); Petro v. Gold, 850 N.E.2d 1218, 1233 (Ohio Ct. App. 2006); McDermott Inc. v. Lewis, 531 A.2d 206, 214–15 (Del. 1987).

14. The most common exception is that in alter ego cases, the law of the jurisdiction where the entity has been formed will most typically apply. *See* REV. UNIF. LTD. LIAB. CO. ACT §104, cmt. ¶ 2.

15. The one exception is that alter ego claims will be tested with reference to the laws of the state of formation. *See* RULLCA § 104, cmt. ¶ 2.

16. Earthgrains Baking Co. v. Sycamore Family Bakery, Inc., D. Utah Case No. 09CV523 (Aug. 21, 2015).

> The Charging Order does not implicate the internal affairs of the Sycamore Family LLC. It merely relates to the LLC's obligations to a third party.
>
> The internal affairs of an LLC are limited only to matters peculiar to the relationships among or between the corporation and its current officers, directors, and shareholders. . . . Many courts have already concluded that claims, such as Earthgrains's, asserted by third party creditors against an LLC fall outside the internal affairs doctrine. . . . Moreover, under a choice of law analysis, Utah law would govern the Charging Order because all of the LLC's activities, dealings, and properties are located in Utah, and Leland Sycamore is a resident of Utah. Therefore, the court concludes that the Charging Order was properly issued under Utah law and is a valid court order for purposes of contempt proceedings. [Internal citations and quotation marks omitted.]

The only remaining question was whether Sycamore Family LLC violated the charging order. Earthgrains claimed that the LLC, just to avoid paying on the judgment, had been making distributions to Jeri Sycamore without making equivalent distributions to Leland.

The LLC responded that it had not made any distributions to Jeri Sycamore, but instead was merely paying her a "management fee" to take care of the affairs of the LLC. However, there was no written agreement to document this arrangement for any amount, much less the large payments made to Jeri, which Earthgrains contended was excessive for her scant management duties.

To resolve this, the court granted the parties 70 days to engage in discovery on the issue and denied EarthGrain's motion without prejudice and subject to possible renewal at the close of such discovery.

Earthgrains also sought a restraining order to keep the Sycamore Family LLC from liquidating property in violation of Leland Sycamore's interest. What happened is that Leland financed the purchase of his codebtor, Sycamore Family Bakery, through a $2.1 million line of credit from Wells Fargo, but the deed of trust listed Sycamore Family LLC as the borrower. A subsequent rider to the deed of trust acted as an amendment and listed Leland as the borrower.

Leland owed about $2 million on the Wells Fargo loan, and the property was listed for sale at around $4 million. Earthgrains argued that allowing Sycamore Family LLC to liquidate the property and let Wells Fargo take $2 million would be the equivalent of a $2 million distribution by the LLC to Leland, which would not go to Earthgrains (but instead to Wells Fargo) and thus violate the charging order.

Sycamore retorted that Wells Fargo was an "indispensable party" to this dispute and should be joined as a party (presumably so that it could join Leland in fighting off Earthgrains).

No sale, sayeth the court, noting that Wells Fargo had not declared the loan in default or attempted to collect against the property. Moreover, Earthgrains was simply trying to preserve the property for later enforcement action and not resolve any issues of whether Wells Fargo had a lien on the property or issues of lien priority. Thus, the court entered an order to prevent the property's sale unless Leland or the Sycamore Family LLC could demonstrate that sufficient other assets were available to satisfy EarthGrain's judgment.

CHAPTER 21

The Foreign LLC Issue

Article 9 of the ULLCA deals with foreign limited liability companies, but does not speak to the topic of charging orders.[1] Section 102 defines a limited liability company as: "except in the phrase 'foreign limited liability company' . . . means an entity formed under this Act . . . ."[2] Section 503 relates only to a "limited liability company," without reference to a foreign limited liability company.[3] Bootstrapping all of this together, arguments have been made that section 503 applies only to limited liability companies that are formed in the state, and not to foreign limited liability companies formed outside the state.

This argument first came up in the *Bay Guardian* litigation, where the debtor defensively argued that under California's Uniform Limited Liability Company Act (CULLCA), the California court lacked the authority to place a charging order on the debtor's interest in various foreign LLCs.[4] To the debtor's great surprise, the creditor gleefully accepted the argument as valid, and then offensively argued that if the charging order section of the CULLCA did not apply to foreign LLCs, then by the same token the statutory restriction to the charging order remedy of that same section similarly did not apply to foreign LLCs. Thus, the creditor could instead levy directly upon and sell the debtor's interests.[5] The debtor attempted to take back its argument, and the court simply ignored the entire issue on its way to issuing the sought charging order (without opinion) against the foreign LLC interests.[6]

Then, the Minnesota Court of Appeals took up the cudgel in *Fannie Mae v. Heather Apartments LP*,[7] where the creditor used the argument offensively to

1. *See* Rev. Unif. Ltd. Liab. Co. Act art. 9 (Unif. Law Comm'n 2016).

2. *Id.* § 102(8).

3. *Id.* § 503.

4. Bay Guardian v. New Times Media, No. CGC-04-435584 (Calif. Super. San Francisco Cty.), Defendants' Opposition to Motion for Charging Order, at 17–18 (Dec. 18, 2009).

5. *Bay Guardian*, Judgment Creditor's Reply to Debtor's Opposition to Motion for Charging Order, at 25–27 (Dec. 23, 2009).

6. *Bay Guardian*, Charging Order (Jan. 6, 2010).

7. Fannie Mae v. Heather Apartments Ltd. P'ship, No. A13-0562, 2013 WL 6223564 (Minn. Ct. App. Dec. 2, 2013).

force a debtor to turn over his interests in Cook Islands LLC. On this issue, the court held *in toto*:

> Finally, Grossman argues that Fannie Mae's only remedy is to obtain a charging order under Minn. Stat. § 322B.32 (2012). But this argument fails because that statute only applies to Minnesota limited liability companies. Chapter 322B defines a "limited liability company" as "a limited liability company, other than a foreign limited liability company, organized or governed by this chapter." Minn. Stat. § 322B.03, subd. 28 (2012). Because LSPG Shoreline was organized in, and is governed by, the laws of the Cook Islands, chapter 322B does not apply.[8]

Certainly, it was not the intent of the ULLCA or RULLCA drafters to exclude a foreign limited liability company from the ambit of the section 503 charging order procedure or exclusive remedy limitation. Professor Carter G. Bishop of Suffolk University Law School, a member of the RULLCA Drafting Committee and an expert on American charging order law (if there is one),[9] unsuccessfully attempted to file an *amicus curiae* brief with the Minnesota Supreme Court which pointed out the error, and ultimately the appeal was denied.[10]

Although this issue has the latent potential for vast procedural confusion, the ultimate effect in terms of what a creditor ends up with should not be significantly different, largely because the only interest the debtor has that is susceptible to being transferred is the debtor's economic right to distributions. If the creditor successfully attaches the debtor's interest, the attachment lien that the creditor receives would not be significantly different than a charging order lien. Likewise, if the creditor levies upon the debtor's interest, and that levy results in a judicial sale, the purchaser at the judicial sale simply becomes an involuntary transferee of the debtor's former interest, and under ULLCA § 502(c), and limited to only the "distributions to which the transferor would otherwise be entitled."[11]

---

8. *Id.* at *6.

9. *See* Carter G. Bishop, *Fifty State Series: LLC Charging Order Case Table* (Suffolk Univ. Law Sch., Legal Research Paper Series, Paper No. 10-15, 2015), *available at* http://ssrn.com/abstract=1565595. Appendix C hereto.

10. Review was denied on February 18, 2014.

11. That a writ of attachment can accomplish the lien aspect of a charging order, and a writ of levy the foreclosure aspect of a charging order, the question arises as to why these traditional enforcement remedies are not used instead of a charging order? The author suggests that there is no good answer to this question other than the historical one.

Case Study: *German American Capital*[12]

In a nutshell, there is an issue as to whether the so-called Harmonized Acts define partnership and companies under those acts.

To illustrate, consider the treatment of LLCs under the ULLCA. Under that act, a "limited liability company" is defined as one that is formed under the laws of the particular state; however, the provision relating to creditors' rights, and thus to charging orders, discusses only a "limited liability company." In the *Heather Apartments* decision, the Minnesota Court of Appeals held that this means—relying on a strict construction of Minnesota's ULLCA—that the provisions relating to charging orders do not apply to a limited liability company not formed in Minnesota (there, the LLC was formed in the Cook Islands). In that case, the creditor was therefore not restricted to a charging order against the debtor's interest in the Cook Islands LLC.

Some courts have rejected this strict construction as nonsensical because there is no sensible reason anybody has yet articulated why in-state and out-of-state LLCs should be treated differently for charging order purposes, such as the *Vision Marketing* court. The *Heather Apartments* glitch, in other words, is little more than a drafting error.

A manifestation of the latter position appeared in a case involving German American Capital Corporation (GACC), which obtained a charging order in Maryland against Dean Morehouse's interest in a Georgia LLC. Morehouse claimed that the charging order should not be entered against the Georgia LLC under Maryland law, but instead Georgia law relating to charging orders should apply. The court rejected this argument:

> In Maryland, a creditor of a debtor who "hold[s] an economic interest in a limited liability company" may request that a court "charge the economic interest of the debtor in the limited liability company for the unsatisfied amount of the debt." Md. Code. Corps. & Ass'ns § 4A-607(b)(1). Because it was formed under the laws of Georgia. ECF No. 40-2, Savannah Harbor is a foreign limited liability company. See Md. Code. Corps. & Ass'ns § 4A-101(j) (defining "foreign limited liability" as a company formed under the laws of a state other than Maryland.). Notably, the charging statute that GACC relies on does not reference foreign limited liability companies and the term, "limited liability company," is defined as an unincorporated business "organized and existing under [the Maryland Limited Liability Company Act]." See id. § 4A-101(k). However, the charging statute also references a debtor's "economic interest," which is defined in the Act's definitional section as the right

12. German Am. Capital Corp. v. Morehouse, 2017 WL 3411941 (D. Md. Aug. 4. 2017), *aff'd* 714 Fed. App'x 286, 2018 WL 1312253 (4th Cir. Mar. 14, 2018) (per curiam) (unpublished).

> of a "member," of either a limited liability company or a foreign limited liability company, to receive distributions from a limited liability company, or a member's share of the profits and losses of such a company. See id. §§ 4A-101(i), (m). Thus, reading the charging statute in conjunction with the definition section, and in the absence of any language specifically barring the entry of charging orders against foreign limited liability companies, the Court concludes that the charging statute does provide for the enforcement of a charging order against a foreign limited liability corporation like Savannah Harbor. Vision Mktg. Res., Inc. v. McMillin Grp., LLC, No. CIV.A. 10-2252-KHV, 2015 WL 4390071, at *6 (D. Kan. July 15, 2015) (reaching same conclusion after interpreting similar Kansas statute).

But every bit as interesting is footnote 2 of the opinion, which addresses whether the Maryland court needed jurisdiction over the Georgia LLC to issue the charging order; the court thought not:

> Morehouse's membership interest in Savannah Harbor is his personal property and the Court's personal jurisdiction over Morehouse extends to his personal property even if it is located outside of Maryland. See e.g. Vision Mktg. Res., Inc., 2015 WL 4390071, at *5 (holding that because the Court had personal jurisdiction over the debtor, the Court could enter judgment against his interest in a foreign limited liability company): Glob. Money Mgmt. v. McDonnold, No. 06CV34 BTM (WMC), 2009 WL 3352574, at *3 (S.D. Cal. Oct. 15, 2009).

This is the correct outcome. The decision in *Heather Apartments* and its progeny is simply wrong, and the courts in those cases should have recognized the drafting error in the ULLCA (and, indeed, in all the Harmonized Acts) instead of blindly applying the statute in a way that makes utterly no sense. Further, so long as the court has personal jurisdiction over the debtor, the court similarly has jurisdiction over the debtor's LLC interest sufficient to place a charging order lien on that interest.[13]

Case Study: *Arayos*[14]

Plaintiff Arayos, LLC won a judgment in the U.S. District Court for the District of Maine. To begin collecting the $1.3 million judgment, Arayos

---

13. As a member's interest in an LLC is in the nature of personal property under ULLCA § 501, and intangible personal property is deemed to "exist," if at all, where the debtor is variously located or resides.

14. Arayos, LLC v. Jimmie Ellis, 2016 WL 1642676 (S.D. Ala. Apr. 25, 2016).

registered the judgment in the U.S. District Court for the Southern District of Alabama, where one of the defendants, John M. Vellianitis, resided.

Arayos then sought charging orders against Vellianitis's interests in four LLCs, the first two formed in Alabama, the third formed in Wyoming, and the fourth formed in Nevada. Like the ULLCA and most states acts, Alabama's charging order establishes a lien for the judgment amount in favor of the creditor against the debtor's economic rights (read: rights to distributions) in the LLC until the judgment has been paid or otherwise discharged. Any distributions after service of the charging order should be re-routed to the creditor.

Arayos's application attached documents from the Alabama Secretary of State's office that showed that Vellianitis had some interest in the two Alabama LLCs. Thus, the Alabama federal court issued the charging orders against those two domestic LLCs.

Curiously, Arayos attached nothing about the Wyoming or Nevada LLC, so Arayos's application failed on that basis. The court could and arguably should have stopped right there. Perhaps, though, in light of the common practice for a court to issue writs of garnishment without any allegation of debt owed by the judgment debtor, the court continued with additional grounds for denying the application:

> [A]s noted supra, plaintiff's filings reflect that Lodge Entertainment is a Wyoming limited liability company, and that Jonesboro Investments is a Nevada limited liability company. Plaintiff has presented no argument explaining why it contends a provision of the Alabama Business and Nonprofit Entities Code would empower this Court to issue a charging order as to a judgment debtor's membership interest in Wyoming and Nevada limited liability companies, as part and parcel of the judgment creditor's efforts to enforce a judgment entered by a federal court in Maine. {Footnote 2} On its face, Alabama Code sec. 10A-5-6.05(a) does not appear to authorize issuance of charging orders relating to foreign limited liability companies. {Footnote 3}

The court then expounds on these two issues in the footnotes; both are important for understanding the scope of charging orders. The first issue is whether a U.S. district court in which a judgment is registered has the ability to issue a charging order, as opposed to the charging order being issued by the U.S. district court which originally issued the judgment. On this point, the court elaborated in footnote 2 (referenced in brackets above):

> To be sure, plaintiff states in conclusory fashion that "[t]his Court has jurisdiction over Vellianitis's interest in his limited liability companies," and cites two cases in which judges of this District Court have entered charging orders pursuant to Alabama law as to foreign limited liability

> companies. However, the cited cases articulate no reasoning for their expansive application of Alabama Code sec. 10A-5-6.05. Besides, both of those cited cases involved judgments issued by the U.S. District Court for the Southern District of Alabama, such that the charging orders were issued by the court to enforce its own judgment. By contrast, this Court—and this jurisdiction—has nothing to do with the underlying judgment that Arayos, LLC, is trying to enforce. Its only connection to this dispute is, ostensibly, that Vellianitis lives in this district (although plainiffs [sic] submits no proof whatsoever to establish such a jurisdictional fact) and is a member of two LLCs organized and formed in the State of Alabama. The Alabama authorities cited by plaintiff cannot persuasively be read as authorizing this Court, based on such a tenuous connection to the dispute and the absence of supporting language in the applicable charging order statute, to issue charging orders under Alabama law as to limited liability companies formed in Wyoming and Nevada. And plaintiff's citations to a pair of unpublished state trial-court opinions interpreting the Connecticut charging order statute to allow charging orders to be applied to foreign LLCs are unavailing absent a showing (which has not been made) that the Connecticut statute is identical or even substantially similar to Alabama Code sec. 10A-5-6.05(a) in all material respects. Even if the two states' statutes were the same, the Connecticut decisions are unhelpful because of the minimalist reasoning employed (which essentially boils down to the state trial judge's assessment that the Connecticut statute does not expressly forbid issuance of charging orders to foreign LLCs).

In *Aryos*, the Alabama federal judge rests his denial of the requests for charging orders against foreign LLCs on his not entering the judgment, partially rescuing two other Alabama federal judges from granting such requests in the face of the plain language of the Alabama charging order statute.

The second issue is whether Alabama's charging order laws authorize a charging order against a "foreign LLC," i.e., an LLC formed in another state than Alabama (an LLC formed outside of the United States would be referred to as an "alien LLC"). On this point, the court commented in footnote 3 (referenced in brackets above):

> The Alabama statute cited by Arayos allows charging orders to issue as to the interest of a "member." Ala. Code sec. 10A-5-6.05. "Member" is statutorily defined as "[a] person reflected in the required records of a limited liability company as the owner of some governance rights of a membership interest in the limited liability company." Ala. Code sec. 10A-5-1.02(7). The term "limited liability company" is likewise defined as "[a]n organization that is formed and existing under this

> chapter," Ala. Code sec. 10A-5-1.02(6), meaning Chapter 5 of Title 10A of the Alabama Code. Neither Lodge Entertainment, LLC, nor Jonesboro Investments, LLC, is an organization "formed and existing" under that chapter; therefore, the charging order provisions of sec. 10A-5-6.05 do not appear to reach those entities because Vellianitis would not qualify as a "member" of a "limited liability company," as those terms are defined by the statute. Again, plaintiff has made no showing to the contrary. Moreover, although there appears to be precious little case authority on this point, at least one appellate decision from a jurisdiction with an analogous statute supports this result. See, e.g., *Fannie Mae v. Heather Apartments Ltd. Partnership*, 2013 WL 6223564, *6 (Minn. App. Dec. 2, 2013) (charging order unavailable because Minnesota charging order statute applies only to a limited liability company "organized or governed by this chapter," whereas subject LLC was organized in and governed by laws of the Cook Islands).

The court then applied the plain meaning of the statute, granting charging orders against the two domestic LLCs and denying charging orders against the foreign LLCs.

Case Study: *Vision Marketing*[15]

Vision Marketing Resources, Inc. (Vision) sued James L. McMillin and McMillin Group LLC in federal court, claiming that Vision has purchased several sets of golf clubs that were neither delivered nor the payment refunded, and that the individual used McMillin Group LLC to conduct his personal business.

The defendants failed to respond, and Vision took a default judgment against the two for $101,500 in compensatory damages and the same amount for punitive damages, for a total judgment of $203,000 plus some costs and interest. This was in 2011, and the default judgment was entered in the U.S. District Court for the District of Kansas.

Vision requested that the court enter a charging order against the defendants' interest in Buffalo Nickel Trading LLC. Both defendants and Buffalo Nickel list Georgia addresses. The court instructed the plaintiff to explain:

> (1) how the U.S. district court in Kansas had jurisdiction over Buffalo Nickel as a Georgia company; and
>
> (2) why Kansas law relating to charging orders against an LLC did not limit its application to only Kansas LLCs and not foreign (i.e., not Kansas) LLCs.

15. Vision Mktg. Res., Inc. v. McMillin Group, LLC, 2015 WL 4390071 (D. Kan. July 15, 2015).

As to the first part, Vision responded that the court needed jurisdiction over only the member(s) of a foreign LLC. As to the second, Vision argued that the Kansas LLC statute did not expressly exclude foreign LLCs from the application of its charging order provisions.

The U.S. district judge referred the matter to a U.S. magistrate judge to sort out, and the magistrate judge submitted a report and recommendation, which was adopted in all respects as the court's opinion.

First, the court addressed the issue of whether it had the jurisdiction to issue a charging order in Kansas against a Georgia LLC. A U.S. district court in post-judgment enforcement proceedings will apply the collection laws of the state in which it sits, unless there is a contrary federal statute as to a particular issue (and no such federal statute controlled here). The Kansas statute provides simply:

> On application by a judgment creditor of a member or of a member's assignee, a court having jurisdiction may charge the limited liability company interest of the judgment debtor to satisfy the judgment.

In this case, the court had personal jurisdiction over the two defendants, but Buffalo Nickel did not have any presence in Kansas, was not doing business there, and really had no connections to the Sunflower State. The court ruled it did not have personal jurisdiction over the foreign LLC.

Similarly, the court did not have *in rem* jurisdiction (which is jurisdiction over property as opposed to jurisdiction over a person or entity) over the interests in Buffalo Nickel that were to be charged by the charging order. An interest in an LLC is considered to be in the nature of intangible property, and intangible property is said to be located where its owner resides, and here the owners of the interests in Buffalo Nickel resided in Georgia.

Vision argued that the *Rockstone Capital*[16] opinion supported its argument that a creditor does not need jurisdiction over the LLC whose interests are charged, but instead needs personal jurisdiction over the defendants holding those interests—of course, a court that has entered a judgment against those defendants has already determined that it has such personal jurisdiction (or it could not have entered the judgment).

Although the court found no Kansas authority on the subject, it did note that *Rockstone Capital* and several other cases, including *Mahalo Investments III, LLC v. First Citizens Bank & Trust Co.* have likewise held that it is not necessary for the particular court that enters the charging order to have jurisdiction over the entity itself. Thus:

---

16. Rockstone Capital, LLC v. Mktg. Horizons, Ltd., 2013 WL 4046597 (Conn. Super. July 17, 2013) (unpublished).

> the Court agrees with the rationale expressed in them. It therefore concludes that it has the requisite jurisdiction needed to issue a charging order against the LLC member interest of Judgment Debtor James McMillin by its continuing jurisdiction over Plaintiff and Defendants/Judgment Debtors. The Court need not have jurisdiction over the LLC entity itself in order to issue a charging order, when it has jurisdiction over the LLC member because the LLC has no right or direct interest affected by the charging order. Rather it is the judgment debtor's interest in and right to future distributions of the LLC that is being charged. As provided by the Kansas charging order statute, the charging order constitutes a lien on the judgment debtor's LLC interest. It only grants Plaintiff the right to receive any distribution or distributions to which the judgment debtor would otherwise have been entitled with respect to such LLC interest. The statute further provides that no creditor of a member or of a member's assignee shall have any right to obtain possession of, or otherwise exercise legal or equitable remedies with respect to, the property of the LLC. These provisions make it clear that it is the judgment debtor's interest in and rights to the LLC interest that are affected by the charging order.

Thus, the court decided that because it had personal jurisdiction over the debtor, the charging order could be properly issued against the judgment debtor's interest in Buffalo Nickel Trading LLC, even though the court did not have personal jurisdiction over that foreign LLC itself.

That left the second issue to be determined, which was whether the charging order provisions of the Kansas Limited Liability Company Act should be applied to a Georgia LLC (a "foreign LLC" in the vernacular of the act). The Kansas Limited Liability Company Act defines a "limited liability company" as one formed in Kansas, and a "foreign limited liability company" as one formed in another jurisdiction. Foreign LLCs are treated in one part of the act, but that part does not mention charging orders. Charging orders are treated in another part of the act[17] but that part only references LLCs and not foreign LLCs. There was an open question as to whether the act's charging order provisions relate only to Kansas LLCs, or whether those provisions should control foreign LLCs as well.

As the court described the issue:

> The definition of "member," which specifically includes a person who is admitted to a foreign LLC, suggests that a court having jurisdiction can issue a charging order against a foreign LLC under K.S.A. 17–76,113. However, because the term "limited liability company" appears to be

17. K.S.A. 17-76,113.

> limited to those "formed under the laws of the state of Kansas," this suggests the opposite—that a court does not have authority to issue a charging order against the interests in LLCs formed under another state's laws. One commentator has remarked on this as a foreign LLC "glitch" in the Revised Uniform Limited Liability Company Act ("RULLCA"). Jay D. Adkisson, in his paper, *Charging Orders, The Misunderstood Theory -vs- The Trenches of Litigation*, has described this as a glitch of statutory drafting resulting from how a "limited liability company" is defined under Section 102 of the RULLCA, the lack of any section authorizing charging orders under Article 8 (applying to foreign LLCs), and because Section 503 (which authorizes charging orders) does not make any reference to a foreign limited liability company.

A strict statutory construction of the act would lead one to conclude that the charging order provisions apply to only Kansas LLCs and not to foreign LLCs. Indeed, that is the result that has been reached by two cases: *Fannie Mae v. Heather Apartments LP* and the aforementioned *Rockstone Capital* case. Is that the right result?

The *Heather Apartments* decision has been subject to academic criticism, not the least of which by Professor Bishop.[18] Here, we finally have a court that makes more than a superficial analysis of the issue, concluding:

> Based upon the inconsistencies in the definitions and absence of any language in K.S.A. 16–76,113 specifically excepting its provisions from applying to a member's interest in a foreign (non-Kansas) LLC, the Court concludes that K.S.A. 16–76,113 is not limited to interests in Kansas LLCs, and a charging order may be issued against an LLC member's interest in a foreign (non-Kansas) LLC. This conclusion is supported by the purpose of a charging order, which is to execute or collect upon a judgment. It is a post-judgment remedy by which the judgment creditor attempts to collect its judgment from future LLC distributions that may flow to the judgment debtor by diverting any such future distributions to the creditor. In the typical case, the debtor remains the owner of the membership interest, with all of the associated rights, except that the creditor is entitled to the member's share of LLC distributions needed to pay the debt if and when the distributions are made. Limiting the issuance of charging orders under K.S.A. 16–76,113 to judgment debtor interests in Kansas-formed LLCs would further significantly hinder a judgment creditor in Kansas from attempting to collect its judgment from a debtor with interests in foreign LLCs. The

18. *See supra* note Ch.21, fn. 9.

> judgment creditor would be forced to investigate where each LLC was formed and seek a charging order against the debtor's interest in each of those states. The Court concludes that the Kansas legislature likely did not intend such a result, which could significantly hinder the ability of a judgment creditor to collect its judgments.

This result was the recommendation of the magistrate judge, which as mentioned above was adopted by the U.S. district court and became its order. The federal court implemented the plain purpose of the statute over its plain language.

CHAPTER 22

The Single-Member Entity

Like a computer program that terminates when an attempt is made to divide something by zero, so does the so-called charging order protection in that it runs into trouble when the LLC has but a single member, i.e., the number of other partners is likewise zero.

We have previously seen that the historical purpose of the charging order is to protect the nondebtor members, not the debtor-member, but where there are no nondebtor members to protect, then we have a situation where the charging order is not serving its intended purpose, but is instead misapplied to protect the assets of the single member from his or her creditors. Note for these purposes that the asset of the single member is his or her interest in the LLC; it is not an interest in the property owned by the LLC. This is all summarized nicely by Gerry Niesar:

> When considering a charging order in the context of a SMLLC it is very important to remember why the procedure was developed. It was not to protect the debtor-partner. The procedure limiting the creditor of a partner to an economic, but not management or control, right was designed to protect the *other* partners and the *partnership* from interference by a creditor, cum partner, whom the other partners had not invited to the management and control table. Viewed in the light of its history, it is easy to see that in a SMLLC context (where there are no partners other than the debtor) the charging order procedure generally will have no *raison d'etre* and, in fact, it could be used unfairly by debtors to prevent creditors from having a way to collect on their judgments.
>
> In a SMLLC there is no other 'partner' to protect, and it would require legerdemain to advance the notion that there is an "entity" that deserves the right to be protected from the creditor. If the judgment creditor is one who obtained a judgment based upon a tort claim, or through an enforcement action relating to the debtor's violation of a law or regulation, it is even more obvious that being limited to a charging order denies the creditor justice. For all of these reasons, the cases addressing this issue of creditors' remedies against a single member are providing

> scant, if any, reason for debtors to believe that a SMLLC will provide much of a shield against creditors.[1]

In at least two reported bankruptcy cases, courts have held that applying charging order protection to single-member LLCs is nonsensical because the purpose of charging orders is to protect the interests of nondebtor members, who do not exist in the context of single-member LLCs and, on such grounds, have allowed the bankruptcy trustee to exercise management control over, and sell for the benefit of the bankruptcy estates, the assets of the subject LLCs.[2]

State Law and the *Olmstead* Patch

Outside of bankruptcy, on a certified question from the Eleventh Circuit, the Florida Supreme Court in *Olmstead v. FTC*[3] answered that a charging order was not the exclusive remedy against a SMLLC under the Sunshine State's laws.[4] The majority in *Olmstead* paid their respects to the logic of *Albright* and *Modanlo*, but instead focused on differences between the language of Florida's LLC statute, which did not clearly limit a creditor's remedy to a charging order, and Florida's partnership and limited partnership statutes, which did.[5] After analogizing an LLC interest to a share of corporate stock, the majority concluded that the Florida legislature must not have meant to make the charging order the exclusive remedy, at least with respect to a SMLLC.[6] Thereafter, the Florida legislature amended the LLC statute (referred to as the *Olmstead* patch).[7] The statute provided that the charging order was indeed the exclusive remedy in Florida—but

1. Gerald V. Niesar, *Charging Orders and the Single-Member LLC*, 65 Consumer Fin. L.Q. Rep. 278, 278 (2011).

2. *In re* Ashley Albright, 291 B.R. 538, 541 (Bankr. D. Colo. 2003); *In re* Nadar Modanlo, 412 B.R. 715, 728 (Bankr. D. Md. 2006). With respect to the *Albright* decision, *see also* Thomas E. Rutledge & Thomas Earl Geu, *The Albright Decision—Why a SMLLC Is Not an Appropriate Asset Protection Vehicle*, 5 Bus. Entities 16 (Sept./Oct. 2003).

3. 44 So. 3d 76 (Fla. 2010).

4. *Id.* at 81–83.

5. *Id.*

6. *Id.* at 80–83. Other and more expansive reviews of the *Olmstead* decision include Carter G. Bishop, *Desiderata: The Single Member Limited Liability Company Charging Order Statutory Lacuna* (Suffolk U. Law School Legal Studies Research Paper 10–59), *available at* SSRN, abstract 1697621; J. William Callison, *Charging Order Exclusivity: A Pragmatic Approach to Olmstead v. FTC*, 66 Bus. Law. (Feb. 2011); Thomas E. Geu, Thomas E. Rutledge & John DeBruyn, *To Be or Not to Be Exclusive: Statutory Construction of the Charging Order in the Single Member LLC*, 9 DePaul Bus. & Comm. L.J. 83 (Fall 2010).

7. *See generally* Louis T. M. Conti, *The New Olmstead Patch: A Case Study in the Art of Compromise for Florida LLC Law*, 85 Fla. B.J. 49 (Dec. 2011) (referring to the Florida statute passed after the *Olmstead* case as the "Olmstead Patch").

only as to multiple-member LLCs.[8] As to SMLLCs, the *Olmstead* patch expressly allows a creditor to foreclose on the single-member's interest in the SMLLC, with the buyer able to take management control of the SMLLC, but only if the creditor first shows that his or her judgment will not be satisfied by distributions from the LLC within a reasonable time.[9]

Other states later took different approaches to addressing the perceived abuse of single-member asset protection LLCs. For example, Kentucky amended its LLC Act to provide that, in the event of the transfer of 100 percent of the member's interest, such as would happen upon foreclosure of the charging order, the member will thereby be dissociated. In that instance, the successor-in-interest to the former sole member—for these purposes the purchaser at the foreclosure sale—may either elect themselves as a member or allow the LLC to proceed to dissolve. By either path, the judgment-creditor, assuming they are the purchaser at the foreclosure sale, may access the LLC's assets.[10]

In 2013, ULLCA was amended to add a new section 503(f) to address the issue of a charging order issued against a SMLLC:

> (f) If a court orders foreclosure of a charging order lien against the sole member of a limited liability company:
>
> > (1) the court shall confirm the sale;
> >
> > (2) the purchaser at the sale obtains the member's entire interest, not only the member's transferable interest;
> >
> > (3) the purchaser thereby becomes a member; and
> >
> > (4) the person whose interest was subject to the foreclosed charging order is dissociated as a member.

The reporter's comments to the new section 503(f) illuminate the reasons for this new provision to the ULLCA:

> The charging order remedy—and, more particularly, the exclusiveness of the remedy—protect the "pick your partner" principle. That principle is inapposite when a limited liability company has only one member. The exclusivity of the charging order remedy was never intended to protect a judgment debtor, but rather only to protect the interests of the judgment debtor's co-owners.

8. *Olmstead*, 44 So. 3d at 80–83.

9. Fla. Stat. Ann. § 605.0503(4) (West 2015).

10. *See* Ky. Rev. Stat. Ann. §§ 275.280(i)(c)3, 275.285(4); *see also* Thomas E. Rutledge, *The 2011 Amendments to Kentucky's Business Entities Laws*, 75 Bench & Bar Hot Topics (July 2011), *available at* http://www.kybar.org/425.

> Put another way, the charging order remedy was never intended as an "asset protection" device for judgment debtors. . . . Accordingly, when a charging order against an LLC's sole member is foreclosed, the member's entire ownership interest is sold and the buyer replaces the judgment debtor as the LLC's sole member.

Statutory Problems with Foreclosure of the Charging Order Lien

Some state legislatures have expressly amended their partnership and LLC laws to provide charging order exclusivity for entities formed in their states for the very purpose of making such entities asset protection vehicles for their single-member owners.[11] Where the legislative history in those states shows that the legislature affirmatively desired that charging order exclusivity should apply to single-member entities, an assertion of the *Albright* rationale to circumvent charging order exclusivity might not hold water.[12] Whether extending such exclusivity to single-member LLCs, thus turning them into asset protection vehicles with creditor-thwarting super powers, is a good idea from a public-policy standpoint is another matter entirely (certainly, it helps marketing the use of LLCs from those states).

Additionally, recall that in *Olmstead* the Florida Supreme Court indicated that the Florida partnership and limited partnership statutes did provide for charging order protection as the exclusive remedy, and thus inferred that if the Florida LLC statute had been similarly drafted, then charging order protection might have applied in that case despite *Albright*.[13] Notably, the 2013 amendments to ULLCA now provide at 503(f) that when a charging order lien against an interest in a single-member LLC is foreclosed upon, the purchaser at the judicial sale takes the entire interest of the debtor and the debtor is thereafter dissociated from the LLC.

Late-Arriving Members

Another "fly in the ointment" goes to the issue of just exactly when the status of an LLC as a single-member or multiple-member entity is tested. Theoretically, it might be possible to add a second member to an LLC to destroy its single-member status and thus prevent the application of *Albright*—the

11. *See* Bishop, Appendix C hereto (providing an exhaustive state-by-state list of jurisdictions that allow or preclude foreclosure).

12. *See, e.g., In re* Desmond, 316 B.R. 593 (Bankr. D. N.H. 2004); *In re* Penn, No. 09-14624-WHD, 2010 WL 9445533 (Bankr. N.D. Ga Apr. 2, 2010); Robucci v. C.I.R., 101 T.C.M. (CCH) 1060 (2011).

13. *See Olmstead*, 44 So. 3d at 81–83.

late-arriving member being the not-so-innocent party crasher who shows up with the intent of spoiling the creditor's party. Consider the following timeline:

- January 12: Debtor forms an LLC, contributes assets to it, and is the single-member of LLC
- February 13: Debtor negligently causes a car accident with multiple injuries
- March 14: Debtor consents to judgment in excess of his net wealth, including Debtor's 100-percent interest in the LLC
- April 15: Debtor's golf buddy acquires a five-percent membership interest in the LLC by contributing the necessary cash
- May 16: Creditor files a motion for turnover order for the assets of the LLC and/or full management control of the LLC
- June 17: Court holds hearing on motion for turnover order

On which date do we "test" whether the LLC is single-member or multiple-member? Possibly the right answer is May 16, the date that the creditor filed the motion for turnover order. That is the date that the creditor first attempted to take enforcement action against the debtor's LLC interest. One may analogize this to other judgment enforcement procedures, such as a writ of levy, which "hits" the value of an asset on the day the writ is served. Thus, a creditor would get whatever shares of corporate stock the debtor owns on the day the writ of levy is served, not the most shares of stock the debtor previously owned.

However, to change the timeline slightly, assume the creditor first filed a motion for charging order against the debtor's LLC interest on April 14—the day before the debtor attempted to sell the interest to his golf buddy. In that case, the "temporary lien" created by the filing of the charging order motion would be created in the debtor's 100-percent interest, and the attempt of the golf buddy to acquire an interest might be defeated.

In addition, there may be fraudulent transfer concerns associated with adding a member late to thwart collections. In *Sardis v. Frankel*,[14] the debtor owned 100 percent of the interest in a profitable LLC, but just days after she lost an arbitration award, she sold a 10-percent interest in the LLC to her son.[15] Although the court never directly reached the issue of whether the transfer of the 10-percent interest was a fraudulent transfer, the court did negatively comment upon it as one in a number of facts that demonstrated the debtor's intent to fraudulently transfer another of her assets to her son:

14. 113 A.D.3d 135 (N.Y. App. Div. 2014).
15. *Id.* at 138–39.

> Finally, the addition of Michael as a member of Applied Medicals LLC, of which Sofia was formerly the sole member, precludes plaintiffs from obtaining an order from a Florida court directing the surrender of her entire interest in the company to satisfy the award against her.[16]

Implicitly, the *Sardis* court was saying that even though the son acquired the 10-percent interest after the debtor had lost the arbitration proceeding, the transfer was effective to "bust" the single-member status of the entity and require the creditor to pursue a charging order. It can be implicitly read within the overall context of the case to suggest that the transfer of the 10-percent interest might be a fraudulent transfer because it had the effect of hindering the creditor.

D. When Is a Peppercorn Not a Peppercorn?

How much interest must another nondebtor-member have to defeat a creditor's argument based on *Albright*? The court addressed the issue, if only to tease us, in footnote 9 of its opinion:

> The harder question would involve an LLC where one member effectively controls and dominates the membership and management of an LLC that also involves a passive member with a minimal interest. If the dominant member files bankruptcy, would a trustee obtain the right to govern the LLC? Pursuant to Colo. Rev. Stat. § 7–80–702, if the non-debtor member did not consent, even if she held only an infinitesimal interest, the answer would be no. The Trustee would only be entitled to a share of distributions, and would have no role in the voting or governance of the company. Notwithstanding this limitation, 7–80–702 does not create an asset shelter for clever debtors. To the extent a debtor intends to hinder, delay or defraud creditors through a multi-member LLC with 'peppercorn' co-members, bankruptcy avoidance provisions and fraudulent transfer law would provide creditors or a bankruptcy trustee with recourse.[17]

The truth is that nobody knows, or will likely ever know, what sort of minimal interest is required to change the characterization of a single-member LLC to a multiple-member LLC for *Albright* purposes because such an issue must fundamentally be resolved upon a facts-and-circumstances evaluation in each particular case. Caution must be given, however, that simply putting in another member who is the *de facto* nominee of the debtor-member risks a court simply collapsing all the interests together and treating them as the debtor-member's interest for purposes of this analysis.

16. *Id.* at 143.
17. *In re* Albright, 291 B.R. at 538, n.9 (citing 11 U.S.C. §§ 544(b)(1), 548(a) (2015)).

For example, it is common for planners to give their clients a 99-percent non-managing interest in an LLC, and then create a new corporation or trust (often a revocable "living" trust), directly or indirectly controlled by the client, to act as the one-percent managing member. In such a case, it would not be too terribly difficult for a court to hold that the one-percent (or 5-, 10-, or even 70-percent) other member is simply the client in a different form in order to trigger relief under *Albright*.[18] Planners should thus quit focusing on the *percentage*, and instead focus on the true substance of the situation because it is the substance of what is really happening on which the court will ultimately cast its focus.

Case Study: *Heckert*[19]

When Clyde and Teresa Heckert divorced in Texas, Clyde ended up owing Teresa $381,324.47. Clyde didn't pay up, and so Teresa sought a turnover order for Clyde's nonexempt assets. Clyde claimed that he didn't have any nonexempt assets, and Teresa was able to get a receiver appointed. The evidence showed that soon after Theresa won her monetary award against Clyde, he started to either cash his paychecks or deposit them into his new wife's account. Some $87,000 of Clyde's money went to pay down his new wife's mortgage, and in return Clyde got a 50-percent interest in his new wife's house. Clyde also transferred shares of investment stock into A2R, Ltd.

Eventually, the court ordered Clyde to turn over to Teresa his Vanguard account, his interest in a limited partnership called A2R Ltd., and his 100-percent interest in Averse 2 Risk, LLC—the latter two entities Clyde created while the litigation was ongoing. However, the court did not order Clyde to turn over his interest in a Fidelity Investment account. Both Teresa and Clyde appealed.

Passing over the Texas Court of Appeals' discussion of the exemption issues, the interesting part of this opinion is whether a court can force a debtor to turn over interests in a limited partnership and an LLC. Clyde quite correctly pointed out that Texas statutory law provides that a charging order is the "exclusive remedy" to collect on a debtor's partnership interests or LLC interests. A charging order essentially puts a lien on the debtor-member's right to distributions, such that any distributions made to that interest will instead be routed to the creditor

---

18. There exists any number of analogies that would justify this treatment. For example, under the Model Business Corporation Act (Third) § 1.42, three or fewer co-owners may be treated as a single shareholder. A husband and wife operating a business in what would otherwise be characterized as a partnership may elect that it be treated as a sole proprietorship. § 761(f). Notwithstanding that for state law purposes they are distinct legal organizations, a grantor trust and its grantor, when operating a partnership, will have a default classification as a disregarded entity. *See also generally* Thomas E. Rutledge, *Regarding the Disregarded Entity*, 14 J. Passthrough Entities 39 (Mar./Apr. 2011).

19. Heckert v. Heckert, 2017 WL 5184840 (Tex. App. Nov. 9, 2017).

until the judgment is satisfied. A charging order does not, however, transfer the ownership of the debtor-member's interest to the creditor, only the right to distributions.

That is true, said the court of appeals, but there are exceptions to that rule, such as where both the creditor and the debtor are members of the same partnership or LLC. Given that the purpose of charging order exclusivity is to protect the nondebtor members from interference with their business, there should be no exclusivity where there are no nondebtor members. Here, Clyde was effectively the only member of A2R Ltd. and Averse 2 Risk LLC, there were no nondebtor members who would be adversely effected, and so it didn't make any sense to limit Theresa to a charging order against Clyde's interests in these companies.

CHAPTER 23

Intra-Member Disputes

The vast bulk of charging order litigation involves creditors that are external to the LLC, which of course is another way of saying that they are not members of the LLC. What happens if there is litigation that arises between two members of the LLC, and one member obtains a judgment against the other?

Lack of Nondebtor Member

Recall that the purpose of the charging order arises from the "pick your partner" principle, which is to prevent an external creditor from interfering with the business of the partnership. Much as with a single-member LLC, this concept is nonsensical as applied to an intra-member dispute, and an argument can be made that the charging order should therefore not be the exclusive remedy, and the prevailing member should be able to simply levy upon the losing member's interest as if it were any other similar asset.

There are at least two counterarguments. First, the Harmonized Acts by their plain text do not distinguish between internal and external creditors (whether this is a drafting omission of those acts will be left to a future time). Second, although the LLC may not be interfered with by an external creditor, there may be a detrimental change to the dynamics of the LLC by way of what amounts to an involuntary change of rights favoring the creditor-member to the potential disadvantage of the remaining members, i.e., the creditor-member might obtain greater voting rights than the rest of the members to which the latter did not agree.[1]

---

1. Note, however, that whether, upon the transfer of a membership interest inter-se, the transferring person will continue to be treated as a member (i.e., have management rights) with respect to the transferred interest is a point highly dependent upon state law with the attendant possibility of modification in the operating agreement. This is a point addressed in Thomas E. Rutledge, *Interest Assignments Among Members,* 18 J. Passthrough Entities 53 (Mar./Apr. 2017) and J. William Callison, Achaian and Interest Transfers among Existing Partners in Members, Research Handbook on Partnerships, LLCs and Alternative Forms of Business Organizations 70 (Robert W. Hillman & Mark J. Lowenstein, eds.).

The Issue May Be Drafted Around

The parties to the LLC may themselves determine the outcome of such a situation one way or the other by drafting appropriate language into the operating agreement. Such language might simply be:

> Intra-member Disputes: Should one member obtain a judgment against another member, to enforce that judgment a charging order [shall or shall not] be the exclusive remedy against the interest of the member against whom the judgment is rendered.

Case Study: *Gillet*[2]

ZUPT, LLC provides undersea surveying services for the oil and gas industry. Joel Gillet was a co-owner of ZUPT to the tune of 45 percent.

Gillet accepted an offer of employment from one of ZUPT's competitors, but without disclosing that he was already heading to work for the competition, Gillet gave notice to ZUPT of his intent to force that company and its remaining members to buy out his interests. This was in March of 2009. By June of 2009, Gillet resigned from ZUPT outright and went to work for the competitor, and at that time still owned his 45-percent interest in ZUPT.

Gillet's buy-out demand triggered an independent appraisal of his interest. The result of this appraisal was a determination that: (1) if ZUPT as a whole were to be sold, it was worth $1.6 million (resulting in $720,000 to Gillet), and (2) the appraisal presumed that Gillet would sign a standard noncompetition agreement with ZUPT.

Herein lies the dispute. Given that Gillet had already gone to work for one of ZUPT's competitors, he could not sign the noncompetition agreement. This, coupled with the fact that ZUPT wasn't being sold as a whole but only Gillet's interest was being sold, reduced the value of Gillet's 45-percent share to $229,000.

Unhappy with this result, Gillet sued ZUPT and its remaining owners for violating his buy-sell agreement and for oppression of a minority interest holder; ZUPT and its remaining shareholders countersued Gillet for breach of fiduciary duty and misappropriation of trade secrets by disclosing information to his new employer.

The dispute proceeded to arbitration. As arbitrators are wont to do, the arbitrator found that nobody was innocent, and more-or-less split the baby. Gillet got the lesser half of the baby, with a determination that his interest in ZUPT was worth $499,050, and the arbitrator ordered him to turnover his interest in ZUPT in exchange for that amount of money, and awarded him $70,060 in attorney's fees.

---

2. Gillet v. ZUPT, LLC, 2017 WL 716633 (Tex. App. 14th Dist. Feb. 23, 2017).

ZUPT got the larger half of the baby, with an award in its favor of $1.869 million for damages caused by Gillet's disclosure of trade secrets, another almost $170,000 in attorney's fees, and $1,000 under the Texas Theft Liability Act.

Both parties were also awarded pre- and post-judgment interest and certain litigation costs. What the arbitrator did not do, however, was to offset the value of the respective judgments, i.e., each side walked out with a judgment in its favor and thereby also faced a judgment against them.

For its part, ZUPT moved to confirm the arbitration award before the Texas District Court, which did so, and appointed a receiver to collect the nonexempt property of both Gillet and ZUPT to satisfy the award. The court also ordered Gillet to turn over his interest in ZUPT. Gillet appealed.

Gillet's first argument, which he won in substantial part, was that the district court should not have authorized a turnover order for all his exempt property without any proof of what the property was or that it was not exempt (remember, this is Texas where quite a bit of stuff is exempt). The Texas Court of Appeals agreed with Gillet, except as to Gillet's interest in ZUPT for which there was an abundance of evidence that he owned that interest, and an LLC interest is not exempt. So, the turnover order was reversed but for Gillet's ZUPT interest.

This brings us to the juicy part of the opinion, which is whether the Texas court could order Gillet to turnover his interest in ZUPT per the arbitrator's award, or whether ZUPT was stuck with a charging order against Gillet's ZUPT interest.

As is the law of most states, a charging order in Texas is the "exclusive remedy" that a creditor may employ against a debtor's interest in an LLC or partnership. The charging order essentially creates a lien on the debtor's right to distributions, often referred to as the "distributional interest" or "economic interest," such that any distributions are diverted to the creditor until the judgment is paid off.

Where Texas law differs from most (but not all) states is that Texas further prohibits the foreclosure (read: sheriff's sale) of the debtor's interest in an LLC. Thus, ordinarily there is no way under Texas law that a creditor can end up with a debtor's interest in an LLC outright, but instead that creditor would be stuck with waiting for distribution to be made until the judgment was paid.

The historic purpose of this so-called charging order exclusivity is to protect the nondebtor members in an LLC or partnership from being forced into what would amount to an involuntary partnership with a member's creditor.

Here we have the situation of the intra-member dispute where there is no outside creditor, but instead it is the other members (via ZUPT) who hold the judgment. Were the court to respect charging order exclusivity, it would lead to the utterly perverse result of that exclusivity thwarting the recovery by the very persons it was intended to protect.

Displaying a level of common sense that seems to be all too uncommon to contemporary appellate courts, the Texas Court of Appeal thus reasoned:

> We hold that requiring turnover of a membership interest under these circumstances is proper for two reasons. First, the reasoning behind requiring a charging order as the exclusive remedy is inapposite when the judgment creditor seeking the membership interest is the entity from which the membership interest derives. Second, unlike a case in which a judgment creditor seeks to collect on its money judgment by forcing a sale of a membership interest, this case involves an explicit award of the membership interest itself from one party to the other as part of the judgment. For these reasons, we conclude that a charging order was not the exclusive remedy available to ZUPT, and the trial court did not abuse its discretion by ordering turnover of Gillet's 45 percent interest in ZUPT.

Finally, Gillet complained that the turnover order required him to give up his interest in ZUPT without being compensated by its value as determined by the arbitrator. The Texas Court of Appeals agreed and essentially held that Gillet had to yield his interest to the receiver, but that he would get a credit for the amount that ZUPT owed him against the larger amount that he owed ZUPT.

Case Study: *Voll*[3]

Joseph Voll and Robert Dunn were business partners in a pair of restaurants in Connecticut called Macdaddy's Macaroni & Cheese Bar. One restaurant was held in what would be known shorthand as the Monroe LLC, and the other similarly as the Fairfield LLC. A third company without a restaurant, the Management LLC, provided operational services to both Monroe LLC and Fairfield LLC.

Voll and Dunn owned all three LLCs as 50-50 members, with the idea that profits would flow up from Monroe LLC and Fairfield LLC into the Management LLC, which would then distribute equally to Voll and Dunn.

Voll was a construction general contractor, and he contributed the moneys and labor to build the first restaurant, which would go into Monroe LLC. For his 50 percent, Dunn contributed the concept, menus, and operational support. Dunn was working as an investment broker then, but soon agreed to give up that job and work at Monroe LLC on a full-time basis.

The first Macdaddy's opened on July 4, 2011, but even before the concept was proven to be viable on a long-term basis, Voll and Dunn started looking for a second location only a few months later. The two decided on a location and cut a deal with the property owner whereby Voll, Dunn, the property owner, and his wife (the latter two, the Swansons, taking profits in lieu of rent) would all be 25-percent owners in the second company, Fairfield LLC. Certain licensing fees

3. Voll v. Dunn, 2014 WL 7461644 (Conn. Super. Nov. 10, 2014) (unpublished).

and royalties would also be paid to Management LLC, which was owned only by Voll and Dunn.

Apparently, there was not enough profit to sustain Dunn's financial needs, and so beginning in January, 2012, Voll started loaning him $4,000 per month.

The second Macdaddy's finally opened in September 2012 and was to be run by the Swansons; however, about the time that Macdaddy's opened, the Swansons had some medical emergency and were unable to manage that restaurant, so Dunn started managing both Macdaddy's locations. (At some point, apparently, the Swansons ceased to be members in Fairfield LLC, leaving only Voll and Dunn as the remaining 50-50 members).

Unbeknownst to Voll, Dunn had never run a restaurant successfully, and he also had sticky fingers. Only 10 days after the July 1, 2011 opening of the first Macdaddy's, Dunn began taking unauthorized withdrawals from Monroe LLC, depositing $21,150 in cash into a TD Bank account from July 2011 to February 2012, and depositing another $17,600 in cash into Jordan's Future, LLC (named for his daughter) from August 2011 to May 2012. Dunn disguised the payments as "management fees" or "consulting fees" on the checks, which were never authorized by the Monroe LLC or Voll.

Dunn also took another $5,750 in unauthorized "draws" from the Monroe LLC and further used Monroe LLC's assets to barter for goods and services for his home, including lawn-care services and firewood deliveries, for $6,320. A later reconciliation of Monroe LLC's books against its point-of-sale system showed a cash shortfall of $39,425 between June 2012 and November 15, 2012. Dunn also diverted the insurance proceeds from Hurricane Sandy's damage into a second bank account that he opened in the name of Monroe LLC but didn't tell Voll.

Dunn's sticky fingers didn't stop with Monroe LLC, but extended to Management LLC as well. Dunn wire transferred $5,500 from Management LLC to Jordan's Future LLC's account, and removed $10,000 in licensee fees from the Management LLC account. This was all on top of checks and at least one use of the company's debit card for personal purposes.

That brings us to Fairfield LLC, which Dunn began looting immediately to the tune of $8,000 taken from the cash register in September 2012. Changing his method, Dunn enrolled Macdaddy's into a Groupon promotion and used it to divert another $7,076 into the Jordan's Future LLC account. Even after Voll figured out what was going on and filed a lawsuit, Dunn withdrew another $16,000 from Fairfield LLC's account.

For his part, Voll received only a single distribution from the Management LLC for $1,500, but ended up with a big mess. Monroe LLC was behind on its rent, utilities, taxes, and payments to its suppliers. Checks were bouncing NSF. Voll was eventually able to right the ship, however, and pursue Dunn.

For his part, Dunn attempted to portray himself as the victim of Voll's "treachery" in trying to steal the Macdaddy's brand and force Dunn out of the business. Dunn justified his defalcations as merely putting food on the table for his family, claiming that he intended to pay Voll back for every last penny as soon as future stores opened, but the court didn't buy any of it:

> In any event, the court does not credit the defendant's testimony. Indeed, the defendant is perhaps the least credible witness this court has ever seen. From early in the life of the restaurant, the defendant reneged on the agreement he had made. He began siphoning cash out of the Monroe restaurant to whatever purpose he saw fit. His effort to justify his use of the Monroe cash register as his own personal piggy bank is frankly, astonishing. He claims he had to take the money because he had no income but this, we know, is not true. He was taking cash and diverting funds for months while he was still employed at [an investment banking firm]. Further, his diverting of funds was a regular and frequent occurrence within months of the Monroe restaurant opening. He also claims he had no choice because he had to take care of his family. However, the amounts taken are well in excess of the amount needed to sustain a small family. Between July 2011 and November 2012, the defendant had siphoned off in excess of $100,000.00 from the Monroe restaurant alone, to include over $6,000 for lawn care and firewood. This is hardly bread and milk money. Finally, and perhaps most importantly, the defendant's after-the-fact explanation that he intended to even things out with the plaintiff once the second and third stores were opened is a self-serving and wholly incredible claim.

Dunn had failed with a previous restaurant prior to meeting Voll, having had a default judgment entered against him in the amount of $132,444. In a very smart strategic move, Voll bought that judgment against Dunn, and in June 2013, Voll had the marshall levy upon Dunn's interest in Management LLC, Monroe LLC, and Fairfield LLCs (the three LLCs). The marshall also gave Dunn an exemption claim form by which Dunn could contest the execution.

The state marshal later published a notice of his intent to auction off Dunn's interest in the three LLCs. Dunn apparently blew all this off and did not file any objection or claim for exemption, instead telling the marshal that he was going to file for bankruptcy before the auction, which he did. The bankruptcy filing caused the auction to be put off several times, but Dunn did not comply with the bankruptcy court's request for certain paperwork, and Dunn's bankruptcy proceeding was dismissed on December 2, 2013.

The next day, December 3, 2013, the marshal finally held the auction. Although given notice of the auction, Dunn did not object. Voll appeared at the auction and "credit bid" $50,000 for Dunn's interests in the three LLCs, meaning that Voll didn't pay cash for the interests but instead credited Dunn with $50,000 against the outstanding judgment (which is common in post-judgment auctions and completely proper).

At some point, and apparently following the maxim that "the best defense is a good offense," Dunn brought lawsuits against Voll asserting various claims relating to the three LLCs.

Now holding the interests in the three LLCs, Voll moved to dismiss Dunn's lawsuits on the basis that Voll no longer had a membership interest in the three LLCs. Dunn responded that the marshal's auction and Voll's purchase of the interests were facially invalid because it was not permitted under Connecticut law—Voll could at best get only a charging order that created a lien on Dunn's distributive rights in the three LLCs, not actual title to them. Before Dunn's motion could be heard, however, Dunn withdrew his lawsuits relating to the three LLCs, thus rendering his motions moot, and they were not heard.

The court set Voll's case against Dunn for trial, and Voll amended his complaint to request a declaration from the court that Voll's purchase of Dunn's interests in the three LLCs was valid. Dunn counterclaimed for a contrary declaration that Voll's purchase of Dunn's interest was invalid because Voll was limited to a charging order. Dunn also sought an order requiring Dunn to fund the building of two additional Macdaddy's, and (this took some chutzpah under the circumstances) for an accounting.

Of most interest here is the court's resolution of the charging order issue, but first it is important to summarize what the court decided preliminarily.

The court found, not surprisingly under these facts, that Dunn had breached his fiduciary duties to the three LLCs, that Dunn's conduct constituted civil theft and conversion, and that Dunn violated the Connecticut Uniform Trade Practices Act (CUPTA). Dunn was thus liable for damages to the three LLCs as follows: (1) to Monroe LLC for $109,021; (2) to Management LLC for $23,948; and to Fairfield LLC for $23,000.

The Connecticut civil theft statute provided for treble damages, and given that Voll proved up his civil theft case, the above damages were trebled; therefore, the judgment was upped to north of $450,000. The court also found that Dunn was directly liable for damages to Voll for violation of CUPTA (for which duties are also owed to members of an LLC that is harmed by conduct). As lagniappe, the court also tacked on interest and Voll's attorney's fees to the judgment against Dunn.

This finally brings us to the charging order issue. Connecticut law allows for a judgment to be enforced against "any property" of the judgment debtor, unless that property is exempt by some specific statute (and there is no exemption for LLC interests there). In this context, the term "property" includes any personal property that the debtor is capable of assigning or transferring. Such property may be levied by the local Marshal (levying officer) and sold at auction, with the net proceeds after the expense of the auction going to the creditor.

An interest in an LLC is an interest in personal property. To determine whether a debtor may assign or transfer his or her interests in an LLC, the court looked to Connecticut's LLC Act, which provides that such interests may be assigned "[e]xcept as provided in writing in an operating agreement."

The LLC Act provides another significant limitation, however, which is that the assignee (i.e., the person to whom an interest is assigned) will not have any rights to participate in the management of the LLC, and therefore is nothing like a full owner of the interest. In other words, the assignee only receives what amounts to the assignor's economic rights, but not the assignor's management rights that the assignor retains.

Here, Dunn argued that because an assignee could not receive the full enchilada, being both the economic rights and management rights, the rights therefore were not capable of assignment, and thus were not personal property that could be levied upon.

The court noted that the provisions of the LLC Act were not dispositive because those provisions could be modified by the parties through the LLC's operating agreement.

The court reviewed the operating agreements for Fairfield LLC and Management LLC and determined that they freely permitted assignment of the full ownership interests in those two LLCs. Further, the "membership interest" was defined in those operating agreements as basically all rights, including management rights. Other provisions required that notice of the assignment be given to the companies and to members (who would then have a right to purchase the interest, almost like a "right of first refusal"), but otherwise Dunn's membership interests were assignable.

Because Dunn's interests in Fairfield LLC and Management LLC were assignable, held the court, they were subject to execution and levy under Connecticut law.[4]

This brings us back to the Connecticut LLC Act, under which Dunn argued that the charging order remedy was "exclusive," meaning that among the various remedies available to creditors to go after assets, the one that a creditor must employ is the charging order remedy, not other remedies such as the levy that Voll pursued instead.

Indeed, the plain text of Connecticut's charging order statute does not, as many other states do, expressly provide that the charging order is the exclusive remedy available to creditors. The legislative history of the Connecticut LLC Act is also silent on the issue. The court interpreted this statutory silence to create

4. Arguably, the court got this part dead wrong, given that whether an LLC's interests is assignable or transferrable normally has nothing to do with whether the interest is subject to execution and levy, or instead is limited in remedy to a charging order. Apples and orangutans.

ambiguity on the issue, and contrasted that with the clear language in Connecticut's Uniform Partnership Act (UPA), which does make clear that the charging order is the exclusive remedy.

A partnership has at least two partners, however, and therefore as the court importantly noted in footnote 28:

> The exclusivity provision prevents the situation of the non-debtor partners having a stranger thrust upon them in the management of the affairs of the partnership. The provisions are designed to protect the debtor's partners from such an occurrence and to preserve the idea that people pick their own partners in matters of business.

The LLC is a different animal, sayeth the court, because it could theoretically have only one member, and to limit the creditors remedy would run against the grain of public policy because it would permit the debtor to stiff the creditor by simply not making distributions to the debtor's 100-percent interest subject to the charging order lien, such that execution and levy in that case would be warranted. This analysis is entirely consistent, the court thought, with the idea that a partnership interest is not "property" because it was not assignable, and thus not subject to the execution and levy procedure. However,

> On the other hand, as noted above, the LLC Act defers, as may be applicable, to the LLC operating agreement on the issue of transferability. Consistent with such a deferral, the Act contains no exclusivity provision with respect to charging orders. In short, the LLC Act gives greater deference to the member's ability to negotiate the terms and conditions of the operating agreement. Therefore, to the extent the operating agreement provides for the transferability of a full membership interest in an LLC, the LLC Act is consistent with the postjudgment procedure statutes but ONLY if the charging order provisions are nonexclusive. If the charging order provisions are an exclusive remedy, the LLC Act becomes inconsistent with the postjudgment procedures statutes in situations such as the one presented here.

In other words, so long as the operating agreement provided that the LLC interests were assignable and transferrable, then the LLC Act and the execution and levy statutes are consistent, but if the LLC interests were made to not be assignable or transferrable in the operating agreement, then a conflict would arise between the LLC Act and the execution and levy statute. Presumably, the court wanted readers to draw the conclusion that because the operating agreements here provided for the LLC interests to be assignable and transferrable, there was thus no conflict between the LLC Act and the execution and levy statute.[5]

Moving on, Dunn next argued that the charging order remedy must be exclusive, or it would violate a fundamental tenant of the LLC Act, which is that members may only freely choose their fellow members and cannot have a creditor thrust upon them as an involuntary member. Voll countered to the effect that although such a concern might be of interest in other cases, it was not a concern here because Voll was already a member of the three LLCs.

Voll's simple argument was spot on, direct hit battleship, checkmate. At this point, the court should have simply have adopted Voll's argument and declared that it's Miller time! Instead, the court began to ramble about how the LLC Act promoted freedom of contract, and here the operating agreements provided that they could accept third-party strangers if a membership interest were assigned or transferred. To bolster this (lame) argument, the court engaged in a long discussion of the holding of the Supreme Court of Florida in *Olmstead v. FTC*,[6] which dealt with a creditor's execution upon the debtor's interest in a single-member LLC, and which of course had nothing to do with the instant case that involved two members in Voll and Dunn.

Apparently, the court was also trying to make the point that so-called reverse veil piercing can also be employed against a debtor's interest in an LLC as proof that the charging order remedy is not really "exclusive," which sort of makes sense in an odd way until one realizes that veil piercing (whether straight or reverse) is not a statutory post-judgment remedy like execution and levy, but rather in the way of court-created doctrine to reach an equitable result in cases where elevating corporate form over economic substance would lead to an unjust result.

In the end, the court granted Voll's request for a declaratory judgment that his levy on Dunn's shares was appropriate and that Voll now owned Dunn's former interests in the three LLCs, and accordingly denied Dunn's claim for the opposite relief.

Case Study: *Young*[7]

Wear It's At LLC (yes, that is an actual name) was doing business in Florida and had two members: Levy, who had a 51-percent membership interest, and Young, who had the other 49-percent membership interest.

At some point, the two ceased to get along, and a business divorce ensued. This was accomplished not in friendly, cheerful, and amicable fashion, but rather Levy locked out Young, took Young's name off the business bank accounts, and

5. This foregoing particular conclusion of the court is quite dubious.
6. 44 So. 3d 76 (Fla. 2010).
7. Young v. Levy, 2014 WL 2741060 (Fla. App. June 18, 2014).

fired Young from the employ of the business. Adios, don't bother to write, and what was in your desk will come in a box shortly.

Not being one to take such matters sitting down, Young sued Levy and sought both an accounting and an injunction against Levy. The latter objected, but the court sided with Young and granted an emergency injunction that gave Young the day-to-day control of the business and its bank accounts. The court also required Young to post a $5,000 bond.

Not being one to go silently into that good night either, Levy moved to dissolve the injunction—and won. Young appealed, and lost.

The trial court then held several hearings, after which it concluded that Levy was in the right and awarded her the $5,000 bond plus another $41,409 in attorney's fees. Young again appealed, and again lost, but she did not pay Levy any of the award.

Levy then moved the court to issue a writ of garnishment, which in English is an order that seizes income and applies it towards the debt. To get the writ issued, Levy represented to the court that the LLC held $44,100 that was otherwise due to Young, and Levy wanted title to that money (Levy already had possession of it through the LLC) to satisfy the debt.

Young filed a claim for exemption against the garnishment and lost. Thus, the court issued the writ of garnishment for the $44,100. Young again appealed, this time asserting that under Florida law (as in the laws of nearly every state), Levy's remedy against Young was limited to a charging order against Young's membership interest, which was different than the moneys owed to her by the LLC.

Indeed, Florida law provides, as does the laws of nearly every state, that a charging order is the exclusive remedy by which a creditor (such as Levy) can get at a debtor-member's interest in an LLC.

Levy attempted to get around this by arguing that the $44,100 represented Young's share of the profits, whereas a charging order would hit only distributions, and Young's profits were not distributions. That didn't make any more sense to the court than it probably just did to readers, with the court pointing out that profit distributions are just the sort of thing that a charging order would pick up.

Although unclear from the opinion, it appears that Levy made a much better argument, which is that the purpose of the so-called charging order exclusivity (i.e., the limitation of the creditor's remedy to a charging order as opposed to some other collection remedy) is not meant to protect the debtor-member's interest, so much as it is to protect the other members of the LLC from interference by an outside creditor.

In this case, given that Levy was the only other member of the LLC, it made no sense to limit Levy's remedy to a charging order because she was the one supposedly "protected" by it, and Levy was the one seeking it.

Be that as it may, the court basically ruled, the Florida statute was clear and unambiguous in limiting a creditor's remedy to a charging order, and thus it was unnecessary for the court to consider that argument no matter how much sense it made. With that, the court held that the writ of garnishment was improper and ruled in favor of Young.

CHAPTER 24

Circumventing Charging Order Exclusivity

Section 503(h) of the RULLCA provides that the charging order is "the exclusive remedy by which a person seeking in the capacity of judgment creditor to enforce a judgment against a member or transferee may satisfy the judgment from the judgment debtor's transferable interest."[1]

They key word here is "remedy," which is a legal term of art that refers to a number of specific legal devices that a creditor may use to enforce a judgment—devices such as levy, attachment, garnishment, etc., that are defined in a state's remedies statutes.[2] The word does not mean, as many planners mistakenly believe, that the outcome should be exclusively that which is set forth in the charging order procedure of RULLCA section 503 generally. Suffice it to say that there are a number of legal strategies that a creditor might employ that

1. Rev. Unif. Ltd. Liab. Co. Act § 503(h), 6B U.L.A. 145–46 (Unif. Law Comm'n Supp. 2015); Madison Hills Ltd. P'ship II v. Madison Hills, Inc., 644 A.2d 363, 367 (Conn. App. Ct. 1994) ("Because the partner's rights in specific property of the partnership cannot be attached or made subject to execution and the partner's management rights cannot be assigned to or conferred on anyone other than a partner the charging order is the sole remedy available to a judgment creditor of a partner.") (citations omitted). *Contra* Nigri v. Lotz, 453 S.E.2d 780, 782 n.2 (Ga. Ct. App. 1995) ("The charging order remedy is not exclusive, and the financial interests of the limited partner may also be reached by the judgment creditor by process of garnishment."). Charging order exclusivity is likewise binding on the federal courts. Lumbermens Mut. Cas. Co. v. Luciano Enters., LLC, No. A01-309 CV JWS, 2005 WL 2340709, at *2 (D. Ala. Sept. 21, 2005) (making charging order the "exclusive remedy" under Alaska law, deemed by federal court to be "a situation in which a state substantive law does in fact limit the court's power to enforce its own judgments . . . ."). It is also effective in divorce cases. Addis v. Addis, 703 S.W.2d 852, 853 (Ark. 1986) ("At divorce, in determining the rights of a husband or wife to a spouse's partnership interest, a court cannot make specific awards of partnership assets. The court must determine the value of the interest in the partnership and then award the spouse an amount equal to one-half of the value of the interest, which may be enforced by a charging order on the partnership interest.") (citing Riegler v. Riegler, 419 S.W.2d 311 (Ark. 1967)).

2. *See also* Sky Cable, LLC v. Direct TV, Inc., 886 F.3d 375 (4th Cir. Mar. 28, 2018) (discussing remedies similar to the charging order and ultimately determining that, notwithstanding charging order "exclusivity," outside reverse piercing is an available remedy).

technically are not "remedies" in the sense of being an enumerated judgment enforcement device under the remedy statutes of the state.[3]

For instance, California enumerates its list of "remedies" that a creditor in a post-judgment enforcement action might employ in the Enforcement of Judgments Law (EJL), as execution, levy, garnishment, written interrogatories to judgment debtor, examination proceedings, creditors suit, charging orders, lien in pending action or proceeding, assignment order, and receiver to enforce judgment.[4] Everything else is not technically a "remedy" under the California EJL.

There are, in fact, other strategies of relief that creditors may pursue to get at the debtor-member's interest, if not of the actual assets of the LLC.[5] A few of those strategies are discussed below.

Case Study: *DeVoll*[6]

Rebecca Demonbreun and William Dowds (Creditors) obtained a judgment in 2010 against Norris DeVoll (Debtor), who resided in Texas.

On March 8, 2011, Creditors applied for a turnover order for Debtor's assets. Texas is a community property state, which means that the community property of a husband and wife is available to the creditors of either or both; this also meant that the community property titled in the name of Debtor's wife (Paulette) was available to Creditors. Paulette owned, as community property, an undivided one-half interest in a partnership known as "206 Camedia Partnership," with the other one-half owned by Debtor's brother, Gene DeVoll (Gene).

Coincidentally, just two days after Creditors made their application for the turnover order, on March 10, Gene suddenly decided that Paulette was in violation of the partnership agreement and sent her a notice of default and demand, by which he asserted his rights to her partnership interest for a nominal sum. Shortly thereafter, Gene purchased Paulette's interest for $5,000.

Creditors' application for a turnover order was finally granted in August of 2011, and the court ordered both Debtor and Paulette not to dispose of their community property. Debtor and Paulette both appealed the turnover order to

---

3. Some reported decisions have language to the contrary. *See, e.g.*, 91st Street Joint Venture v. Goldstein, 691 A.2d 272, 276 (Md. Ct. Spec. App. 1997) ("[T]here is general agreement that the charging order is now the judgment creditor's exclusive method of reaching a partner's interest in a partnership and that the creditor may no longer execute directly on partnership property."); Dispensa v. Univ. State Bank, 951 S.W.2d 797, 800 (Tex. App. 1997) ("A charging order is the sole means by which a judgement creditor can reach an individual debtor's partnership interest.").

4. Cal. Civ. Proc. § 708-9 (West 2015).

5. It may also be that a creditor might employ some other writ to circumvent charging order exclusivity. *See, e.g.*, MacDonald v. MacDonald, 1986 WL 5480, at *3 (Del. Ch. 1986) (declining to address "the question whether a writ of *fieri facias* is effective to seize a limited partnership interest in a Delaware limited partnership . . .").

6. Devoll v. Demonbreun, 2016 WL 4538805 (Tex. App. Aug. 31, 2016).

the Texas Court of Appeals and lost—or "were poured out," to use the quaint Texas litigators' phrase—in an opinion dated November 21, 2012.

Soon thereafter in March of 2013, Creditors brought a fraudulent transfer case against Gene, alleging that the "default" and subsequent $5,000 sale of Paulette's interest in the partnership was simply a scam to transfer her partnership interest out of Creditors' reach. Creditors also sought a temporary injunction to keep Gene from disposing of the partnership's principal asset: a parcel of real estate found at 466 Adrian Drive.

The Texas District Court agreed with Creditors about their need for a temporary injunction and granted it, but the temporary injunction was reversed on a technicality. Creditors reapplied for a second temporary injunction, which was granted on May 1, 2014. The temporary injunction forbade Gene from disposing of 466 Adrian Drive pending the outcome of the fraudulent transfer lawsuit.

Gene appealed, which resulted in the following opinion of the Texas Court of Appeals. First, however, understand that Texas partnership law, like the partnership law of pretty much every other state, restricts the creditor of a partner to a charging order against the partner's interest as the single remedy. Texas also follows the Uniform Fraudulent Transfer Act (TUFTA), however, which allows a creditor to avoid a transfer made by the debtor with the intent of defeating creditors, as well as transfers that are made while the debtor is insolvent. Other Texas law allows a court to enjoin the transferee from further disposing of assets while the fraudulent transfer lawsuit is percolating toward trial.

The conflict in this case was between Texas partnership law and Texas fraudulent transfer law. Gene argued that the temporary injunction violated Texas partnership law, which provides that the charging order is the "exclusive remedy" available to a creditor of a partner in relation to that partner's interest in a partnership. Gene further argued that the temporary injunction keeps him from dealing with the partnership's property in the ordinary course of business, something the Texas partnership law expressly disallows. Finally, Gene argued that his $5,000 buyout of Paulette left her with no interest in the partnership.

Creditors countered that Paulette transferred her interest for $5,000 to Gene only to avoid her interest being subject to enforcement by Creditors, and TUFTA works to avoid such a transfer as a nullity. Avoidance of the $5,000 transfer would leave Paulette still holding her 50-percent interest in the partnership, which effectively means that she would still own through the partnership a one-half interest in 566 Adrian Drive.

Not finding any helpful precedent, the court of appeals considered the issue to be a case of first impression and proceeded to analyze the relevant statutes. The court first considered Texas partnership law (technically, Texas general partnership law, although if this case had involved a limited partnership, it probably would not have made any difference—the same is also likely true if the partnership here had been organized as an LLC instead).

After reviewing the law's legislative history and purposes, the court concluded that the purpose of its charging order provisions was: (1) to allow a creditor to satisfy its judgment from the debtor's partnership interest (but not its assets), while (2) protecting the business of the partnership from interference by the creditor. The charging order provision accomplishes this by restricting a creditor's remedy against the debtor-partner by placing a lien on the debtor-partner's interest.

Importantly, another benefit of the charging order is that a creditor has no rights against partnership property, but not against the partnership's property itself. The charging order provision does this by prohibiting other remedies, including equitable remedies such as an injunction, against the partnership property.

It was this last benefit of a charging order—to exclude other remedies such as an injunction—that created a conflict with TUFTA because TUFTA expressly allows a creditor to obtain an injunction to prohibit a transferee from disposing of an asset. This can be necessary in a given case so that the creditor can obtain meaningful relief, and not just become the owner of yet another uncollectable judgment, this time against the transferee.

Was there really a conflict? The court turned its attention to the two portions of Texas partnership law[7] that restricts a creditor's remedy to a charging order:

> (d) The entry of a charging order is the exclusive remedy by which a judgment creditor of a partner or of any other owner of a partnership interest may satisfy a judgment out of the judgment debtor's partnership interest.
>
> . . .
>
> (f) A creditor of a partner or of any other owner of a partnership interest does not have the right to obtain possession of, or otherwise exercise legal or equitable remedies with respect to, the property of the partnership.

The key takeaway here is that subparagraph (d) does not prohibit the court from using remedies other than the charging order in all circumstances, but only those that would allow the creditor to "satisfy the judgment" from partnership property. Thus, the court held that:

> [S]ubparagraph (f) of the charging order statute strips a creditor of the right to exercise an equitable remedy against the partnership's property. . . .

7. Tex. Bus. Orgs. § 152.308(d), (f).

> But we must read (f) not as an isolated provision but in conjunction with (d).... Subparagraph (d) makes the charging order an exclusive remedy, but it does not say the charging order is the exclusive remedy for all purposes; it says the charging order is "the exclusive remedy by which a judgment creditor . . . may satisfy a judgment out of the judgment debtor's partnership interest." ... When we read (f) together with (d), we conclude (f) deprives a creditor of the right to an equitable remedy against partnership property to satisfy the judgment....
>
> In light of TUFTA's express remedies for creditors, we do not interpret section 152.308 to mean a judgment creditor has no right to any equitable remedy against any partnership property under any circumstance.

The court added that this construction as also necessary to avoid an absurd result, which would be the clearly incorrect conclusion that the Texas legislature intended to promote fraudulent transfers by carving out an exception to TUFTA via Texas partnership law.

Thus, the court held that Texas partnership law's restriction of a creditor's remedy to a charging order did not prevent the entry of an injunction against the dissipation of assets under the TUFTA, so long as the injunction was only as broad as strictly necessary to prevent the partnership interest from being dissipated. Applied to this case, given that 566 Adrian Drive was essentially the only valuable asset of the partnership, the injunction was necessary to preserve Paulette's partnership interest pending resolution of Creditors' fraudulent transfer lawsuit.

The panel of the Texas Court of Appeals that heard this matter had three justices. The majority opinion consisted of two of the justices; the third (Marion, S.B., who just happened to be the Chief Justice) filed a dissent.

Justice Marion was of the opinion that Texas partnership law restricted remedies that may be employed by a creditor to the partnership interest itself, and not to partnership assets. Given that the majority's opinion allowed Creditors to enjoin the sale of 566 Adrian Drive and thus directly interfere with the partnership's business—one of the primary purposes of so-called charging order exclusivity—this violated Texas partnership law, TUFTA notwithstanding.

Case Study: *Wilhite*[8]

In *U.S. v. Wilhite*, a federal court addressed a debtor's argument that the U.S. government's fraudulent transfer was time-barred under Colorado law, and that Colorado law restricted the U.S. government to a charging order against the debtor's interests in an LLC.

8. U.S. v. Wilhite, 2017 WL 5517410 (D. Colo. Nov. 17, 2017).

The court held that the limitations provisions (actually, extinguishment provisions, which are slightly different, but everybody gets this wrong) of Colorado law were not applicable in this case where the U.S. government pursues a claim under the Federal Debt Collection Practices Act (FDCPA), which in this particular case involved a criminal restitution order. The court held that a criminal restitution award was in the nature of a tax, and that contrary state law simply does not apply to actions by the U.S. government to collect a tax. Additionally, the court noted that the FDCPA's six-year limitations period does not apply to criminal restitution awards, but instead there is a 20-year period available to the U.S. government.

The court applied this same rationale, i.e., the FDCPA overrides contrary state law as to the debtor's claim that the U.S. government should have been limited to a charging order, stating only that:

> For the same reasons, the Court likewise rejects Mr. Wilhite's argument that Colorado law requiring the issuance of a charging order before levying interest in an LLC limits the Government's ability to collect Mr. Wilhite's restitution here.

The court thus allowed the U.S. government to levy upon a $200,000 distribution that had been made from an LLC in which the debtor owned an interest.

CHAPTER 25

Other Creditor Remedies

Reverse Veil Piercing

In a traditional veil-piercing case, the LLC has a judgment against it, and the creditor seeks to disregard the LLC's separateness from its member to enforce the judgment directly against the member's assets. By contrast, in a reverse veil-piercing case, the creditor has a judgment against a member of the LLC and attempts to disregard the LLC's separateness from its member to enforce the judgment directly against the LLC's assets—thereby circumventing charging order exclusivity. Veil piercing and reverse veil piercing are merely different sides of the same coin, with the coin being to disregard the separateness for liability purposes of the LLC and its member.

The term "member" is used in the singular because the vast bulk of veil-piercing and reverse veil-piercing cases either involve one member or a dominant member. This is a result of the alter-ego analysis that typically goes into a veil-piercing case, which—despite the multitude of factors that may be considered[1]—usually boils down to the creditor proving two elements: (1) there exists a *unity of ownership* between the LLC and the member against which veil-piercing is asserted; and (2) the separateness of the LLC was used to *commit some wrong.*[2]

Assuming the creditor can prove the "commit some wrong" element, which is so facts-and-circumstances dependent as to be far beyond the scope of this book, the creditor must still prove the unity of ownership element. This is basically that the LLC and the member are so closely intertwined that equitable prin-

1. Such factors may include: commingling of funds and other assets, failure to segregate funds, diversion of funds or assets for nonbusiness uses, holding out to others that a person is individually liable, the failure to observe formalities and failure to adequately capitalize the entity. *See* Ridgerunner, LLC v. Meisinger, 297 P.3d 110, 115 (Wyo. 2013); Inter-Tel Tech., Inc. v. Lynn Station Prop., LLC, 360 S.W.3d 152 (Ky. 2012).

2. *See, e.g.*, GreenHunter Energy, Inc. v. W. Ecosystems Tech., Inc., 337 P.3d 454, 462 (Wyo. 2014).

ciples demand that they be treated as one and the same person (and that their separateness be disregarded).[3]

In the law of corporations, the unity of ownership element historically was met by the creditor proving that corporate formalities of the entity had not been observed.[4] This often led to some poor, first-year associate having to stay up the night before document production was due, drafting minutes "memorializing" board meetings from years past. These days, strict compliance with corporate formalities carries less weight, with the court instead examining the totality of the circumstances to make this determination.[5]

What of the case of the LLC, a supposed advantage of which is its lack of statutory and management formalities? Here, too, the court will most likely look past the strict observance of such formalities, or lack thereof, and instead look to whether the member is treating the LLC as an independent commercial enterprise, or instead as a personal appendage.[6] It may be much easier, for example, for a creditor to prove unity of ownership in the case of the single-member LLC because of the complete control exercised by the member.[7] By the same token, if there are many more-or-less equal members in an LLC, the unity of ownership element will likely be more difficult for a creditor to prove.

Returning to reverse veil piercing, creditors in some states were able to convince courts that reverse veil piercing was warranted in some cases, as discussed (but not successfully applied) by the Third Circuit in *In re Blatstein*.[8] In a more recent decision from the 4th Circuit, *Sky Cable, LLC v. Direct TV, Inc.*,[9] it was held that a single-member LLC organized in Delaware could be pierced in order to access its assets to satisfy a judgment against the member. Other courts rejected the notion and pointed out that the creditor could always get at the entity's assets by enforcing the judgment against the debtor's membership interest, and then use the management power conferred by such membership interests (if any) to do what needed to be done with the assets of the entity.[10]

Reverse veil piercing has thus been widely neutered, but is not quite dead. In the case of a partnership or LLC where the creditor's remedy is restricted to the charging order, a creditor may be able to persuade the court in a particular case that the equitable solution of reverse veil piercing may be warranted. The critical

3. *Id.*
4. *See, e.g.*, Browning-Ferris Indus. of Ill., Inc. v. Ter Maat, 195 F.3d 953, 49 (7th Cir. 1999).
5. *See* Pamperin v. Streamline Mfg., Inc., 276 S.W.3d 428, 437 (Tenn. Ct. App. 2008).
6. *See* Hollowell v. Orleans Reg'l Hosp., 1998 WL 283298 (E.D. La. 1998).
7. 2 Ribstein & Keatinge on Ltd. Liab. Cos. § 12:3 Veil-piercing.
8. *In re* Blatstein, 192 F.3d 88, 100–01 (3d Cir. 1999).
9. 886 F.3d 375 (4th Cir. Mar. 28, 2018).
10. *See, e.g.*, Postal Instant Press, Inc. v. Kaswa Corp., 77 Cal. Rptr. 3d 96, 105 (Cal. Ct. App. 2008); Comm'r of Envtl. Prot. v. St. Five Indus. Park, Inc., 37 A.3d 724, 733–34 (Conn. 2012).

thing for planners in advising their clients is that any protection afforded by the exclusivity of the charging order may only be as good as they strictly maintain separation between the operations of the LLC and their personal activities. As discussed above, this is particularly true with single-member entities.

Distribution Clawbacks

Assume that an LLC has several more-or-less equal members, but one of the members is a debtor, and a charging order has been entered. This places a lien on the debtor-member's interest. Further, assume that the other members decide to distribute the LLC's assets out to themselves (and that the LLC's governing documents would permit such unequal distribution), thus leaving the LLC with no assets available to make distributions to the debtor-member.

The growing theory involving corporations is that the creditor might be able to bring a derivative suit on behalf of the entity to make the nondebtor shareholders return their distributions (known as a clawback) so that an equal distribution could be made to the debtor-shareholder for the benefit of the creditor. The viability of this approach was tested in *CML, LLC v. Bax,*[11] where the Delaware Court of Chancery held that the creditor lacked standing under Delaware's LLC statute to bring such an action. The court commented, however, that such an action was authorized under Delaware's corporate statute.[12] How the theory will be treated in other states under their LLC statutes remains to be seen. It should be noted, however, that a creditor might be able to assert a fraudulent transfer theory[13] to obtain relief in such a case, although that theory remains to be tested as well.

Voidable Transactions

There is a theory circulating that a debtor in financial distress can transfer certain of his or her valuable assets to an LLC without that transfer being held to be a fraudulent transfer because the debtor is receiving "reasonably equivalent value" in return in the form of an equally valued membership interest.

The logic behind this theory is that a debtor can convert his or her valuable assets into a LLC interest, and thus protect those assets from creditors, who can't collect against those assets because they are now owned by the LLC and not the

11. 6 A.3d 238, 249–54 (Del. Ch. 2010). *Contra* Beach Park Assoc. v. Heron, No. H023320, 2003 WL 22000591, at *24 (Cal. Ct. App. Aug. 25, 2003) (nondebtor partners who caused a loan from partnership that reduced the partnership's liquidity such that it could not pay on charging order "perpetrated a fraud on the judgment creditor" and a breach of their fiduciary duties to the partnership.).

12. *CML*, 6 A.3d at 249–54.

13. Although a discussion of such theory is beyond the scope of this book, *see generally* Avoidance and Recovery of Fraudulent Transfers, Am. Jur. Proof of Facts 3d 591.

debtor. Instead, the creditor is limited to a charging order against the debtor's LLC interest, which is really just a lien that catches distributions when and if made (and of course none will be made for the creditor to pick up).

In the end of this theoretical analysis, the creditor goes from being able to collect against valuable assets to being stuck with a lien of dubious value against the debtor's new LLC interest. However, in reality, it is precisely this result that blows up "reasonably equivalent value" and makes the transfer relatively easy for a creditor to set aside as a fraudulent transfer.

In *Interpool Ltd. v. Patterson,*[14] just a week before the debtor went to trial in New York in a civil case against him, the debtor and his wife, both Florida residents, transferred just over $1.4 million in assets to RMC Holdings LP, a limited partnership controlled by the debtor and his wife.

The debtor lost his trial, and a judgment against him for over $4.8 million was entered. Shortly thereafter the creditor moved to void the transfers in violation of New York's fraudulent conveyances laws.

Noting that "reasonably equivalent value" is always measured from the perspective of creditors, the court held that the debtor (Cuneo) and his wife had committed a fraudulent transfer and thus rendered themselves judgment proof:

> Cuneo has done just that by rendering his $1.4 million in property virtually unreachable by the judgment creditor. Cuneo exchanged $1.4 million in cash and securities for general and limited partnership interests in RMC in which he received essentially three rights—the right to receive income and capital distributions from the partnership, the rights in the specific partnership property, and the right to participate in management. Creditors can reach only Cuneo's right to the receipt of whatever distributions that the partnership—consisting only of Cuneo and his wife—chooses to make, but cannot reach his rights in specific partnership property or, far more important, his right to participate in management. Viewing the transfer from the standpoint of Cuneo's creditors and their legal rights vis-a-vis Cuneo's partnership interests, the conveyance was not an exchange for equivalent value.

The debtor argued that Florida law, not New York law, should apply, but the court held that it didn't make any difference because the transfers would have been voidable under Florida fraudulent transfer law as well. In the end, the court entered a turnover order for the property that the debtor and his wife transferred to RMC Holdings LP.

---

14. 890 F. Supp. 259 (S.D.N.Y. 1995).

The *Interpool* result is consistent with rulings in cases arising under section 548 of the U.S. Bankruptcy Code, which is bankruptcy's fraudulent transfer provision.

In *Schaefer v. G.R.D. Investments LLC*,[15] an Iowa farming couple were sued in Oklahoma for breach of a grain contract, losing the case to the tune of $127,125. Wife filed for bankruptcy, but it was dismissed, and thereafter the couple sought the services of an Iowa attorney who helped them form G.R.D. Investments LLC and transfer all their nonhomestead real property to the company in exchange for a 15-year "employment agreement" that paid them a small wage each year and guaranteed health care benefits.

The bankruptcy trustee then filed an adversary action to avoid the transfers under both Iowa's Uniform Fraudulent Transfers Act and section 548 of the Bankruptcy Code.

The court noted that because the couple managed G.R.D., it was a statutory insider under the Iowa UFTA. The court also noted the absence of anything like an arm's-length sale of the property to G.R.D., and that the couple (the Schaefers) would earn equal salaries even if they put in unequal labor; plus, the healthcare benefits would be provided to them regardless of cost. Thus:

> Notwithstanding Schaefers' failure to prove that any portion of the stream of benefits is not truly wages, there are aspects of the arrangement which support an inference that the intent of the agreement was to defraud creditors. The qualitative terms of the employment agreement were not based on the value of Larry and Elaine's services in the marketplace. Larry and Elaine received identical salaries, without regard to whether they performed different tasks or worked different numbers of hours. Larry said that if he and his wife were unable to perform the physical work of managing the properties, they could hire someone else to do it. The agreement guaranteed Schaefers' wage income at a higher level than they had ever had before, regardless of whether G.R.D. would continue to own the properties transferred to it in 2001. The agreement guaranteed health care coverage without regard to cost. The term of the contract was based on Schaefers' desire to have regular, substantial income and guaranteed health insurance coverage until they received Social Security benefits.
>
> Schaefers cannot have it both ways. If the value of their promise to provide labor to G.R.D. was economically equivalent to the compensation to be paid them, the compensation should not be attributed to the real estate transfer in determining whether they received reasonably equiv-

15. 331 B.R. 401 (Bankr. N.D. Iowa 2005).

> alent value for their property . . . . However, if it was not economically equivalent, the transfer was structured by Schaefers to put their non-exempt property out of the reach of their creditors, and in the hands of their sons, while Schaefers were financially distressed. The court concludes that the transfers to G.R.D. were a fraudulent arrangement between Schaefers and their sons to shield non-exempt assets from the parents' creditors by converting them to "exempt wages."

The Schaefers also argued that they were acting in good faith in regard to the transfers to G.R.D. because they had acted on the advice of their counsel, but after reviewing several pertinent prior court opinions on the subject, the court concluded:

> The sense of the cases is not that a debtor will be excused from actual fraudulent intent if he has sought legal advice for the execution of a fraudulent scheme. A defense of advice of counsel may overcome an inference of fraud or willful misconduct, but the defendant must show a full disclosure of all relevant facts to the attorney and a reasonable belief that he was receiving reliable advice.

Given that the debtors failed to make any showing regarding G.R.D. as to what they told their lawyer and what he told them, the court rejected this defense.

These cases are just examples of how the courts have dealt with the assets-for-interest exchange in the fraudulent transfer context. The issue is important because the concept of "reasonably equivalent value" plays a critical role in a fraudulent-transfer analysis.

There are several tests as to whether a given transfer is a fraudulent transfer,[16] but there are two main tests that encompass the majority of reported cases. The first test is an intent test under section 4 of the Uniform Voidable Transactions Act (formerly called the Uniform Fraudulent Transfers Act). The intent test, referred to as the "actual fraudulent transfer" test, is erroneously named because no proof of fraudulent intent is required to establish liability under this section. This test has two alternative elements (the second with multiple subparts): (1) the debtor made the transfer with the intent to defeat creditors, or (2) the transfer was without "reasonably equivalent value" and the debtor "(i) was engaged or was about to engage in a business or a transaction for which the remaining assets

16. For instance, section 5(b) applies to transfer made to an insider in exchange for an antecedent debt to an insolvent debtor and the insider knew or should have been aware that the debtor was insolvent. Given that an LLC of which the debtor is a member is likely to be considered an "insider" of the debtor, and given that knowledge of the debtor may be imputed to the LLC, this section presents particular hazards for LLCs that deal with financially distressed members.

of the debtor were unreasonably small in relation to the business or transaction; or (ii) intended to incur, or believed or reasonably should have believed that the debtor would incur, debts beyond the debtor's ability to pay as they became due." Section 4 goes on to identify factors to consider when determining actual intent and confirms that the burden of proof is by a preponderance of the evidence, not a clear-and-convincing standard as some courts erroneously applied prior to the adoption of the UVTA.

The second test is a balance-sheet test under section 5(a) of the UVTA, which has nothing to do with the debtor's intent, but instead looks exclusively to two elements: (1) the debtor was insolvent at the time or the transfer or made insolvent because of the transfer; and (2) the transfer was without "reasonably equivalent value." This test is the so-called and even more erroneously named constructive fraudulent transfer test.

Note that both of these tests require the creditor to prove that the transfer was without "reasonably equivalent value." This is always proved from the viewpoint of creditors, and the consideration paid to the debtor for the transfer must have what is known as "utility to creditors," meaning that the creditor can get the same value out of what was received as what was transferred.

This is not to suggest that all transfers by a debtor to an LLC, even one in deep financial distress, will *ipso facto* fail to rise to the level of reasonably equivalent value. Assume a debtor transfers $1 million in cash for a like value in a privately traded hedge fund organized as an LLC and managed by a reputable third-party manager. On the day after the transfer, the debtor could easily cash out his interests for about the same $1 million. In such a case, that transfer probably constituted "reasonably equivalent value."

Of course, this is very different from the typical distressed debtor case as described above. The transfer is usually to an LLC that is owned or controlled either by the debtor or by an insider. The LLC usually has no or minimal other assets, and often the ink of the formation papers filed with the Secretary of State hasn't fully dried.

Then, there is the transfer. The transfer is usually dollar-for-dollar, meaning $1 of assets for $1 of interests. Estate planners should immediately recognize the problem with this, which is that with an LLC, $1 of assets isn't worth for tax purposes $1 interest in the LLC. Estate planners take the position with great frequency that $1 of assets is not worth $1 of interests in the LLC for the precise reason involved here: the interest received is subject to various restrictions, such as lack of marketability and lack of control, etc. This is exactly what torpedoes the transfer for reasonably-equivalent-value purposes as shown by the above cases.

These cases almost always involved a debtor who panics when he or she realizes that creditors might come knocking at the door and doesn't just make a transfer to an LLC, but also makes other contemporaneous transfers that belie whatever excuse the debtor has made for making the transfer to the LLC. In analyzing the section 4 actual intent (actual fraudulent transfer) cases, the court doesn't look at particular transfer in a vacuum, but rather looks at the totality of the circumstances surrounding the transfer to divine the debtor's real purpose, with those circumstances expressed as the so-called badges of fraud.

The point is that these late transfers to a LLC will usually be set aside as a fraudulent transfer.

CHAPTER 26

Bankruptcy Issues with Charging Orders

One of the most difficult issues for practitioners and judges has been the treatment of LLC interests in bankruptcy. The Bankruptcy Code does not have any specific provisions for dealing with LLCs and LLC interests. Rather, the provisions of the Bankruptcy Code dealing with "corporations" and "partnerships" are applied to LLCs by analogy. The absence of specific provisions in the Bankruptcy Code about LLCs creates numerous problems.

If the debtor-member commences a case under the Bankruptcy Code, there are two distinct paths (or rabbit holes) down which creditor must travel. The split in the paths is ultimately determined by whether the creditor's charging order has survived bankruptcy, meaning that the lien created by charging order has not been set aside as a preferential transfer or on some other grounds. If the charging order lien has survived, then the creditor will go down the path of a secured creditor, like any other secured creditor. If the charging order lien is set aside by the bankruptcy trustee, however, then the creditor will go down the uncertain path of an unsecured creditor.

The debtor's member interest (subject to a valid charging order lien or not) becomes property of the estate under section 541(a) of the Bankruptcy Code. The automatic stay of section 362(a) of the Bankruptcy Code immediately halts all further collection activity against the debtor.

A caution here for those who might focus only on the actions of the creditor as potentially violating the automatic stay: The stay applies to anybody who takes any action that would affect the debtor's (now the debtor's estate's) property. Thus, if the other members of an LLC attempt to take some action that would diminish the debtor's interest, such as attempting to enforce a buy-out provision, those members could be held in contempt for violating the stay.

The Debtor's Interest as to Secured Creditors

The path of a creditor holding a charging order is that of a secured creditor. Under section 101(37) of the Bankruptcy Code, a "lien" means "a charge against or interest in property to secure payment of a debt or performance of an obligation." Under section 101(36), "judicial lien" is a "lien that is obtained by judgment, levy, sequestration, or other legal or equitable process or proceeding." The lien created by a charging order should be considered a judicial lien under section 101(36).

The creditor is entitled to apply to the bankruptcy court to lift the stay under section 362(d) to continue to receive distributions from the charged interest, and even to foreclose the lien if state law allows. In other words, a creditor who holds a "seasoned" charging order, i.e., a charging order that has existed long enough so as avoid a challenge as a preference, is essentially in the same position as any other consensual secured creditor. A creditor who holds a consensual security interest in a debtor's LLC interest may apply to the bankruptcy court to lift the stay to enforce whatever rights that consensual creditor has in the interest, including nonjudicial foreclosure. The creditor, like any consensual secured creditor, must meet the requirements of section 362(d) for the stay to be lifted.

The Debtor's Interest as to Unsecured Creditors

Unsecured creditors, including creditors whose charging order has been invalidated by an avoidance action, must look to recovery through the trustee's efforts. As mentioned above, the debtor's interest comes into the bankruptcy estate under section 541(a), and thus is part of the assets that are marshaled by the trustee. Now we go down the rabbit hole.

The trustee holds the debtor's member interest, but what the trustee can do with that interest is first determined by an analysis under section 365, which applies to executory contracts. An executory contract is one in which material performance is still due by both parties to the contract. In contrast, a nonexecutory contract is one in which one party has fully performed and the other has not yet fully performed.

Analysis under section 365 applies to the LLC's operating agreement,[1] or more specifically the debtor's rights and obligations under that operating agreement. As to the debtor, the operating agreement is executory if the debtor as a member must perform additional material duties not yet performed as of the time of bankruptcy, such as to make a capital contribution or perform some duties on behalf of the LLC. An operating agreement will be nonexecutory as to the debtor if the debtor does not need to satisfy further material obligations, as with an investor interest in a mutual fund that is organized as an LLC, for example.

If the Interest Is Executory

If the debtor's member interest is executory, then under section 365(a) the trustee may either assume or reject the contract, i.e., the operating agreement.

1. Note that because there is no real bilateral "agreement" by a debtor with a single-member LLC wholly owned by the debtor, the operating agreement in such a case should never be considered an executory contract.

If the trustee assumes the operating agreement, then the trustee essentially "steps into the shoes" of the debtor as member for all purposes of that agreement, both good and bad. If the debtor had a majority interest and the operating agreement or applicable law permitted the debtor to do so, the trustee may vote the debtor's right to dissolve the entity, which would have the effect of flushing the debtor's share of the assets into the trustee's direct control for later liquidation. On the other hand, if the trustee assumes the operating agreement, the trustee is also subject to any duties arising from that agreement, including the duty to satisfy calls for capital contributions from other property of the debtor's estate.

If the trustee rejects the operating agreement, the rejection order is deemed to be a pre-petition breach of the contract by the debtor. The member interest would still be part of the bankruptcy estate, and the trustee would still be entitled to receive distributions on the member interest, but any damage claims by the LLC itself arising from the breach, to the extent that they exist, may be subject to recoupment or setoff against the distributions to be made to the debtor.

To reduce the risk that the operating agreement could be assumed by the trustee as an executory contract, the operating agreement could define the unperformed duties as being capable of or appropriate to being performed only by debtor personally, per sections 365(c)(1) and (e)(2)(A) of the Bankruptcy Code. This technique is likely to work only if the debtor as member is providing unique or specialized services that are so personal to the debtor's relationship with the other members that the other members should not be compelled to accept substituted performance by a third party assignee of the debtor (including the Trustee).

If the Interest Is Nonexecutory

If the interest is nonexecutory, then the trustee is entitled to exercise the debtor's rights as a member in respect of the member interest. Those rights may be broader than an ordinary creditor would have if the creditor had obtained a charging order lien. Here, the trustee, like a charging order creditor, can monetize the asset by selling the interest, but the trustee can also exercise voting and other rights that the debtor as a member would have had. If the trustee determines that it is not worth the trouble for the bankruptcy estate to retain the membership interest, the trustee may, with bankruptcy court approval, abandon the interest back to the debtor.

Ipso Facto Clauses

Operating agreements often contain provisions to the effect that if the debtor becomes insolvent or an involuntary petition is filed against the debtor, then either the LLC or the other members may buy back the debtor's interest. In fact, some LLC planners draft lengthy and meticulous provisions to attempt to bring about this result.

At least in bankruptcy, these provisions, which are known as *ipso facto* clauses, are little more than a waste of otherwise good space in the operating agreement. The reason is that such provisions do not prevent the debtor's LLC interest from coming into the estate under section 541(c)(1) of the Bankruptcy Code and are not otherwise effective to modify the debtor-member's rights existing before the commencement of the bankruptcy case.[2]

Case Study: *Cleveland*[3]

Charles and Ellerie Cleveland (Debtors), residents of Nevada, were the 100-percent owners and managers of two Nevada LLCs: PFG Advisors, LLC, a Las Vegas insurance agency, and PFG Properties, LLC, which owned the building from which PFG Advisors operated.

By 2012, Debtors were having financial troubles, including a foreclosure that year on their PFG Properties office building. In February 2013, Debtors filed a joint Chapter 7 bankruptcy petition in Nevada. By filing a joint petition, Debtors' LLC interests, if included in the estate, would become the property of a single bankruptcy estate.

Debtors fully disclosed their 100-percent interests in the two LLCs and claimed that the LLC interests were exempt under Nevada law. A Chapter 7 trustee was appointed, and he objected to the claim of exemptions. The trustee also sought to take ownership of the LLCs in order ultimately to reach the assets of the two LLCs.

The bankruptcy court held the LLC interests were not exempt and comprised property of the estate, but "the trustee has no right to sell or otherwise take ownership of any assets of those companies." Unwilling to take "no" for an answer, the trustee appealed to the U.S. District Court.[4]

The trustee argued that that the bankruptcy court botched the case by holding he had no right to sell or take possession of the LLCs' assets. From the trustee's view, when Debtors filed for bankruptcy, the LLC interests became property of Debtors' bankruptcy estate. Thus, the trustee "stepped into the shoes" of Debtors and could exercise whatever control Debtors had over the two LLCs and their assets—which of course was all control.

Debtors conceded that 100 percent of the LLC interests were part of the bankruptcy estate. Instead, they argued that the trustee's sole remedy under Nevada

---

2. *But see* Bankruptcy Code § 365(e)(1) described above as to executory contracts.

3. *In re* Cleveland, 2014 WL 4809924 (D. Nev. 2014).

4. Debtors and the trustee seem to have been battling about PFG Advisors' insurance commissions. Debtors claimed 75 percent of the commissions payable to PFG Advisors as exempt, which would track with the 25-percent federal limitation on collection against wages, which include commission income. The trustee originally objected to that exemption, but apparently abandoned that objection.

law was a charging order against their interests in the LLCs. The argument went like this: the trustee might have the right to receive whatever distributions were made to Debtors by the LLCs, if any, but the trustee has no powers regarding the management of the LLCs or their assets.

The district court held in favor of the bankruptcy trustee:

> Numerous bankruptcy courts have held, and the Court agrees, that where a debtor has a membership interest in a single-member LLC and files a petition for bankruptcy under Chapter 7, the Chapter 7 trustee succeeds to all of the debtor's rights, including the right to control that entity, and a trustee need not take any further action to comply with state law before exercising such control. See, e.g., In re First Protection, Inc., 440 B.R. 821, 830 (B.A.P. 9th Cir. 2010); In re B & M Land & Livestock, LLC, 498 B.R. 262, 267 (Bankr. D. Nev. 2013); In re Albright, 291 B.R. 538, 541 (Bankr. D. Colo. 2003). Furthermore, the Court agrees that "[s]tate law does not control the administration of property interests that are part of the bankruptcy estate." In re B & M, 498 B.R. at 268. Accordingly, [trustee] is not limited to a charging order under Nevada law, and succeeds to all of [debtors'] rights in the LLCs, including the right to control those entities.

Now for the curveball thrown by Debtors, which makes this case really interesting—the same curveball that got Debtors past the bankruptcy court: Debtors argued that a trustee should not be allowed to step into the shoes of a debtor-member of an LLC through which the members render personal services, particularly professional services requiring a license (such as law, medicine, insurance, etc.) because the bankruptcy trustee is not qualified or licensed to engage in the LLC's business.

The district court skirted this issue, pointing out that if the trustee could not own or manage an LLC providing professional or personal services, the trustee still could liquidate the assets of such an LLC. The district court held in favor of the trustee on this issue.

Case Study: *Denman*[5]

Derek Denman and his wife Marie jointly filed a Chapter 13 bankruptcy petition in the Western District of Tennessee.

Denman owned a 70-percent interest in Opus Medical Management, LLC. Section 13.4 of Opus' operating agreement provided for a "Sale on Triggering Event," which here meant that when Denman filed for bankruptcy, any other member of Opus could exercise their option to purchase Denman's interest in

5. *In re* Denman, 513 B.R. 720 (W.D. Tenn. July 24, 2014).

Opus. The option was open for 60 days after the filing of the bankruptcy petition and could be made by giving written notice to Opus that the option was being exercised.

Dr. Michael Rack was another member in Opus—a 25-percent member to be exact. Within the 60 days, Dr. Rack filed an emergency motion to lift automatic stay so that he could exercise the option to purchase Denman's 70-percent interest.

Fighting to keep his interest in Opus, Denman objected to Dr. Rack's motion on the ground that the option provision, section 13.4, amounted to an impermissible ipso facto clause (i.e., a clause that only becomes effective upon the debtor's bankruptcy) that is negated by either section 365(e)(1) or 541(c)(1)(B) of the Bankruptcy Code, and that Denman's 70-percent interest therefore was and remained in his bankruptcy estate under section 541(c)(1)(B) despite the 60-day option.

Dr. Rack retorted that the option did not fall under section 365(e)(1), thus attempting to force the court to consider whether the option was an executory contract, but apparently did not dispute that the option died as an ipso facto clause under section 541(c)(1)(B).

The opinion of the bankruptcy court resolves this issue, and in a way that may result in some consternation to planners. If the options clause amounts to an executory contract under section 365, then the options clause is valid, and Denman's 70-percent interest in Opus did not become a part of his bankruptcy estate under 541 (and Dr. Rack could properly exercise the option and take Denman's interest). If the options clause amounts to a nonexecutory contract, however, then section 365 doesn't apply, and Denman's 70-percent interest in Opus passes into his bankruptcy estate under 541 and is protected from Dr. Rack's option.

Denman's 70-percent interest in Opus passes into Denman's bankruptcy estate under section 541 regardless of what happens on the resolution of executory vs. nonexecutory issue under section 365. That is clear. The real question is what the trustee can do with Denman's 70-percent interest in Opus. If section 365 does not apply, then the trustee could theoretically assume all of Denman's rights under the operating agreement, which would include Denman's ability to vote to wind up and dissolve Opus, meaning that Denman's share of Opus' assets would pass to the trustee, and the other members of Opus wouldn't have any say about this result (and they may not want Opus dissolved).

Under *Ehmann* (which the *Denman* court arguably should have followed), the salient inquiry is whether Opus' operating agreement amounts to an executory or nonexecutory agreement. In a typical display of its genius, Congress turns these issues on whether an agreement is executory or nonexecutory, without telling us what an executory or nonexecutory agreement is. Therefore, the courts look outside the Bankruptcy Code to case law, and here to case law that developed from a 1973 *Minnesota Law Review* article entitled "Executory Contracts in

Bankruptcy" that eventually came to be known as the "Countryman standard." In legalese, the Countryman standard says something to the effect that if the contract has been so far performed by one party such that the full obligation to perform has arisen in another party, the contract is nonexecutory.

In English, the Countryman standard basically is that an executory agreement means that somebody must take some material action before they reap the benefit of the agreement, whereas a nonexecutory agreement means that not much more needs to be done before that same somebody gets their promised benefits. A way to think about this is that an interest can be active in the sense that somebody must undertake some activity to earn their payment (i.e., executory), or it can be passive in the sense that their payment is coming in no matter what (i.e., nonexecutory).

As a predicate, however, there must be an "agreement" because section 365 applies only to executory agreements. Is an operating agreement therefore an "agreement" under section 365? Please clear the liquids from your mouth before reading the next paragraph that gives the answer.

The *Denman* court answers this question in the negative—that's right, an LLC's operating agreement is not the type of "agreement" contemplated by section 365. In other words, section 365 has utterly no application to the operating agreements of LLCs (or the partnership agreements of general and limited partnerships). Forget 365 entirely, sayeth the *Denman* court, effectively meaning that a bankruptcy trustee can exercise all the debtor's rights in a partnership agreement or operating agreement, including vote to dissolve the entity.

The *Denman* court reaches this remarkable result through some contorted reasoning. A summary of what the court said follows, as well as what a critic of the court's decision might retort.

First, the court pointed out that an "agreement" typically requires a party's assent to the terms, but with an LLC, if a party becomes a member, then that party automatically becomes subject to the operating agreement if they did not negotiate it.

The critic would point out that the party does have a choice as to whether to become a member in the first place, and exercising that choice is the assent—not too differently from a person who pulls up to a gas pump and starts to fill up, there is an implied assent to the terms of the sale and the price (if you don't want the terms and the price, go to another gas station). That a new member to a partnership effectively assents to the existing terms of a partnership agreement by joining the partnership has been an integral part of partnership law for centuries, and that law was explicitly carried over into the new LLC laws as well.

Second, the court points out that because not all members are required to amend the operating agreement, there is no assent to the change by the minority members who did want the change. The critic would point out that the minority members assented to this possibility when they choose to become members.

Third, the court puts a lot of weight on the fact that an LLC needs only one member, and that one member has nobody else to agree with. The critic would point out that while that is true, that is not the same with multiple-member LLCs (as here).

Fourth, the court looked to the requirement that LLC members respond to cash calls, even if they are unable to perform, as well as the requirement that the other members respond greater if another member fails to respond. Thus:

> A single member LLC operating agreement does not have multiple members and, therefore, can satisfy neither the mutual assent element nor the exchange of consideration element of contract law. This simple problem highlights the underlying problem with considering LLC operating agreements as executory contracts because it demonstrates that LLC members are not contracting amongst themselves but instead are organizing and structuring a new entity to receive their contributions, whether cash, services to be performed, or otherwise. Applying contract logic, the single member LLC seemingly becomes an absurdity.

The critic would again point out that this rationale doesn't apply to multiple-member LLCs and here Opus had multiple members.

Based on all these points, the court then concluded that operating agreements are not "agreements" under section 365, at least under the Countryman standard:

> Based on the foregoing, the court finds here that Tennessee LLC operating agreements are not per se executory contracts governed by sec. 365 of the Bankruptcy Code because of their unique elements and features under state law that are inconsistent with contract law. Such operating agreements, for example, may lack mutual assent, consideration, and privity amongst the parties. Furthermore, a member's failure to perform under an LLC operating agreement does not excuse the other members' performance under the LLC operating agreement, which contradicts the Sixth Circuit and Countryman standards for executory contracts. Tennessee LLC operating agreements cannot satisfy the Sixth Circuit and Countryman standards for executory contracts, and, thus, Tennessee LLC operating agreements are not executory contracts as contemplated under sec. 365 of the Bankruptcy Code.

Aware that the court's conclusion would raise eyebrows, the court reflected that this area of law is at best confused. Although the "overwhelming majority" had determined that LLC operating agreements were nonexecutory contracts under section 365, at least three other courts had found that they were executive contracts, but these cases were just wrong:

> In reviewing these cases, the court believes there may have been some confusion or difference of opinion as to the obligations, duties, and rights that existed under an LLC operating agreement. These courts determined that the existence of "executory obligations" that could be "breached" caused the agreements detailing these obligations to be executory contracts. However, these courts arguably failed to consider that executory obligations can arise under numerous types of legal instruments and not just ordinary contracts. Also, the executory obligations and hypothetical breaches discussed therein were not subject to ordinary contract law but rather to the LLC entity laws of their respective states. Unilateral executory obligations like those found in operating agreements are not executory contractual obligations under either the Sixth Circuit standard or the Countryman standard. These standards require bilateral future obligations and not merely unilateral obligations to contribute to the LLC entity. Furthermore, a member's breach or default of its duties and obligations under an LLC operating agreement does not necessarily excuse the future performance of other members. To qualify as an executory contract, the breach must excuse the other parties' future performance as discussed in the Countryman standard. These three courts apparently failed to fully consider that an LLC operating agreement is a distinct legal instrument apart from contract instruments.

With regard to Opus' operating agreement, the court held that the only duty of the members was to make their initial contribution, after which they had little duties. Strangely, and although professing to have scrutinized Opus' operating agreement, the court apparently missed numerous duties that the members had, turning a Nelsonian blind eye to the provisions creating duties that ran afoul of the court's desired storyline. Thus, partially blinded, the court concluded:

> These membership interests are personal property of the individual members analogous to shares of corporate securities. Mr. Denman's Membership Interest became property of the sec. 541(a) estate upon the filing of his Chapter 13 petition. 11 U.S.C. sec. 541(a). In conclusion, the LLC operating agreement here is not an executory contract and is more appropriately classified as a business formation and governance instrument; therefore, the Opus Operating Agreement here is not an executory contract under sec. 365, however, Mr. Denman's Membership Interest is sec. 541 property of the estate.

The court then turned to section 541, or more specifically to 541(c)(1)(B), which basically provides that if a provision in an agreement is triggered by the insolvency or bankruptcy of the debtor, the court may ignore that provision.

Recalling that the debtor, Denman, was trying to fight off the attempt of Dr. Rack to exercise his option to purchase Denman's interest for $10,000, Denman argued that Dr. Rack's option was precisely the type of provision that is invalidated by 541(c)(1)(B) because Dr. Rack's option did not vest until Denman filed for bankruptcy.

This is the so-called *ipso facto* clause, and the court noted that such clauses are triggered by some external event (usually the filing for bankruptcy) and not by any normal operation of the operating agreement:

> [I]t is well-established that ipso facto clauses are unenforceable as a matter of law under the Bankruptcy Code. This is because the whole purpose of filing for bankruptcy is to provide the debtor with a 'fresh start,' and enforcement of ipso facto clauses would punish debtors by negating this central purpose. . . . Section 541(c) provides that, despite [a] provision between the parties to the contrary, a debtor's interest becomes property of the bankruptcy estate upon the filing of a bankruptcy petition and the debtor does not lose the property due to its bankruptcy petition.[6]

Here, Dr. Rack's option to purchase Denman's stock only arose upon Denman's bankruptcy; thus, it constituted an impermissible *ipso facto* clause. Given that Dr. Rack was attempting to get relief from the automatic stay just to enforce this unenforceable clause, he loses, and the court so ruled.

6. Quoting *In re* W.R. Grace & Co., 475 B.R. 34, 152–53 (D. Del. 2012).

CHAPTER 27

Tax Issues

Once a charging order has been entered, certain tax issues arise.[1] As will be discussed, the treatment of these issues differs between the stage at which the charging order has simply been issued but prior to foreclosure (preforeclosure) and after the creditor's charging order lien has been foreclosed upon by the creditor (post-foreclosure). Due to the fact that these issues may impact the creditor, the debtor, the entity itself, and the buyer at a judicial sale (who might not be the creditor), consideration of the effect upon these parties at each phase is likewise necessary.[2]

Here, we must be reminded that a charging order is merely the legal vehicle by which a lien is placed by the creditor upon the debtor's economic right to distributions from the entity. Foreclosure of a charging order correspondingly means that the creditor has liquidated its lien only in the debtor's economic right to distributions, and whoever ends up owning that interest merely takes that right without more.

Pre-Foreclosure

Tax Implications to the Creditor

After the issuance of a charging order, the creditor becomes a mere lienholder of the debtor's economic right to distributions;—no more, no less.[3] As such, the creditor will treat the cash received as a result of the charging order lien no differently than other money the creditor might receive as a result of other collection efforts. In other words, if the creditor would be taxed on the money that it receives through other collection efforts (such as arising from an action

1. For these purposes, it is assumed that the LLC in question is, for purposes of federal tax classification regulations, a "partnership" and not a "disregarded entity" or a "corporation."

2. *See also* Thomas E. Rutledge & Sarah Sloan Wilson (now Sarah Sloan Reeves), *An Examination of the Charging Order Under Kentucky's LLC and Partnership Acts (Part II)*, 99 Ky. L.J. 107, 108–13 (2010–11).

3. *See* Ky. Rev. Stat. Ann. § 275.260(3) (charging order is not an assignment); *accord* § 362.285(4) (KyUPA); § 362. 481(3) (KyRULPA); § 362.1-504(4) (KyRUPA); § 362.2-703(3) (KyULPA).

sounding in contract), then it will be taxed on the money that it receives pursuant to a charging order as well. Conversely, if the creditor would not pay tax on the money that it receives (such as from a personal injury award), then it should not be taxed on the charging order money either.

As a mere lienholder, the creditor in the preforeclosure stage is not an "assignee" of the interest for tax purposes and therefore for tax purposes is not treated as a partner. As discussed further below, this treatment will change if the creditor obtains the debtor's interest through foreclosure.

It is not uncommon in charging order proceedings, however, for the entity or the judgment-debtor to attempt to treat the judgment-creditor as a partner for tax purposes preforeclosure, and to send the creditor a K-1 for the moneys that the creditor received pursuant to the charging order. In such an event, the creditor must take action to advise the IRS that the K-1 has not been properly issued to it.

Tax Implications to the Debtor

For the debtor in the preforeclosure phase, the debtor remains the partner for tax purposes and remains responsible for his or her allocated share of the entity's tax items, including income and gain, even if he or she never receives a distribution, it being diverted to the judgment-creditor by the charging order.[4] It is the debtor who properly receives the K-1 showing the allocation of income from the LLC and is responsible for the tax liability generated thereby.[5]

Even as the debtor recognizes the allocated portion of the LLC's income and other tax items, in certain circumstances the judgment-debtor may also have a deduction in the amount diverted to the creditor consequent to the charging order.

---

4. *See* GCM 36960 (1977), Rev. Rul. 77-137, 1977-1 C.B. 178; *see also* Treas. Reg. § 1.704-1(e)(2)(ix); Robert R. Keatinge, *Transfers of Partnership and LLC Interests-Assignees, Transferees, Creditors, Heirs, Donees, and Other Successors* in PROCEEDINGS OF THE 32ND ANNUAL PHILIP E. HECKERLING INSTITUTE ON ESTATE PLANNING (1998), at § 504.3; Priv. Ltr. Rul. 8434047 (where assignee of interests in limited partnership may vote and in so voting bind assignor to vote in accordance thereto, and assignees are otherwise granted rights to information, assignee treated as a "partner" for purposes of the Code); Priv. Ltr. Rul. 8440081.

5. *See also* Keatinge, *supra* note Ch.27, fn. 4. ("Where the charging order is similar to a garnishment, the debtor/partner will probably be treated as the partner, required to include the distributive share of income and loss and entitled to a deduction if the payment of the judgment would give rise to a deduction."); Christopher M. Riser, *Tax Consequences of Charging Orders*, 1 ASSET PROTECTION J. 14 (Winter 2000); CARTER G. BISHOP & DANIEL S. KLEINBERGER, LIMITED LIABILITY COMPANIES-TAX AND BUSINESS LAW ¶ 8.07[1][a][ii].

Tax Reporting Implications for the Entity

At the preforeclosure stage, the entity essentially takes no notice of the creditor for tax purposes and continues to issue K-1s to the debtor in the normal course, even though distributions are redirected to the creditor. At this stage, the entity must reject the almost-inevitable entreaties by the debtor that the K-1 be issued to the creditor. The entity must reject those requests; issuing the K-1 to the creditor would be improper.

POST-FORECLOSURE

Tax Implications to the Creditor

The foreclosure of the interest presumably will result in a cash payment to the creditor (otherwise, as discussed in Chapter 18 relating to foreclosures, there really is little incentive to even seek foreclosure in the first place). The cash payment received by the creditor should be treated for tax purposes as any other payment received from the debtor, i.e., it may or may not be taxable to the creditor because of the nature of the underlying dispute, but that has nothing to do with the charging order or foreclosure.

While there is essentially no guidance specifically with respect to the foreclosure of a charging order, the creditor should undertake a careful analysis before making a credit bid at a foreclosure sale. For example, if the credit bid is below market, is there a non-taxable bargain purchase? If the LLC has made a Code § 754 election, how will that apply? The creditor should consider Form 1099 reporting obligations with respect to the receipt of the foreclosure proceeds. Also, a creditor purchasing at a foreclosure sale, whether pursuant to a credit bid or otherwise, should consider in advance the implications of a subsequent sale of the interest at fair market value.

Tax Implications to the Purchaser

The purchaser is the winning bidder at the judicial sale, which takes place as part of the foreclosure of the creditor's charging order lien on the debtor's interest. The purchaser may be the creditor (who can make a "credit bid" of part or all of the outstanding judgment, or pay in cash like any other bidder), or it can be some third-party buyer at the judicial sale who pays cash.

Regardless, the purchaser at the judicial sale becomes an "assignee" of the debtor's now-former interest. As an assignee of the interest, the purchaser effectively becomes a partner of the entity for tax purposes, and this is so even though the purchaser is simply taking the debtor's economic rights to distributions but does take any other rights, such as voting or management rights.[6] The upshot is

6. REV. RUL. 77-137, 1977-1 C.B. 178. *See also* Rev. Rul. 77-332, 1977-2 C.B. 483 (discussing non-CPAs in accounting firms who for state law purposes are not partners but who are partners

that the purchaser at the judicial sale should thereafter receive a K-1 for taxable distributions from the entity so long as the purchaser holds that interest.

Tax Implications to the Debtor

Presumably, the foreclosure will as to the debtor be treated as a sale of a partnership interest, with the debtor recognizing gain or loss, and being treated as having surrendered the sale proceeds to the creditor in either partial or full satisfaction of the underlying judgment, with the tax treatment thereof the equivalent to any payment the debtor might make to the creditor of funds generated other than from the LLC and the charged interest.

Given that the judicial sale has the effect of entirely severing the debtor's economic interest in the entity, the debtor should from that date no longer receive any allocation of entity tax items (income, gain, loss, deduction, or credit).

In considering the tax implications of the foreclosure, the debtor should consider a variety of factors including his/her/its basis in its interest, the deemed treatment of the proceeds of the foreclosure sale and the deemed distribution to the debtor resulting from the reduction in the debtor's share of LLC's liabilities.

Tax Reporting Implications for the Entity

As noted, following the judicial sale, it is the purchaser of the interest who is treated as a partner for tax purposes. The entity should therefore provide the purchaser with a K-1 reflecting appropriate tax allocations from that date forward. Correspondingly, the debtor should no longer receive tax allocations from that date, nor receive a K-1 for the post-judicial sale period.

---

for tax purposes). Assuming the foreclosure sale takes place during the LLC's/partnership's tax year, there will be issues as to how the allocations of tax items is over the course of that year allocated between the judgment-debtor and the acquirer by foreclosure. The treatment of the debtor's right to participate in the venture's management is as provided for in the controlling agreement and organizational act.

Appendix A: Additional Resources

1 Larry E. Ribstein & Robert R Keatinge, Ribstein and Keatinge on Limited Liability Companies § 7.9 (Dec. 2017).

1 Carter G. Bishop and Daniel S. Kleinberger, Limited Liability Companies, Tax & Business Law, ¶¶ 1.03[4], 2.07(1)(j), 2.07(1)(m).

Callison & Sullivan, Partnership Law and Practice: General and Limited Partnerships §§ 7:20, 21:3 (Thomson Reuters).

Callison & Sullivan, Limited Liability Companies § 4:5 (Thomson Reuters).

1 Christine Hurt & Gordon Smith, Bromberg and Ribstein on Partnership § 3.05(D).

J. Gordon Gose, *The Charging Order Under the Uniform Partnership Act*, 28 Wash. L. Rev. & St. B. J. 1 (1953).

Thomas E. Rutledge & Sarah S. Wilson, *An Examination of the Charging Order under Kentucky's LLC and Partnership Acts (Part I)*, 99 Kentucky L.J. Online 85 (2011); *An Examination of the Charging Order under Kentucky's LLC and Partnership Acts (Part II)*, 99 Kentucky L.J. Online 107 (2011).

Appendix B: Model Charging Order Documents

STATE OF CONFUSION
District Court of Bloom County

<table>
<tr><td>Creditor Corp.,</td><td>Case No. 2018-CV-1234-A</td></tr>
<tr><td>Plaintiff,</td><td>NOTICE OF MOTION AND</td></tr>
<tr><td>— vs. —</td><td>MOTION FOR CHARGING ORDER</td></tr>
<tr><td>Danny Debtor,</td><td>with Memorandum of Law Incorporated</td></tr>
<tr><td>Defendant.</td><td>Date/Time: 7/14/2018 at 9:00 a.m.</td></tr>
<tr><td></td><td>Judge: Hon. Marla Marlborough</td></tr>
<tr><td></td><td>Location: Annex Courthouse, Dept. 11</td></tr>
</table>

NOTICE IS HEREBY GIVEN, that the Plaintiff, Creditor Corp., has filed a Motion for Charging Order in this matter, and that said Motion for Charging Order will be heard on the 14th day of July, 2018, at 9:00 a.m., or as soon thereafter as said Motion may be heard, before the Hon. Marla Marlborough, Judge of the District Court, in Department 11 at the Annex Courthouse.

MOTION FOR CHARGING ORDER

Plaintiff, Creditor Corp., hereby moves the Court to enter a Charging Order against the interest of the Defendant, Danny Debtor, in Largess LLC, and shows as follows:

(1) Judgment was entered against the Defendant on May 1, 2018, for $543,897.45, Dkt. 654;
(2) The judgment is unpaid in any part, Ex. A at ¶ 1;
(3) Largess LLC is a limited liability company that was formed in the State of Confusion, and its Registered Agent is Cheapo Registered Agents, Inc., facts of which this Court is hereby requested to take Judicial Notice thereof, and see also Ex. A at ¶ 2;

(4) The Defendant has admitted that he owns a ten-percent (10%) interest in Largess LLC, Ex. A at ¶ 3(a);
(5) The Defendant has admitted that he has previously taken loans from Largess LLC, Ex. A at ¶ 3(b); and
(6) The Defendant has admitted that Largess LLC has, for the past three years, made payments to reduce the balance of the Defendant's personal credit cards, and attributed these payments as "distributions" made to the Defendant, Ex. A at ¶ 3(c).

WHEREFORE, Plaintiff respectfully moves the Court for the entry of a Charging Order against the Defendant's interest in Largess LLC.

INCORPORATED MEMORANDUM OF LAW

The State of Confusion has adopted the Uniform Limited Liability Company Act (ULLCA), as last amended in 2013. Section 503(a) of that Act provides *in toto*:

> On application by a judgment creditor of a member or transferee, a court may enter a charging order against the transferable interest of the judgment debtor for the unsatisfied amount of the judgment. Except as otherwise provided in subsection (f), a charging order constitutes a lien on a judgment debtor's transferable interest and requires the limited liability company to pay over to the person to which the charging order was issued any distribution that otherwise would be paid to the judgment debtor.

The Reporter's Comment to Section 503 further explains:

> Under this section, the judgment creditor of a member or transferee is entitled to a charging order against the relevant transferable interest. While in effect, that order entitles the judgment creditor to whatever distributions would otherwise be due to the member or transferee whose interest is subject to the order. However, the judgment creditor has no say in the timing or amount of those distributions. The charging order does not entitle the judgment creditor to accelerate any distributions or to otherwise interfere with the management and activities of the limited liability company.

Section 503(h) states why the particular remedy of a charging order is *required* to be used in the instant circumstances:

> This section provides the exclusive remedy by which a person seeking in the capacity of judgment creditor to enforce a judgment against a member or transferee may satisfy the judgment from the judgment debtor's transferable interest.

The ancillary provisions sought by the Plaintiff are similarly justified. Although the State of Confusion does not appear to have any opinions on the subject, an opinion from the State of Oregon, Law v. Zemp, 362 Or. 302 (Jan. 11, 2018), held to the effect that ancillary provisions in charging orders are appropriate if the record evidence supports the inclusion of such provisions.

Here, the record evidence shows that Largess LLC has passed money to the Defendant by way of "loans," and also that Largess LLC has paid down the debtor's credit cards and treated those payments as distributions to the Defendant. *See* Ex. A hereto. Therefore, the inclusion of additional provisions in the proposed charging order to henceforth treat "loan" moneys and credit-card payments made by Largess LLC in favor of the Defendant are wholly appropriate.

A proposed Charging Order is submitted herewith.
Respectfully submitted this 6th day of June, 2018, by:

/s/ Bill Barrister
Bill Barrister

Counsel for Creditor Corp.

CERTIFICATE OF SERVICE

The following certifies that on this 6th day of June, 2018, a full, true, and correct copy of the above and foregoing document was deposited in the U.S. mail, with correct first-class postage affixed thereto, and addressed to the following:

Mr. Dan Dealy
SMITH, DEALY, *et al.*
123 Main Street
Applegate, CF 99999
Counsel for Defendant

Largess LLC
c/o Cheapo Registered Agents, Inc.
321 Oak Street
Capitol City, CF 99888
Registered Agent for Largess LLC

/s/ Bill Barrister
Bill Barrister

Counsel for Creditor Corp.

STATE OF CONFUSION
District Court of Bloom County

Creditor Corp.,	Case No. 2018-CV-1234-A
Plaintiff,	EXHIBIT "A"
— vs. —	DECLARATION OF BILL BARRISTER
Danny Debtor,	Date/Time: 7/14/2018 at 9:00 a.m.
Defendant.	Judge: Hon. Marla Marlborough
	Location: Annex Courthouse, Dept. 11

Bill Barrister, upon his oath, declares as follows:

1. The Judgment was entered against the Defendant on May 1, 2018, Dkt. 654, for $543,897.45 and is as of this date unpaid in part;
2. Largess LLC is a limited liability company that was formed in the State of Confusion, and its Registered Agent is Cheapo Registered Agents, Inc.;
3. On May 10, 2018, I personally made an examination upon oral testimony of the Defendant as to his assets, and the Defendant then admitted that:
   (A) The Defendant owns a ten-percent (10%) interest in Largess LLC;
   (B) The Defendant has previously taken loans from Largess LLC; and
   (C) Largess LLC has, for the past three years, made payments to the reduce the balance of the Defendant's personal credit cards, and attributed these payments as "distributions" made to the Defendant.
4. Attached hereto are full, true and correct copies of the following documents:
   (A) Exhibit A-1: A copy of the Defendant's Subscription Agreement in Largess LLC, which was provided to me in post-judgment discovery by the Defendant, and which he stated to me was the same;
   (B) Exhibit A-2: A copy of the Loan Agreement between the Defendant and Largess LLC, which was provided to me in post-judgment discovery by the Defendant, and which he stated to me was the same; and
   (C) Exhibit A-3: Transcript of the third-party examination of the Defendant's tax preparer, who testified that Largess LLC paid certain of the Defendant's credit-card billings, and treated those payments as taxable distributions to the Defendant.

Further Declarant sayeth not.

I declare under the laws of the State of Confusion that the foregoing statements are true and correct.

Dated this 6th day of June, 2018, by:

/s/ Bill Barrister
Bill Barrister

STATE OF CONFUSION
DISTRICT COURT OF BLOOM COUNTY

Creditor Corp.,	Case No. 2018-CV-1234-A
Plaintiff,	[Proposed]
— vs. —	CHARGING ORDER
Danny Debtor,	Date/Time: 7/14/2018 at 9:00 a.m.
Defendant.	Judge: Hon. Marla Marlborough
	Location: Annex Courthouse, Dept. 11

CAME ON FOR HEARING this 14th day of July, 2018, the Motion for Charging Order of the Plaintiff, Creditor Corp., with the supporting Declaration of Bill Barrister, which seeks to charge the interest of the Defendant, Danny Debtor, in Largess LLC, and for other relief. Based upon the Plaintiff's evidentiary submissions, the Court hereby finds:

(1) Judgment was entered against the Defendant on May 1, 2018 for $543,897.45;
(2) The judgment is unpaid in any part;
(3) The Court takes Judicial Notice that Largess LLC is a limited liability company that was formed in the State of Confusion, and its Registered Agent is Cheapo Registered Agents, Inc.;
(4) The Defendant owns a ten-percent (10%) interest in Largess LLC;
(5) The Defendant has previously taken loans from Largess LLC; and
(6) Largess LLC has, for the past three years, made payments to the reduce the balance of the Defendant's personal credit cards, and attributed these payments as "distributions" made to the Defendant.

Based upon these findings, and good cause having been shown, the Court hereby Orders as follows:

(1) The Defendant's ten-percent (10%) interest in Largess LLC is hereby charged with a lien in favor of the Plaintiff, Creditor Corp., until the Judgment herein has been paid in full;
(2) Until the Judgment herein has been paid in full, any payments made or any other consideration (whether cash or otherwise) passing to the Defendant by Largess LLC, which are characterized by either of the parties as "loans" or the incurring of other indebtedness by the Defendant to Largess LLC, shall

henceforth be treated as distributions from Largess LLC to the Defendant, and subject to the Plaintiff's charging order lien herein;

(3) Until the Judgment herein has been paid in full, any payments made by Largess LLC to credit-card companies on behalf of the Defendant, shall henceforth be treated as distributions from Largess LLC to the Defendant, and subject to the Plaintiff's charging order lien herein; and

(4) Any distributions from Largess LLC to the Defendant shall, until the Judgment herein is satisfied in full, shall be paid not to the Defendant or to any third-party, but instead shall only and exclusively be paid by check drawn on the account of Largess LLC, and made to, and mailed to, the following:

Barrister Law Firm Client Trust Account IOLTA
The Barrister Law Firm
567 Hilldale Road, Suite 8
Hilldale, CF 99844

SO ORDERED this 14th day of July, 2018, by:

/s/ Marla Marlborough
Hon. Marla Marlborough

Judge of the District Court, Dept. 11

STATE OF CONFUSION
District Court of Bloom County

Creditor Corp., Plaintiff, — vs. — Danny Debtor, Defendant.	Case No. 2018-CV-1234-A NOTICE OF ENTRY OF CHARGING ORDER

TO: Danny Debtor and Largess LLC

NOTICE IS HEREBY GIVEN that on this 14th day of July, 2018, the Hon. Marla Marlborough, Judge of the District Court of Bloom County, State of Confusion, did enter the attached Charging Order, a full, true, and correct copy of which is attached hereto. You are hereby on notice of the terms of that Charging Order.

PLEASE TAKE FURTHER NOTICE that the amount necessary to satisfy the Judgment is presently $543,897.45 plus post-judgment interest on the unpaid balance and post-judgment costs to be further sought.

Take due notice thereof and conduct yourself accordingly.

Dated this 14th day of July, 2018, by:

/s/ Bill Barrister
Bill Barrister

Counsel for Creditor Corp.

STATE OF CONFUSION
DISTRICT COURT OF BLOOM COUNTY

Creditor Corp.,	Case No. 2018-CV-1234-A
Plaintiff,	PROOF OF SERVICE OF
— vs. —	NOTICE OF ENTRY
Danny Debtor,	OF CHARGING ORDER
Defendant.	

The following certifies that on this 17th day of July, 2018, I personally served the following with a full, true and correct copy of the Notice of Entry of Charging Order, with the Charging Order dated July 14, 2018, attached thereto, upon the parties and at the addresses which follow:

Mr. Danny Debtor
789 Deadbeat Ave.
Inarrears, CF 99871

Largess LLC
c/o Cheapo Registered Agents, Inc.
321 Oak Street
Capitol City, CF 99888

/s/ Sid Server
Sid Server

Registered Process Server, Lic# 321

Appendix C: Carter Bishop Charts

Suffolk University Law School

Table updated version available at: http://ssrn.com/abstract=1542244

FIFTY STATE SERIES: LLC CHARGING ORDER STATUTE TABLE

Professor Carter G. Bishop
Suffolk University Law School, Boston, MA

State	Citation	Present Statute	Amendments	Category
RULLCA	UNIF. LTD. LIAB. CO. ACT § 503 (2006), 6B U.L.A. 498 (2008)	**§ 503. Charging Order.** (a) On application by a judgment creditor of a member or transferee, a court may enter a charging order against the transferable interest of the judgment debtor for the unsatisfied amount of the judgment. A charging order constitutes a lien on a judgment debtor's transferable interest and requires the limited liability company to pay over to the person to which the charging order was issued any distribution that would otherwise be paid to the judgment debtor. (b) To the extent necessary to effectuate the collection of distributions pursuant to a charging order in effect under subsection (a), the court may: (1) appoint a receiver of the distributions subject to the charging order, with the power to make all inquiries the judgment debtor might have made; and (2) make all other orders necessary to give effect to the charging order. (c) Upon a showing that distributions under a charging order will not pay the judgment debt within a reasonable time, the court **may foreclose** the lien and order the sale of the transferable interest. The purchaser at the foreclosure sale only obtains the transferable interest, does not thereby become a member, and is subject to Section 502. (d) At any time before foreclosure under subsection (c), the member or transferee whose transferable interest is subject to a charging order under subsection (a) may extinguish the charging order by satisfying the judgment and filing a certified copy of the satisfaction with the court that issued the charging order.		CAT I **Exclusive**

CAT I – Expressly permits foreclosure; CAT II – Expressly precludes foreclosure; CAT III – Silent by amendment eliminating foreclosure; CAT IV – Silent from the beginning

For additional information, see BISHOP & KLEINBERGER: LIMITED LIABILITY COMPANIES (available in print and via Westlaw (WGL-LLC Database); updated semi-annually).

Table Current as of September 6. 2017

State	Citation	Present Statute	Amendments	Category
		(e) At any time before foreclosure under subsection (c), a limited liability company or one or more members whose transferable interests are not subject to the charging order may pay to the judgment creditor the full amount due under the judgment and thereby succeed to the rights of the judgment creditor, including the charging order. (f) This [act] does not deprive any member or transferee of the benefit of any exemption laws applicable to the member's or transferee's transferable interest. (g) This section provides the exclusive remedy by which a person seeking to enforce a judgment against a member or transferee may, in the capacity of judgment creditor, satisfy the judgment from the judgment debtor's transferable interest.		
UPA	UNIF. P'SHIP ACT § 28 (1914), 6 U.L.A. Pt. II 341 (2001)	**§ 28. Partner's Interest Subject to Charging Order.** (1) On due application to a competent court by any judgment creditor of a partner, the court which entered the judgment, order, or decree, or any other court, may charge the interest of the debtor partner with payment of the unsatisfied amount of such judgment debt with interest thereon; and may then or later appoint a receiver of his share of the profits, and of any other money due or to fall due to him in respect of the partnership, and make all other orders, directions, accounts and inquiries which the debtor partner might have made, or which the circumstances of the case may require. (2) The interest charged may be redeemed at **any time before foreclosure,** or in case of a sale being directed by the court may be purchased without thereby causing a dissolution: (a) With separate property, by any one or more of the partners, or (b) With partnership property, by any one or more of the partners with the consent of all the partners whose interests are not so charged or sold. (3) Nothing in this act shall be held to deprive a partner of his right, if any, under the exemption laws, as regards his interest in the partnership.		**CAT I** **Not Exclusive**
RUPA	REV. UNIF. P'SHIP ACT § 504 (1997), 6 U.L.A. Pt. I 160 (2001)	**§ 504. Partner's Transferable Interest Subject to Charging Order.** (a) On application by a judgment creditor of a partner or of a partner's transferee, a court having jurisdiction may charge the transferable interest of the judgment debtor to satisfy the judgment. The court may appoint a receiver of the share of the distributions due or to become due to the judgment debtor in respect of the partnership and make all other orders, directions, accounts, and inquiries the judgment debtor might have made or which the circumstances of the case may require.	The exclusive remedy language first appeared in RUPA and was designed to reflect that the charging order procedure replaced earlier creditor procedures designed to	**CAT I** **Exclusive**

State	Citation	Present Statute	Amendments	Category
		(b) A charging order constitutes a lien on the judgment debtor's transferable interest in the partnership. The court **may order a foreclosure** of the interest subject to the charging order at any time. The purchaser at the foreclosure sale has the rights of a transferee. (c) At any time before foreclosure, an interest charged may be redeemed: (1) by the judgment debtor; (2) with property other than partnership property, by one or more of the other partners; or (3) with partnership property, by one or more of the other partners with the consent of all of the partners whose interests are not so charged. (d) This [Act] does not deprive a partner of a right under exemption laws with respect to the partner's interest in the partnership. (e) This section provides the exclusive remedy by which a judgment creditor of a partner or partner's transferee may satisfy a judgment out of the judgment debtor's transferable interest in the partnership.	reach a partner's interest in the partnership. RUPA Comment 5. "Subsection (e) provides that the charging order is the judgment creditor's exclusive remedy. Although the UPA nowhere states that a charging order is the exclusive process for a partner's individual judgment creditor, the courts have generally so interpreted it. See, e.g., Matter of Pischke, 11 B.R. 913 (E.D. Va. 1981); Baum v. Baum, 51 Cal. 2d 610, 335 P.2d 481 (1959); Atlantic Mobile Homes, Inc. v. LeFever, 481 So. 2d 1002 (Fla. App. 1986)."	
ULPA	UNIF. LTD. P'SHIP ACT § 703 (1976, amended 1985), 6B U.L.A. 313 (2008)	**§ 703. Rights of Creditor.** On application to a court of competent jurisdiction by any judgment creditor of a partner, the court may charge the partnership interest of the partner with payment of the unsatisfied amount of the judgment with interest. To the extent so charged, the judgment creditor has only the rights of an assignee of the partnership interest. This [Act] does not deprive any partner of the benefit of any exemption laws applicable to his [or her] partnership interest.		**CAT I** (ULPA drag-in clause § 1105, permits by reference to UPA) **Not Exclusive**

State	Citation	Present Statute	Amendments	Category
ULPA 2001	UNIF. LTD. P'SHIP ACT § 703 (2001), 6A U.L.A. 463 (2008)	**§ 703. Rights of Creditor of Partner or Transferee.** (a) On application to a court of competent jurisdiction by any judgment creditor of a partner or transferee, the court may charge the transferable interest of the judgment debtor with payment of the unsatisfied amount of the judgment with interest. To the extent so charged, the judgment creditor has only the rights of a transferee. The court may appoint a receiver of the share of the distributions due or to become due to the judgment debtor in respect of the partnership and make all other orders, directions, accounts, and inquiries the judgment debtor might have made or which the circumstances of the case may require to give effect to the charging order. (b) A charging order constitutes a lien on the judgment debtor's transferable interest. The court **may order a foreclosure** upon the interest subject to the charging order at any time. The purchaser at the foreclosure sale has the rights of a transferee. (c) At any time before foreclosure, an interest charged may be redeemed: (1) by the judgment debtor; (2) with property other than limited partnership property, by one or more of the other partners; or (3) with limited partnership property, by the limited partnership with the consent of all partners whose interests are not so charged. (d) This [Act] does not deprive any partner or transferee of the benefit of any exemption laws applicable to the partner's or transferee's transferable interest. (e) This section provides the exclusive remedy by which a judgment creditor of a partner or transferee may satisfy a judgment out of the judgment debtor's transferable interest.		CAT I **Exclusive**

Suffolk University Law School

Table updated version available at:
http://ssrn.com/abstract=1542244

State	Citation	Present Statute	Amendments	Category
Alabama	ALA. CODE § 10A-5A-5.03. Charging order.	(a) On application to a court of competent jurisdiction by any judgment creditor of a member or transferee, the court may charge the transferable interest of the judgment debtor with payment of the unsatisfied amount of the judgment with interest. To the extent so charged and after the limited liability company has been served with the charging order, the judgment creditor has only the right to receive any distribution or distributions to which the judgment debtor would otherwise be entitled in respect of the transferable interest. (b) A limited liability company, after being served with a charging order and its terms, shall be entitled to pay or deposit any distribution or distributions to which the judgment debtor would otherwise be entitled in respect of the charged transferable interest into the hands of the clerk of the court so issuing the charging order, and the payment or deposit shall discharge the limited liability company and the judgment debtor from liability for the amount so paid or deposited and any interest that might accrue thereon. Upon receipt of the payment or deposit, the clerk of the court shall notify the judgment creditor of the receipt of the payment or deposit. The judgment creditor shall, after any payment or deposit into the court, petition the court for payment of so much of the amount paid or deposited as is held by the court as may be necessary to pay the judgment creditor's judgment. To the extent the court has excess amounts paid or deposited on hand after the payment to the judgment creditor, the excess amounts paid or deposited shall be distributed to the judgment debtor and the charging order shall be extinguished. The court, may in its discretion, order the clerk to deposit, pending the judgment creditor's petition, any money paid or deposited with the clerk, in an interest bearing account at a bank authorized to receive deposits of public funds. (c) A charging order constitutes a lien on the judgment debtor's transferable interest. (d) Subject to subsection (c):		CAT II EXCLUSIVE

CAT I – Expressly permits foreclosure; CAT II – Expressly precludes foreclosure; CAT III – Silent by amendment eliminating foreclosure; CAT IV – Silent from the beginning

For additional information, see BISHOP & KL EI NBERGER: LIMITED LIABILITY COMPANIE'S (available in print and via Westlaw (WGL-LLC Database); updated semi-annually).

Table Current as of September 6. 2017

State	Citation	Present Statute	Amendments	Category
		(1) a judgment debtor that is a member retains the rights of a member and remains subject to all duties and obligations of a member; and (2) a judgment debtor that is a transferee retains the rights of a transferee and remains subject to all duties and obligations of a transferee. (e) This chapter does not deprive any member or transferee of the benefit of any exemption laws applicable to the member's or transferee's transferable interest. (f) This section provides the exclusive remedy by which a judgment creditor of a member or transferee may satisfy a judgment out of the judgment debtor's transferable interest and the judgment creditor shall have no right to foreclose, under this chapter or any other law, upon the charging order, the charging order lien, or the judgment debtor's transferable interest. A judgment creditor of a member or transferee shall have no right to obtain possession of, or otherwise exercise legal or equitable remedies with respect to, the property of a limited liability company. Court orders for actions or requests for accounts and inquiries that the judgment debtor might have made, are not available to the judgment creditor attempting to satisfy the judgment out of the judgment debtor's transferable interest and may not be ordered by a court.		
Alaska	ALASKA STAT. § 10.50.380	(a) If a judgment creditor of a limited liability company member applies to a court of competent jurisdiction, the court may charge the member's limited liability company interest for payment of the unsatisfied amount of the judgment. (b) To the extent a limited liability company interest is charged under (a) of this section, the judgment creditor has only the rights of an assignee of the member's interest. (c) This section provides the exclusive remedy that a judgment creditor of a member or a member's assignee may use to satisfy a judgment out of the judgment debtor's interest in the limited liability company. Other legal or equitable remedies, including foreclosure on the member's limited liability company interest and a court order for directions, accounts, and inquiries that the debtor member might have made, are not available to the judgment creditor attempting to satisfy a judgment out of the judgment debtor's interest in the limited liability company and may not be ordered by a court. (d) This section does not deprive a member of the benefit of an exemption applicable to the member's membership interest. (e) This section applies to limited liability companies with only one member as well as to limited liability companies with more than one member.		CAT II EXCLUSIVE

State	Citation	Present Statute	Amendments	Category
Arizona	ARIZ. REV. STAT. ANN. § 29-655	A. On application to a court of competent jurisdiction by any judgment creditor of a member, the court may charge the member's interest in the limited liability company with payment of the unsatisfied amount of the judgment plus interest. To the extent so charged, the judgment creditor has only the rights of an assignee of the member's interest. B. This chapter1 does not deprive any member of the benefit of any exemption laws applicable to his interest in the limited liability company. C. This section provides the exclusive remedy by which a judgment creditor of a member may satisfy a judgment out of the judgment debtor's interest in the limited liability company.		CAT IV EXCLUSIVE
Arkansas	ARK. CODE ANN. § 4-32-705	On application to a court of competent jurisdiction by any judgment creditor of a member, the court may charge the member's limited liability company interest with payment of the unsatisfied amount of judgment with interest. To the extent so charged, the judgment creditor has only the rights of an assignee of the member's limited liability company interest. This chapter does not deprive any member of the benefit of any exemption laws applicable to his or her limited liability company interest.		CAT IV NOT EXCLUSIVE
California	CAL. CORP. CODE § 17705.03. Charging order	(1) Appoint a receiver of the distributions subject to the charging order, with the power to make all inquiries the judgment debtor might have made. (2) Make all other orders necessary to give effect to the charging order. (3) Upon a showing that distributions under a charging order will not pay the judgment debt within a reasonable time, foreclose the lien and order the sale of the transferable interest. The purchaser at the foreclosure sale obtains only the transferable interest, does not thereby become a member, and is subject to Section 17705.02. (c) At any time before foreclosure under paragraph (3) of subdivision (b), the member or transferee whose transferable interest is subject to a charging order under subdivision (a) may extinguish the charging order by satisfying the judgment and filing a certified copy of the satisfaction with the court that issued the charging order. (d) At any time before foreclosure under paragraph (3) of subdivision (b), a limited liability company or one or more members whose transferable interests are not subject to the charging order may pay to the judgment creditor the full amount due under the judgment and thereby succeed to the rights of the judgment creditor, including the charging order.		CAT I EXCLUSIVE

State	Citation	Present Statute	Amendments	Category
		(e) This title does not deprive any member or transferee of the benefit of any exemption laws applicable to the member's or transferee's transferable interest. (f) This section provides the exclusive remedy by which a person seeking to enforce a judgment against a member or transferee may, in the capacity of judgment creditor, satisfy the judgment from the judgment debtor's transferable interest.		
Colorado	COLO. REV. STAT.			
Connecticut	CONN. GEN. STAT. 34-171	New Sec. 51 (eff. July 1, 2017). (a) On application by a judgment creditor of a member or transferee, a court may enter a charging order against the transferable interest of the judgment debtor for the unsatisfied amount of the judgment. Subject to subsection (e) of this section, a charging order constitutes a lien on a judgment debtor's transferable interest and requires the limited liability company to pay over to the person to which the charging order was issued any distribution that otherwise would be paid to the judgment debtor. To the extent that the transferable interest of the judgment debtor is so charged, the judgment creditor has only the right to receive any distribution or distributions to which the judgment debtor would otherwise have been entitled in respect of such transferable interest. (b) To the extent necessary to effectuate the collection of distributions pursuant to a charging order in effect under subsection (a) of this section, the court may: (1) Appoint a receiver of the distributions subject to the charging order, with the power to make all inquiries the judgment debtor might have made; and (2) make all other orders necessary to give effect to the charging order. (c) The member or transferee whose transferable interest is subject to a charging order under subsection (a) of this section may extinguish the charging order by satisfying the judgment and filing a certified copy of the satisfaction with the court that issued the charging order. (d) A limited liability company or one or more members whose transferable interests are not subject to the charging order may pay to the judgment		CAT I EXCLUSIVE

State	Citation	Present Statute	Amendments	Category
		(e) The entry of a charging order is the exclusive remedy by which a person seeking to enforce a judgment against a member or transferee may, in the capacity of judgment creditor, satisfy the judgment from the judgment debtor's transferable interest. With respect to the judgment debtor's transferable interest, attachment, garnishment, foreclosure or other legal or equitable remedies are not available to the judgment creditor, whether the limited liability company has one member or more than one member. (f) Sections 1 to 102, inclusive, of this act do not deprive any member or transferee of the benefit of any exemption laws applicable to the transferable interest of the member or transferee.		
Deleware	DEL. CODE. ANN. § 18-703.	(a) On application by a judgment creditor of a member or of a member's assignee, a court having jurisdiction may charge the limited liability company interest of the judgment debtor to satisfy the judgment. To the extent so charged, the judgment creditor has only the right to receive any distribution or distributions to which the judgment debtor would otherwise have been entitled in respect of such limited liability company interest. (b) A charging order constitutes a lien on the judgment debtor's limited liability company interest. (c) This chapter does not deprive a member or member's assignee of a right under exemption laws with respect to the judgment debtor's limited liability company interest. (d) The entry of a charging order is the exclusive remedy by which a judgment creditor of a member or a member's assignee may satisfy a judgment out of the judgment debtor's limited liability company interest and attachment, garnishment, foreclosure or other legal or equitable remedies are not available to the judgment creditor, whether the limited liability company has 1 member or more than 1 member. (e) No creditor of a member or of a member's assignee shall have any right to obtain possession of, or otherwise exercise legal or equitable remedies with respect to, the property of the limited liability company. (f) The Court of Chancery shall have jurisdiction to hear and determine any matter relating to any such charging order.		CAT II EXCLUSIVE

State	Citation	Present Statute	Amendments	Category
D.C.	D.C. CODE ANN.	(a) On application by a judgment creditor of a member or transferee, the Superior Court may enter a charging order against the transferable interest of the judgment debtor for the unsatisfied amount of the judgment. Except as otherwise provided in subsection (f) of this section, a charging order constitutes a lien on a judgment debtor's transferable interest and requires the limited liability company to pay over to the person to which the charging order was issued any distribution that would otherwise be paid to the judgment debtor. (b) To the extent necessary to effectuate the collection of distributions pursuant to a charging order in effect under subsection (a) of this section, the Superior Court may: (1) Appoint a receiver of the distributions subject to the charging order, with the power to make all inquiries the judgment debtor might have made; and (2) Make all other orders necessary to give effect to the charging order. (c) Upon a showing that distributions under a charging order will not pay the judgment debt within a reasonable time, the Superior Court may foreclose the lien and order the sale of the transferable interest. Except as otherwise provided in subsection (f) of this section, the purchaser at the foreclosure sale shall obtain the transferable interest, shall not thereby become a member, and shall be subject to § 29-805.02. (d) At any time before foreclosure under subsection (c) of this section, the member or transferee whose transferable interest is subject to a charging order under subsection (a) of this section may extinguish the charging order by satisfying the judgment and filing a certified copy of the satisfaction with the Superior Court. (e) At any time before foreclosure under subsection (c) of this section, a limited liability company or one or more members whose transferable interests are not subject to the charging order may pay to the judgment creditor the full amount due under the judgment and thereby succeed to the rights of the judgment creditor, including the charging order. (f) If a court orders foreclosure of a charging order lien against the sole member of a limited liability company: (1) The court shall confirm the sale;		CAT I EXCLUSIVE

State	Citation	Present Statute	Amendments	Category
		(2) The purchaser at the sale obtains the member's entire interest, not only the member's transferable interest; (3) The purchaser thereby becomes a member; and (4) The person whose interest was subject to the foreclosed charging order is dissociated as a member. (g) This chapter shall not deprive any member or transferee of the benefit of any exemption laws applicable to the member's or transferee's transferable interest. (h) This section provides the exclusive remedy by which a person seeking to enforce a judgment against a member or transferee may, in the capacity of judgment creditor, satisfy the judgment from the judgment debtor's transferable interest.		
Florida	FL. STAT. ANN.	(1) On application to a court of competent jurisdiction by a judgment creditor of a member or a transferee, the court may enter a charging order against the transferable interest of the member or transferee for payment of the unsatisfied amount of the judgment with interest. Except as provided in subsection (5), a charging order constitutes a lien upon a judgment debtor's transferable interest and requires the limited liability company to pay over to the judgment creditor a distribution that would otherwise be paid to the judgment debtor. (2) This chapter does not deprive a member or transferee of the benefit of any exemption law applicable to the transferable interest of the member or transferee. (3) Except as provided in subsections (4) and (5), a charging order is the sole and exclusive remedy by which a judgment creditor of a member or member's transferee may satisfy a judgment from the judgment debtor's interest in a limited liability company or rights to distributions from the limited liability company. (4) In the case of a limited liability company that has only one member, if a judgment creditor of a member or member's transferee establishes to the satisfaction of a court of competent jurisdiction that distributions under a charging order will not satisfy the judgment within a reasonable time, a charging order is not the sole and exclusive remedy by which the judgment creditor may satisfy the judgment against a judgment debtor who is the sole member of a limited liability company or the transferee of the sole member, and upon such showing, the court may order the sale of that interest in the limited liability company pursuant to a foreclosure sale. A judgment creditor may make a showing to the court that distributions under a charging order will not satisfy the judgment within a reasonable time at any time after the entry of the judgment and may do so at the same time that the judgment creditor applies for the entry of a charging order.		CAT II Exclusive (excluding single-member LLCs)

State	Citation	Present Statute	Amendments	Category
		(5) If a limited liability company has only one member and the court orders a foreclosure sale of a judgment debtor's interest in the limited liability company or of a charging order lien against the sole member of the limited liability company pursuant to subsection (4): (a) The purchaser at the court-ordered foreclosure sale obtains the member's entire limited liability company interest, not merely the rights of a transferee; (b) The purchaser at the sale becomes the member of the limited liability company; and (c) The person whose limited liability company interest is sold pursuant to the foreclosure sale or is the subject of the foreclosed charging order ceases to be a member of the limited liability company. (6) In the case of a limited liability company that has more than one member, the remedy of foreclosure on a judgment debtor's interest in the limited liability company or against rights to distribution from the limited liability company is not available to a judgment creditor attempting to satisfy the judgment and may not be ordered by a court. (7) This section does not limit any of the following: (a) The rights of a creditor who has been granted a consensual security interest in a limited liability company interest to pursue the remedies available to the secured creditor under other law applicable to secured creditors. (b) The principles of law and equity which affect fraudulent transfers. (c) The availability of the equitable principles of alter ego, equitable lien, or constructive trust or other equitable principles not inconsistent with this section. (d) The continuing jurisdiction of the court to enforce its charging order in a manner consistent with this section.		
Georgia	GA. CODE. ANN.	(a) On application to a court of competent jurisdiction by any judgment creditor of a member or of any assignee of a member, the court may charge the limited liability company interest of the member or such assignee with payment of the unsatisfied amount of the judgment with interest. To the extent so charged, the judgment creditor has only the rights of an assignee of the limited liability company interest. This chapter does not deprive any member of the benefit of any exemption laws applicable to his or her limited liability company interest.		CAT II NOT EXCLUSIVE

State	Citation	Present Statute	Amendments	Category
		(b) The remedy conferred by this Code section shall not be deemed exclusive of others which may exist, including, without limitation, the right of a judgment creditor to reach the limited liability company interest of the member by process of garnishment served on the limited liability company, provided that, except as otherwise provided in the articles of organization or a written operating agreement, a judgment creditor shall have no right under this chapter or any other state law to interfere with the management or force dissolution of a limited liability company or to seek an order of the court requiring a foreclosure sale of the limited liability company interest.		
Hawaii	HAW. REV. STAT. ANN. § 428-504	(a) On application by a judgment creditor of a member of a limited liability company or a member's transferee, a court having jurisdiction may order that the distributional interest of the judgment debtor be used to satisfy the judgment. The court may appoint a receiver to carry out the provisions of the charging order. (b) A charging order constitutes a lien on the judgment debtor's distributional interest. The court may order a foreclosure of a lien on a distributional interest subject to the charging order at any time. A purchaser at the foreclosure sale has the rights of a transferee. (c) At any time before foreclosure, a distributional interest in a limited liability company which is charged may be redeemed: (1) By the judgment debtor; (2) With property other than the company's property, by one or more of the other members; or (3) With the company's property, but only if permitted by the operating agreement. (d) This chapter does not affect a member's right under exemption laws with respect to the member's distributional interest in a limited liability company. (e) This section provides the exclusive remedy by which a judgment creditor of a member or a transferee may satisfy a judgment out of the judgment debtor's distributional interest in a limited liability company.		CAT I Not Exclusive (single- member LLCs)

State	Citation	Present Statute	Amendments	Category
Idaho	IDAHO CODE ANN. § 30-25-503.	all LLcs on and after 1/1/17.) (a) On application by a judgment creditor of a member or transferee, a court may enter a charging order against the transferable interest of the judgment debtor for the unsatisfied amount of the judgment. Except as otherwise provided in subsection (f) of this section, a charging order constitutes a lien on a judgment debtor's transferable interest and requires the limited liability company to pay over to the person to which the charging order was issued any distribution that otherwise would be paid to the judgment debtor. (b) To the extent necessary to effectuate the collection of distributions pursuant to a charging order in effect under subsection (a) of this section, the court may: (1) Appoint a receiver of the distributions subject to the charging order, with the power to make all inquiries the judgment debtor might have made; and (2) Make all other orders necessary to give effect to the charging order. (c) Upon a showing that distributions under a charging order will not pay the judgment debt within a reasonable time, the court may foreclose the lien and order the sale of the transferable interest. Except as otherwise provided in subsection (f) of this section, the purchaser at the foreclosure sale obtains only the transferable interest, does not thereby become a member, and is subject to section 30-25-502, Idaho Code. (d) At any time before foreclosure under subsection (c) of this section, the member or transferee whose transferable interest is subject to a charging order under subsection (a) of this section may extinguish the charging order by satisfying the judgment and filing a certified copy of the satisfaction with the court that issued the charging order. (e) At any time before foreclosure under subsection (c) of this section, a limited liability company or one (1) or more members whose transferable interests are not subject to the charging order may pay to the judgment creditor the full amount due under the judgment and thereby succeed to the rights of the judgment creditor, including the charging order. (f) If a court orders foreclosure of a charging order lien against the sole member of a limited liability company: (1) The court shall confirm the sale; previous Act & created Idaho Uniform Business Organization Code, eff. July 1, 2015.		CAT I EXCLUSIVE

State	Citation	Present Statute	Amendments	Category
		New § 30-25-503 renumbers the existing section and adds new paragraph (f) relating to foreclosure against the sole member of an LLC. (2) The purchaser at the sale obtains the member's entire interest, not only the member's transferable interest; (3) The purchaser thereby becomes a member; and (4) The person whose interest was subject to the foreclosed charging order is dissociated as a member. (g) This chapter does not deprive any member or transferee of the benefit of any exemption laws applicable to the transferable interest of the member or transferee. (h) This section provides the exclusive remedy by which a person seeking in the capacity of judgment creditor to enforce a judgment against a member or transferee may satisfy the judgment from the judgment debtor's transferable interest.		
Indiana	IND. CODE. ANN.	Sec. 7. (a) On application to a court with jurisdiction by a judgment creditor of a member, the court may charge the interest of the member in the limited liability company with the payment of the unsatisfied amount of the judgment with interest. (b) To the extent the court charges under subsection (a), the judgment creditor has only the rights of an assignee of the member's interest in the limited liability company. (c) This article does not deprive a member of the benefit of any exemption laws applicable to the member's interest in the limited liability company.		CAT IV NOT EXCLUSIVE
Iowa	IOWA CODE ANN. § 489.503	1. On application by a judgment creditor of a member or transferee, a court may enter a charging order against the transferable interest of the judgment debtor for the unsatisfied amount of the judgment. A charging order constitutes a lien on a judgment debtor's transferable interest and requires the limited liability company to pay over to the person to which the charging order was issued any distribution that would otherwise be paid to the judgment debtor. 2. To the extent necessary to effectuate the collection of distributions pursuant to a charging order in effect under subsection 1, the court may do all of the following: a. Appoint a receiver of the distributions subject to the charging order, with the power to make all inquiries the judgment debtor might have made. b. Make all other orders necessary to give effect to the charging order.		CAT I EXCLUSIVE

State	Citation	Present Statute	Amendments	Category
		3. Upon a showing that distributions under a charging order will not pay the judgment debt within a reasonable time, the court may foreclose the lien and order the sale of the transferable interest. The purchaser at the foreclosure sale only obtains the transferable interest, does not thereby become a member, and is subject to section 489.502. 4. At any time before foreclosure under subsection 3, the member or transferee whose transferable interest is subject to a charging order under subsection 1 may extinguish the charging order by satisfying the judgment and filing a certified copy of the satisfaction with the court that issued the charging order. 5. At any time before foreclosure under subsection 3, a limited liability company or one or more members whose transferable interests are not subject to the charging order may pay to the judgment creditor the full amount due under the judgment and thereby succeed to the rights of the judgment creditor, including the charging order. 6. This chapter does not deprive any member or transferee of the benefit of any exemption laws applicable to the member's or transferee's transferable interest. 7. This section provides the exclusive remedy by which a person seeking to enforce a judgment against a member or transferee may, in the capacity of judgment creditor, satisfy the judgment from the judgment debtor's transferable interest.		
Kansas	KAN. STAT. ANN. 17-76,113	(a) On application by a judgment creditor of a member or of a member's assignee, a court having jurisdiction may charge the limited liability company interest of the judgment debtor to satisfy the judgment. To the extent so charged, the judgment creditor has only the right to receive any distribution or distributions to which the judgment debtor would otherwise have been entitled in respect of such limited liability company interest. (b) A charging order constitutes a lien on the judgment debtor's limited liability company interest. (c) This act does not deprive a member or member's assignee of a right under exemption laws with respect to the judgment debtor's limited liability company interest. (d) The entry of a charging order is the exclusive remedy by which a judgment creditor of a member or of a member's assignee may satisfy a judgment out of the judgment debtor's limited liability company interest.		CAT IV EXCLUSIVE

State	Citation	Present Statute	Amendments	Category
		(e) No creditor of a member or of a member's assignee shall have any right to obtain possession of, or otherwise exercise legal or equitable remedies with respect to, the property of the limited liability company. (f) The district court shall have jurisdiction to hear and determine any matter relating to any such charging order.		
Louisiana	LA. REV. STAT. ANN. § 1331	On application to a court of competent jurisdiction by any judgment creditor of a member, the court may charge the membership interest of the member with payment of the unsatisfied amount of judgment with interest. To the extent so charged, the judgment creditor shall have only the rights of an assignee of the membership interest. This Chapter shall not deprive any member of the benefit of any exemption laws applicable to his membership interest.		CAT IV NOT EXCLUSIVE
Maine	ME. REV. STAT. ANN. tit. 31 § 1573	1. Transferable interest of judgment debtor. On application to a court of competent jurisdiction by any judgment creditor of a member or transferee, the court may charge the transferable interest of the judgment debtor with payment of the unsatisfied amount of the judgment with interest. To the extent so charged and after the limited liability company has been served with the charging order and its terms, the judgment creditor has only the right to receive any distribution or distributions to which the judgment debtor would otherwise be entitled in respect of such transferable interest. 2. Payment to clerk of court. A limited liability company, after being served with the charging order and its terms, is entitled to pay or deposit any distribution or distributions to which the judgment debtor would otherwise be entitled in respect of the charged transferable interest into the hands of the clerk of the court issuing the charging order, and the payment or deposit has the effect of discharging the limited liability company and the judgment debtor from liability for the amount so paid and any interest that might accrue thereon. Upon receipt of the payment, the clerk of the court shall notify the judgment creditor of the receipt of the payment. The judgment creditor shall, after the payment or deposit into the court, petition the court for payment of so much of the amount paid or deposited as is held by the court as may be necessary to pay the judgment creditor's judgment. To the extent the court has excess amounts paid or deposited on hand after the payment to the judgment creditor, the excess amounts paid or deposited must be distributed to the judgment		CAT II EXCLUSIVE

State	Citation	Present Statute	Amendments	Category
		debtor and the charging order must be extinguished. The court may in its discretion order the clerk to deposit, pending the judgment creditor's petition, any money paid or deposited with the clerk in an interest-bearing account at a bank authorized to receive deposits of public funds. 3. Lien. A charging order constitutes a lien on the judgment debtor's transferable interest. The charging order lien may not be foreclosed upon under this chapter or any other law. 4. Judgment debtor. Subject to subsection 3: A. A judgment debtor that is a member retains the rights of a member and remains subject to all duties and obligations of a member; and B. A judgment debtor that is a transferee retains the rights of a transferee and remains subject to all duties and obligations of a transferee. 5. Exemptions apply. This chapter does not deprive any member or transferee of the benefit of any exemption laws applicable to the member's or transferee's transferable interest. 6. No right to property. Subject to the laws against fraudulent conveyances, a judgment creditor of a judgment debtor who is a member or transferee has no right to obtain possession of, or otherwise exercise legal or equitable remedies with respect to, the property of a limited liability company. 7. Exclusive remedy. This section provides the exclusive remedy by which a judgment creditor of a member or transferee may satisfy a judgment out of the judgment debtor's transferable interest, and the judgment creditor may not foreclose upon the charging order or the judgment debtor's transferable interest. Court orders for actions or requests for accounts and inquiries that the judgment debtor might have made are not available under this chapter to the judgment creditor attempting to satisfy the judgment out of the judgment debtor's transferable interest and may not be ordered by a court.		
Maryland	MD. CODE. ANN. CORPS. & ASS'NS § 4A-607	(a)(1) In this section the following words have the meanings indicated. (2) "Creditor" means a person for whom a court may issue an attachment under Title 3, Subtitle 3 of the Courts Article. (3) "Debtor" means a person whose property or credits are subject to attachment under Title 3, Subtitle 3 of the Courts Article.		CAT I EXCLUSIVE

State	Citation	Present Statute	Amendments	Category
		(b)(1) On application by a creditor of a debtor holding an economic interest in a limited liability company, a court having jurisdiction may charge the economic interest of the debtor in the limited liability company for the unsatisfied amount of the debt. (2) The court may appoint a receiver for the distributions due or to become due to the debtor with respect to the limited liability company and make all other orders, directions, accounts, and inquiries that the debtor would have been entitled to make or that the circumstances of the case may require. (c)(1) A charging order constitutes a lien on the economic interest of the debtor in the limited liability company and requires the limited liability company to pay over to the creditor only any distributions that would otherwise be payable to the debtor whose economic interest is charged. (2) Subject to paragraph (3) of this subsection, the noneconomic interest of a debtor whose economic interest is subject to a charging order is unaffected and is retained by the debtor. (3)(i) Unless otherwise agreed, on a showing that the distributions under a charging order will not pay the amount owed to the creditor within a reasonable time, the court may order foreclosure of the economic interest subject to the charging order and order the sale of the economic interest of the debtor. (ii) The purchaser of the economic interest of the debtor at the foreclosure sale is an assignee as provided in §§ 4A-603 and 4A- 604 of this subtitle. (d) Before a foreclosure under this section, an economic interest charged may be redeemed with property: (1) Other than property of the limited liability company, by the debtor; (2) Other than property of the limited liability company, by one or more of the members other than the debtor; or (3) Of the limited liability company, with the consent of the members as provided in the operating agreement or, if the operating agreement does not so provide, with the consent of all of the members whose economic interests are not so charged. (e) This title does not deprive a debtor of a right under exemption laws with respect to the economic interest of the debtor in the limited liability company. (f) This section provides the exclusive remedy by which a creditor of a member may attach the membership interest of the member or otherwise satisfy the outstanding debt of the member out of the membership interest of the member.		

State	Citation	Present Statute	Amendments	Category
Massachusetts	MA. GEN. LAWS ANN. Ch 156C, § 40	On application to a court of competent jurisdiction by any judgment creditor of a member, the court may charge the limited liability company interest of the member with payment of the unsatisfied amount of the judgment with interest. To the extent so charged, the judgment creditor has only the rights of an assignee of the limited liability company interest. This chapter does not deprive any member of the benefit of any exemption laws applicable to his limited liability company interest.		CAT IV NOT EXCLUSIVE
Michigan	MICH. COMP. LAWS 450.4507	Sec. 507. (1) If a court of competent jurisdiction receives an application from any judgment creditor of a member of a limited liability company, the court may charge the membership interest of the member with payment of the unsatisfied amount of judgment with interest. (2) If a limited liability company is served with a charging order and notified of the terms of that order, then to the extent described in the order, the member's judgment creditor described in the order is entitled to receive only any distribution or distributions to which the judgment creditor is entitled with respect to the member's membership interest. (3) This act does not deprive any member of the benefit of any exemption laws applicable to the member's membership interest. (4) Unless otherwise provided in an operating agreement or admitted as a member under section 501,1 a judgment creditor of a member that obtains a charging order does not become a member of the limited liability company, and the member that is the subject of the charging order remains a member of the limited liability company and retains all rights and powers of membership except the right to receive distributions to the extent charged. (5) A charging order is a lien on the membership interest of the member that is the subject of the charging order. However, a person may not foreclose on that lien or on the membership interest under this act or any other law, and the charging order is not an assignment of the member's membership interest for purposes of section 505(4).2		CAT II NOT EXCLUSIVE

State	Citation	Present Statute	Amendments	Category
		(6) This section provides the exclusive remedy by which a judgment creditor of a member may satisfy a judgment out of the member's membership interest in a limited liability company. A court order to which a member may have been entitled that requires a limited liability company to take an action, provide an accounting, or answer an inquiry is not available to a judgment creditor of that member attempting to satisfy a judgment out of the member's membership interest, and a court may not issue an order to a judgment creditor.		
Mississippi	MISS. CODE. ANN. § 79-29-705	(1) On application to a court of competent jurisdiction by a judgment creditor of a member, referred to in this section as the "judgment debtor," the court may charge the financial interest of the judgment debtor with payment of the unsatisfied amount of the judgment, with interest (referred to in this section as a "charging order"). To the extent so charged, the judgment creditor has only the rights of an assignee of the financial interest, however, the judgment creditor shall have no rights to bring a proceeding under Article 11 of this chapter. This article does not deprive any judgment debtor of the benefit of any exemption laws applicable to the judgment debtor's financial interest. (2) A charging order constitutes a lien on the judgment debtor's financial interest. (3) The entry of a charging order is the exclusive remedy by which a judgment creditor of a judgment debtor or its assignee may satisfy a judgment out of the judgment debtor's financial interest. (4) No creditor of a judgment debtor or its assignee shall have any right to obtain possession of, or otherwise exercise legal or equitable remedies with respect to, the property of the limited liability company. (5) The chancery court shall have jurisdiction to hear and determine any matter relating to any such charging order.		CAT IV
Missouri				CAT IV NOT EXCLUSIVE

State	Citation	Present Statute	Amendments	Category
Montana	MONT. CODE. ANN. 35-8-705	(1) On application to a court of competent jurisdiction by any judgment creditor of a member, the court may charge the distributional interest of the member with payment of the unsatisfied amount of judgment, with interest. To the extent charged, the judgment creditor has only the rights of an assignee of the distributional interest. This chapter does not deprive a member of the benefit of any exemption laws applicable to a distributional interest. (2) The court may appoint a receiver of the share of the distributions due or to become due to a judgment debtor and make all other orders, directions, accounts, and inquiries that the judgment debtor may have made or that the circumstances require to give effect to the charging order. (3) A charging order constitutes a lien on the judgment debtor's distributional interest. The court may order a foreclosure of a lien on a distributional interest subject to the charging order at any time. A purchaser of the distributional interest at a foreclosure sale has the rights of a transferee. (4) At any time before foreclosure, a distributional interest that is charged may be redeemed: (a) by the judgment debtor; (b) by one or more of the other members with property other than the company's; or (c) with the company's property if permitted by the operating agreement. (5) This section provides the exclusive remedy by which a judgment creditor of a member or a transferee may satisfy a judgment out of the judgment debtor's distributional interest in a limited liability company.		CAT I
Nebraska	NEB. REV. STAT. § 21-142	(ULLCA 503) (a) On application by a judgment creditor of a member or transferee, a court may enter a charging order against the transferable interest of the judgment debtor for the unsatisfied amount of the judgment. A charging order constitutes a lien on a judgment debtor's transferable interest and requires the limited liability company to pay over to the person to which the charging order was issued any distribution that would otherwise be paid to the judgment debtor. (b) To the extent necessary to effectuate the collection of distributions pursuant to a charging order in effect under subsection (a) of this section, the court may: (1) appoint a receiver of the distributions subject to the charging order, with the power to make all inquiries the judgment debtor might have made; and (2) make all other orders necessary to give effect to the charging order.		CAT I EXCLUSIVE

State	Citation	Present Statute	Amendments	Category
		(c) Upon a showing that distributions under a charging order will not pay the judgment debt within a reasonable time, the court may foreclose the lien and order the sale of the transferable interest. The purchaser at the foreclosure sale only obtains the transferable interest, does not thereby become a member, and is subject to section 21-141. (d) At any time before completion of the foreclosure sale under subsection (c) of this section, the member or transferee whose transferable interest is subject to a charging order under subsection (a) of this section may extinguish the charging order by satisfying the judgment and filing a certified copy of the satisfaction with the court that issued the charging order. (e) At any time before completion of the foreclosure sale under subsection (c) of this section, a limited liability company or one or more members whose transferable interests are not subject to the charging order may pay to the judgment creditor the full amount due under the judgment and thereby succeed to the rights of the judgment creditor, including the charging order. (f) The Nebraska Uniform Limited Liability Company Act does not deprive any member or transferee of the benefit of any exemption laws applicable to the member's or transferee's transferable interest. (g) This section provides the exclusive remedy by which a person seeking to enforce a judgment against a member or transferee may, in the capacity of judgment creditor, satisfy the judgment from the judgment debtor's transferable interest.		
Nevada	NEV. REV. STAT. 86.401	1. On application to a court of competent jurisdiction by any judgment creditor of a member, the court may charge the member's interest with payment of the unsatisfied amount of the judgment with interest. To the extent so charged, the judgment creditor has only the rights of an assignee of the member's interest. 2. This section: (a) Provides the exclusive remedy by which a judgment creditor of a member or an assignee of a member may satisfy a judgment out of the member's interest of the judgment debtor, whether the limited- liability company has one member or more than one member. No other remedy, including, without limitation, foreclosure on the member's interest or a court order for directions, accounts and inquiries that the debtor or member might have made, is available to the judgment creditor attempting to satisfy the judgment out of the judgment debtor's interest in the limited- liability company, and no other remedy may be ordered by a court.		CAT III EXCLUSIVE

State	Citation	Present Statute	Amendments	Category
		(b) Does not deprive any member of the benefit of any exemption applicable to his or her interest. (c) Does not supersede any written agreement between a member and a creditor if the written agreement does not conflict with the limited-liability company's articles of organization or operating agreement.		
New Hampshire	N.H. REV. STAT. § 304-C:126	I. On application to a court of competent jurisdiction by any judgment creditor of (a) a member of a limited liability company (the "debtor-member") or (b) a transferee of all or any part of a member's limited liability company interest (a "transferee"), the court may enter a charging order against the limited liability company in respect of the limited liability company interest of the debtor-member or the transferee for the unsatisfied amount of the judgment plus interest. II. (a) A charging order constitutes a lien on a debtor-member's or transferee's limited liability company interest. (b) Under a charging order, a judgment creditor has only the right to receive distributions to which the debtor-member or transferee would otherwise have been entitled from the limited liability company, and only to the extent of the judgment, including interest. (c) A judgment debtor that obtains a charging order does not thereby become the holder of the debtor-member's or transferee's limited liability company interest. III. This section does not deprive any judgment debtor of the benefit of any exemption law applicable to the judgment debtor's membership rights. IV. Except as provided in paragraphs VI and VII, a charging order is the sole and exclusive remedy by which a judgment creditor of a debtor-member may satisfy a judgment from a debtor-member's membership rights or from the assets of a limited liability company. This section is not exclusive as to the rights of creditors with respect to the limited liability company interests of transferees. V. (a) The remedy of execution upon a debtor-member's membership rights shall be unavailable to a judgment creditor attempting to satisfy a judgment against a debtor-member of a multi-member limited liability company. (b) Except as provided in paragraph VI, the remedy of execution upon a debtor-member's membership rights shall be unavailable to a judgment creditor attempting to satisfy a judgment against a debtor-member of a single-member limited liability company.		CAT II EXCLUSIVE

State	Citation	Present Statute	Amendments	Category
		VI. (a) If a judgment creditor shows to the satisfaction of a court of competent jurisdiction that distributions under a charging order in respect of the limited liability company interest of a debtor- member of a single-member limited liability company will not satisfy the judgment within a reasonable time, a charging order shall not be the sole and exclusive remedy by which the judgment creditor may satisfy the judgment against the member. (b) Upon such a showing, the court may order the sale of the debtor-member's membership rights under an execution sale. (c) A judgment creditor may make a showing to the court under subparagraph (a) that distributions under a charging order will not satisfy a judgment either (1) when the judgment creditor applies for the entry of a charging order under a member of a single-member limited liability company or (2) at any time thereafter. VII. If, under paragraph VI, a court orders an execution sale of the membership rights of a debtor-member that is the member of a single-member limited liability company: (a) The purchaser shall obtain all of the member's membership rights and not merely the rights of an transferee; (b) The purchaser shall become the member of the limited liability company; and (c) The debtor-member whose membership rights have been sold shall cease to be a member. VIII. Nothing in this section shall limit: (a) The rights of a creditor that has been granted a consensual security interest in the limited liability company interest or other membership rights of a member to pursue the remedies available to the secured creditor under other law applicable to secured creditors; (b) The principles of law and equity which affect fraudulent transfers; (c) The availability of the equitable principles of veil-piercing, equitable lien, or constructive trust, or other equitable principles not inconsistent with this section; or (d) The continuing jurisdiction of the court to enforce its charging order in a manner consistent with this section. IX. In any action in a court of this state in which a judgment creditor seeks a charging order against a member or transferee of a foreign limited liability company, this section shall apply.		

State	Citation	Present Statute	Amendments	Category
New Jersey	N.J.S.A. 42:2C-43	On application by a judgment creditor of a member , a court may charge the transferable interest of the member with payment of the unsatisfied amount of the judgment with interest. To the extent so charged, the judgment creditor has only the rights of an assignee of the limited liability company interest. An action by a court pursuant to this section does not deprive any member of the benefit of any exemption laws applicable to his transferable interest. A court order charging the transferable interest of a member pursuant to this section shall be the sole remedy of a judgment creditor, who shall have no right under 42:2C-1 et seq. or any other State law to interfere with the management or force dissolution of a limited liability company or to seek an order of the court requiring a foreclosure sale of the transferable interest. Nothing in this section shall be construed to affect in any way the rights of a judgment creditor of a member under federal bankruptcy or reorganization laws.		CAT II EXCLUSIVE
New Mexico	N.M. STAT. § 53-19-35.	On application to a court by any judgment creditor of a member, the court may charge the interest of the member with payment of the unsatisfied amount of the judgment, with interest. To the extent so charged, the judgment creditor has no more rights than those to which an assignee of the member's limited liability company interest would be entitled under the provisions of Section 32 of the Limited Liability Company Act. That act does not deprive any member of the benefit of any exemption laws applicable to his membership interest.		CAT IV NOT EXCLUSIVE
New York	N.Y. Ltd. Liab. Co. Law § 607	(a) On application to a court of competent jurisdiction by any judgment creditor of a member, the court may charge the membership interest of the member with payment of the unsatisfied amount of the judgment with interest. To the extent so charged, the judgment creditor has only the rights of an assignee of the membership interest. This chapter does not deprive any member of the benefit of any exemption laws applicable to his or her membership interest. (b) No creditor of a member shall have any right to obtain possession of, or otherwise exercise legal or equitable remedies with respect to, the property of the limited liability company.		CAT IV NOT EXCLUSIVE

State	Citation	Present Statute	Amendments	Category
North Carolina	N.C. GEN. STAT. § 57D-5-03	(a) On application to a court of competent jurisdiction by any judgment creditor of an interest owner, the court may charge the economic interest of an interest owner with the payment of the unsatisfied amount of the judgment with interest. To the extent so charged, the judgment creditor has only the right to receive the distributions that otherwise would be paid to the interest owner with respect to the economic interest. (b) A charging order is a lien on the judgment debtor's economic interest to the extent provided in this section from the time that such charging order is served upon the LLC in accordance with Rule 4(j)(8) of the Rules of Civil Procedure. If more than one charging order is properly served upon the LLC with respect to an economic interest, the liens shall have priority in the order in which the charging orders were served, except that a charging order in favor of a judgment creditor that has previously delivered to the LLC garnishment process relating to an economic interest pursuant to G.S. 1-440.25 shall relate back to the date of service of the garnishment process. (c) This Chapter does not deprive any interest owner of a right, including any benefit of any exemption law applicable to the interest owner's ownership interest. (d) The entry of a charging order is the exclusive remedy by which a judgment creditor of an interest owner may satisfy the judgment from or with the judgment debtor's ownership interest.		CAT IV NOT EXCLUSIVE
Ohio	OHIO REV. CODE ANN. § 1705.19	(A) If any judgment creditor of a member of a limited liability company applies to a court of common pleas to charge the membership interest of the member with payment of the unsatisfied amount of the judgment with interest, the court may so charge the membership interest. To the extent the membership interest is so charged, the judgment creditor has only the rights of an assignee of the membership interest as set forth in section 1705.18 of the Revised Code. Nothing in this chapter deprives a member of the member's statutory exemption. (B) An order charging the membership interest of a member of a limited liability company is the sole and exclusive remedy that a judgment creditor may seek to satisfy a judgment against the membership interest of a member or a member's assignee.		CAT IV EXCLUSIVE

State	Citation	Present Statute	Amendments	Category
		(C) No creditor of a member of a limited liability company or a member's assignee shall have any right to obtain possession of, or otherwise exercise legal or equitable remedies with respect to, the property of the limited liability company. (D) A limited liability company or one or more members of a limited liability company who are not subject to a charging order entered in favor of a judgment creditor may at any time pay to the judgment creditor the full amount then still due under the judgment and by that payment succeed to the rights of that judgment creditor.		
Oregon	OR. REV. STAT. § 63.259	On application to a court of competent jurisdiction by any judgment creditor of a member, the court may charge the membership interest of the member with payment of the unsatisfied amount of the judgment with interest. To the extent so charged, the judgment creditor has only the rights of an assignee of the membership interest. This chapter shall not deprive any member of the benefit of any exemption laws applicable to the member's membership interest.		CAT IV NOT EXCLUSIVE
Rhode Island	R.I. GEN. LAWS § 7-16-37	On application to a court of competent jurisdiction by any judgment creditor of a member, the court may charge the membership interest of the member with payment of the unsatisfied amount of judgment with interest. To the extent charged, the judgment creditor has only the rights of an assignee of the membership interest. This chapter does not deprive any member of the benefit of any exemption laws applicable to that member's membership interest.		CAT IV NOT EXCLUSIVE
South Dakota	S.D. CODIFIED LAWS § 47-34A-504	(a) On application by a judgment creditor of a member of a limited liability company or of a member's transferee, and following notice to the limited liability company of such application, a court having jurisdiction may charge the distributional interest of the judgment debtor to satisfy the judgment. (b) A charging order constitutes a lien on the judgment debtor's distributional interest. (c) A distributional interest in a limited liability company which is charged may be redeemed: (1) By the judgment debtor; (2) With property other than the company's property, by one or more of the other members; or		CAT II EXCLUSIVE

State	Citation	Present Statute	Amendments	Category
		(3) With the company's property, but only if permitted by the operating agreement. (d) This chapter does not affect a member's right under exemption laws with respect to the member's distributional interest in a limited liability company. (e) This section provides the exclusive remedy that a judgment creditor of a member's distributional interest or a member's assignee may use to satisfy a judgment out of the judgment debtor's interest in a limited liability company. No other remedy, including foreclosure on the member's distributional interest or a court order for directions, accounts, and inquiries that the debtor, member might have made, is available to the judgment creditor attempting to satisfy the judgment out of the judgment debtor's interest in the limited liability company. (f) No creditor of a member or a member's assignee has any right to obtain possession of, or otherwise exercise legal or equitable remedies with respect to, the property of the company. (g) This section applies to single member limited liability companies in addition to limited liability companies with more than one member.		
Tennesee	T. C. A. § 48-249-509	On application to a court of competent jurisdiction by any judgment creditor of a member or holder of financial rights, the court may charge such person's financial rights with payment of the unsatisfied amount of the judgment with interest. To the extent so charged, the judgment creditor has only the rights of a transferee of such person's financial rights under § 48-249-507. This section does not deprive any member, holder or transferee of financial rights of the benefit of any exemption laws applicable to the membership interest or financial rights. This section is the sole and exclusive remedy of a judgment creditor with respect to the judgment debtor's membership interest or financial rights.		CAT IV EXCLUSIVE
Texas	V.T.C.A., BUS. ORG. COD. § 101.112	(a) On application by a judgment creditor of a member of a limited liability company or of any other owner of a membership interest in a limited liability company, a court having jurisdiction may charge the membership interest of the judgment debtor to satisfy the judgment. (b) If a court charges a membership interest with payment of a judgment as provided by Subsection (a), the judgment creditor has only the right to receive any distribution to which the judgment debtor would otherwise be entitled in respect of the membership interest.		CAT II EXCLUSIVE

State	Citation	Present Statute	Amendments	Category
		(c) A charging order constitutes a lien on the judgment debtor's membership interest. The charging order lien may not be foreclosed on under this code or any other law. (d) The entry of a charging order is the exclusive remedy by which a judgment creditor of a member or of any other owner of a membership interest may satisfy a judgment out of the judgment debtor's membership interest. (e) This section may not be construed to deprive a member of a limited liability company or any other owner of a membership interest in a limited liability company of the benefit of any exemption laws applicable to the membership interest of the member or owner. (f) A creditor of a member or of any other owner of a membership interest does not have the right to obtain possession of, or otherwise exercise legal or equitable remedies with respect to, the property of the limited liability company.		
Virginia	VA CODE ANN § 13.1-1041.1	A. On application by a judgment creditor of a member or of a member's assignee, a court having jurisdiction may charge the transferable interest of the judgment debtor to satisfy the judgment. To the extent so charged, the judgment creditor has only the right to receive any distribution or distributions to which the judgment debtor would otherwise have been entitled in respect of the interest. B. A charging order constitutes a lien on the judgment debtor's transferable interest in the limited liability company. C. This chapter does not deprive a member or a member's assignee of a right under exemption laws with respect to the judgment debtor's interest in the limited liability company. D. The entry of a charging order is the exclusive remedy by which a judgment creditor of a member or of a member's assignee may satisfy a judgment out of the judgment debtor's transferable interest in the limited liability company. E. No creditor of a member or of a member's assignee shall have any right to obtain possession of, or otherwise exercise legal or equitable remedies with respect to, the property of the limited liability company.		CAT III EXCLUSIVE

State	Citation	Present Statute	Amendments	Category
West Virginia	W. VA. CODE § 31B-5-504	(a) On application by a judgment creditor of a member of a limited liability company or of a member's transferee, a court having jurisdiction may charge the distributional interest of the judgment debtor to satisfy the judgment. The court may appoint a receiver of the share of the distributions due or to become due to the judgment debtor and make all other orders, directions, accounts and inquiries the judgment debtor might have made or which the circumstances may require to give effect to the charging order. (b) A charging order constitutes a lien on the judgment debtor's distributional interest. The court may order a foreclosure of a lien on a distributional interest subject to the charging order at any time. A purchaser at the foreclosure sale has the rights of a transferee. (c) At any time before foreclosure, a distributional interest in a limited liability company which is charged may be redeemed: (1) By the judgment debtor; (2) With property other than the company's property, by one or more of the other members; or (3) With the company's property, but only if permitted by the operating agreement. (d) This chapter does not affect a member's right under exemption laws with respect to the member's distributional interest in a limited liability company. (e) This section provides the exclusive remedy by which a judgment creditor of a member or a transferee may satisfy a judgment out of the judgment debtor's distributional interest in a limited liability company.		CAT I EXCLUSIVE
Wisconsin	W.S.A. 183.0705	On application to a court of competent jurisdiction by any judgment creditor of a member, the court may charge the member's limited liability company interest with payment of the unsatisfied amount of the judgment. To the extent so charged, the judgment creditor has only the rights of an assignee of the member's limited liability company interest. This section does not deprive any member of the benefit of any exemption laws applicable to the limited liability company interest.		CAT IV NOT EXCLUSIVE

State	Citation	Present Statute	Amendments	Category
Wyoming	WYO. STAT. ANN.	(a) On application by a judgment creditor of a member or transferee, a court may enter a charging order against the transferable interest of the judgment debtor for the unsatisfied amount of the judgment. A charging order requires the limited liability company to pay over to the person to which the charging order was issued any distribution that would otherwise be paid to the judgment debtor. (b) Reserved. (c) Reserved. (d) The member or transferee whose transferable interest is subject to a charging order under subsection (a) of this section may extinguish the charging order by satisfying the judgment and filing a certified copy of the satisfaction with the court that issued the charging order. (e) A limited liability company or one (1) or more members whose transferable interests are not subject to the charging order may pay to the judgment creditor the full amount due under the judgment and thereby succeed to the rights of the judgment creditor, including the charging order. (f) This article does not deprive any member or transferee of the benefit of any exemption laws applicable to the member's or transferee's transferable interest. (g) This section provides the exclusive remedy by which a person seeking to enforce a judgment against a judgment debtor, including any judgment debtor who may be the sole member, dissociated member or transferee, may, in the capacity of the judgment creditor, satisfy the judgment from the judgment debtor's transferable interest or from the assets of the limited liability company. Other remedies, including foreclosure on the judgment debtor's limited liability interest and a court order for directions, accounts and inquiries that the judgment debtor might have made are not available to the judgment creditor attempting to satisfy a judgment out of the judgment debtor's interest in the limited liability company and may not be ordered by the court.		CAT II EXCLUSIVE

Suffolk University Law School

Updated table available: http://ssrn.com/abstract=1565595

Fifty State Series: LLC Charging Order Case Table

Professor Carter G. Bishop
Suffolk University Law School, Boston, MA

State	Cases	Remedy	Jurisdiction	State Law Applied
Alabama **CAT IV*** **Exclusive**	Regions Bank v. Stewart, 2011 WL 1827453 (S.D. Ala., May 10, 2011) **Note:** The Official Commentary states that this section is based on ABA Prototype Act § 705 and Uniform Act § 508. The Uniform Act terminology "financial rights" is used to assure that the judgment creditor does not assert any rights to participate in management.	**Charging order/LLC:** The LLC is not a necessary party to a charging order action, which can proceed ex parte, especially when the judgment member owned a majority of the economic interests of the LLC.		
Alaska **CAT II *** **Exclusive**	LumbermensMut. Cas. Co. v. Luciano Enterprises, LLC, No. A01-309 CV JWS, 2005 WL 2340709, (D. Alaska, Sept. 21, 2005)	**Charging order/LP:** Charging order is exclusive remedy under applicable statute, which limits the court's power to enforce its own judgments; therefore, defendant's limited partnership interest is subject to a lien of judgment, and until satisfied, his share in any distribution of money, other personal property, any real property or the proceeds of any sale, transfer, assignment or conveyance of		

* See Carter G. Bishop, Fifty State Series: LLC Charging Order Statute Table http://ssrn.com/abstract=1542244 (full text of LLC charging order statutes classifying statutes into four categories relative to the availability of foreclosure). CAT I – Expressly permits foreclosure; CAT II – Expressly precludes foreclosure; CAT III – Silent by amendment eliminating foreclosure; and CAT IV – Silent from the beginning.

For additional information, see Bishop & Kleinberger: Limited Liability Companies (available in print and via Westlaw (WGL-LLC Database); updated semi-annually).

Table Current as of September 6. 2017

State	Cases	Remedy	Jurisdiction	State Law Applied
		his interest in the partnership itself shall be paid to plaintiff; request for regular financial disclosure denied. Does not address foreclosure but quotes statutory language that foreclosure or other remedies not available to judgment creditor.		
Arizona **CAT IV* Exclusive**	In re Breland, __ Bankr. ___, 2017 WL 1628880 (SD ALA 2017). In re Marriage of Dimitri Rozenman, 2014 WL 2211398 (Az. Ct. App. May 27, 2014).	Debtor filed Chapter 11 petitions but creditors sought to appoint an independent trustee to replace the debtor in possession under 11 USC § 1104(a). The motion was granted, in part, because of numerous Breland prepetition transfers to affiliated persons denying creditor direct access to the transferred assets in exchange for a charging order. In essence, the court replaced a DIP that refused to assert fraudulent transfers that would ultimately preclude debtor from a discharge. **SMLLC/Receiver.** A family court issued a divorce along with property division and other asset support orders. The husband's sole asset was an interest in a SMLLC operating a cigar business. Within a month, husband was convicted of attempted murder of his ex-wife and sentenced to twenty-five years in prison. He then appointed his girlfriend as the business manager who was not paying the divorce payments. The family court then ordered the appointment of a receiver. The husband unsuccessfully argued the appointment of a receiver was invalid because a charging order was the exclusive remedy.		

State	Cases	Remedy	Jurisdiction	State Law Applied
	Merchant Transaction Systems, Inc. v. Nelcela, Inc., 2011 WL 4625716 (D. Ariz., Sept. 6, 2011	The LLC is not a necessary party to a charging order action, especially where a judgment debtor is the manager of the LLC.		
	In re First Protection, Inc., --- B.R.---, 2010 WL 5059589 (9th Cir. BAP Ariz. Nov. 22, 2010)	**SMLLC/bankruptcy:** Debtor owning a SMLLC filed for bankruptcy and trustee sought SMLLC assets. Court rejected debtor's argument that the trustee acquired only the rights of a transferee in the SMLLC because the SMLLC interest was not acquired by transfer or assignment under Arizona law, but rather by operation of law under Federal Bankruptcy law. More importantly, the Court also rejected the debtor's argument that the operating agreement constituted a personal services executor contract because (i) the agreement was not a contract, executor or otherwise because there was only one party, and (ii) even if it were an executor contract it was impossible to affect the rights of others by assuming the contract.		
	Gecko Pools & Spas, v. Blackhawk Holdings, LLC, No. 1 CA-CV 08-0757, 2010 WL 785875 (Ariz. App. Div. 1 March 9, 2010)	**LLC/attorney's charging lien:** Judgment debtor's (Blackhawk's) attorney moved to intervene in judgment creditor's (Gecko's) garnishment action against Blackhawk's third party settlement, in order to assert an attorney's charging lien against the settlement funds that would be superior to Gecko's claim. Court upheld sanctions against attorney, finding that he failed to cite any evidence that he and Blackhawk looked to the settlement funds as a source of payment of the attorneys' fees, and that his motion to intervene was not well- grounded in fact or law.		

State	Cases	Remedy	Jurisdiction	State Law Applied
	Gecko Pools & Spas v. Blackhawk Holdings, LLC, Nos. 1 CA-CV 06-0659, 1 CA-CV 07-0253, 2007 WL 5448130 (Ariz. App. Div. 1 Oct. 11, 2007)		**LLC/charging order/jurisdiction:** Judgment debtor (Blackhawk) reached settlement with third party for payments due to Blackhawk for services rendered, and stipulated to entry of judgment against third party. Judgment creditor (Gecko) moved to intervene in the action, and received a charging order against Blackhawk and a judgment of garnishment in favor of Gecko and against third party. On appeal, Gecko argued that Blackhawk's failure to appeal the charging order led to a lack of subject matter jurisdiction. The court found that the failure to appeal the issue did not affect jurisdiction, although it would limit Blackhawk's arguments on appeal. Blackhawk argued that Gecko's failure to plead in its complaint that it was a duly licensed contractor as required by statute deprived the superior court of subject matter jurisdiction. The court found that Gecko's failure to comply with the statute did not deprive the superior court of jurisdiction; it merely subjected the complaint to a motion to dismiss.	

State	Cases	Remedy	Jurisdiction	State Law Applied
	In re Ehmann, 319 B.R. 200, (Bankr. D. Ariz. Jan. 13, 2005)	**LLC/Bankruptcy:** Court found that specific Operating Agreement for defendant LLC was not an executory contract; therefore, trustee in bankruptcy had broad rights under Bankruptcy Code § 541(c)(1), and could continue suit seeking declaration that he had the status of a member in the LLC. Under these circumstances, restrictions in the LLC Operating Agreement and the state charging order provision do not apply.		
Arkansas **CAT IV* Not Exclusive**	AmerisourceBergen Drug Corp. v. Meier, 2007 WL 1560012 (W.D. Ark. May 29, 2007)	**Charging Order/LLC & LP:** Where a U.S. District Court judgment entered in Pennsylvania is properly registered in Arkansas, the Arkansas federal court will grant judgment creditor's motion for charging orders against debtor's interest in a family (debtor and his wife) LLC, LP and revocable trust.		
California	Curci Investments, LLC v. Baldwin, 2017 WL 3431457 (CA Ct App 2017).	Creditor held a judgment against Baldwin and later sought to add an LLC in which he held a 99% interest and his wife the remaining 1%. The creditor argued the LLC was an alter ego. The court denied the motion but also concluded that neither that fact nor that the charging order was an exclusive remedy, precluded the creditor from asserting reverse veil piercing to attack the assets of the LLC directly. The court also determined this was appropriate in a multi-member LLC where there were no innocent members who would be adversely affected and where adding another creditor to the liabilities of the entity would not		

State	Cases	Remedy	Jurisdiction	State Law Applied
		harm other creditors of the entity. The court noted that reverse veil piercing may be more appropriate for LLCs than for corporations because a creditor of a shareholder that exercises remedies against the stock typically may exercise all of the shareholder's rights, while a creditor of a member of an LLC may be precluded from exercising those rights under LLC law.		
	Airport Blvd. Reality, LLC v. HB&C Associates, LLC, 2017 WL 3700803 (CA. D. Ct. 2017).	HBC agreed to make a $750,000 capital contribution to ABC but later refused to contribute more than $350,000.. The other members therefore completed the remaining $400,000 contribution. Later ABC received an arbitration award of $867,485, a charging order against HBC's remaining interest, foreclosure, and purchased the remaining interest for a $25,000 credit bid. HBC set aside the sale because of deficiencies in the notice of execution and sale.		
CAT I* Exclusive	Gwartz v. Weilert, 2014 WL 6436185 (CA Ct. App. 3rd Dist. November 3, 2014).	**Disentitlement Doctrine.** Post judgment, defendant made several transfers in violation of court orders including a charging order and then appealed the judgments. The defendant failed to post an appeal bond and so the court of appeals dismissed the appeal under its discretionary power referred to as a disentitlement doctrine.		
	Jay Bharat Developers, Inc. v. Minidis, Not Reported in Cal. Rptr.3d, 2014 WL 6765611 (2014).	**LLC/Standing.** An LLC does not have standing to challenge a charging order against its owner.		

State	Cases	Remedy	Jurisdiction	State Law Applied
	Choice Hotels International, Inc. v. Penta Denver LLC, Not Reported in F.Supp.2d, 2014 WL 458069 (N. D. Cal., Jan. 27, 2014) (NO. C 13-80249 WHA).	**Charging order/lien created.** Judgment creditor sought a charging order in California after registering a Maryland judgment. In California, a lien on a judgment debtor's interest in a partnership or LLC is created by service of a notice of motion for a charging order on the judgment debtor and either (1) all partners or the partnership, or (2) all members or the LLC. The judgment creditor served the members, partners and entities with a copy of the motion for a charging order. Absent objection, the motion was granted.		
	La Jolla Bank, FSB v. Tarkanian, 2013 WL 3717108 (E.D. Cal., July 12, 2013)	**Charging order/filing requirement.** As receiver for the La Jolla Bank, FDC filed a motion for a charging order against Tarkanian's interest in, inter alia, Tark, LLC. Vegas Diamond Properties, LLC ("VDP") borrowed $14.75 million dollars from La Jolla Bank, and Tarkanian personally guaranteed the loan. VDP defaulted, as did guarantors. A bank FDIC receiver sued the guarantor Tarkanian and obtained a judgment. Collection efforts failed so a charging order was sought. Motion for charging order denied because California law requires "all" partners or LLC members be served with a charging order motion against one of the partners or LLC members. Further, the receiver sought but was not granted a motion to require the entities submit to an audit to assure proper distributions to the bank.		

State	Cases	Remedy	Jurisdiction	State Law Applied
	Webb & Carey, P.C. v. Keenan, 2012 WL 1944839 (Cal.App. 4 Dist., Unpublished, May 30, 2012).	**Receiver.** The issue was whether the trial court was justified in determining that a postjudgment appointment of a receiver was a reasonable method to obtain the fair and orderly satisfaction of Webb's judgments. Receivers, under the control of the court, are afforded the power to take and keep possession of the property, to receive rents, collect debts, to compound for and compromise the same, to make transfers, and generally to do such acts respecting the property as the court may authorize. As the hand of the court, the receiver thus aids the court in preserving and managing the property involved in the suit for the benefit of those to whom it may ultimately be determined to belong. The appointment was affirmed and the receiver was able to gain access to partnership assets to satisfy the judgments.		
	Litke O'Farrell v. Tipton, 204 Cal. App. 4th 1178, 139 Cal. Rptr. 3d 548, Cal. App. 1 Dist. (April 10, 2012).	**Charging order/Marital settlement agreement.** Husband's judgment creditor sought charging orders against LLC and partnership interests owned by husband and wife with service on 1/24/2011. However, prior to that date on 1/18/2011, the husband and wife entered into a binding marital settlement agreement (MSA) with a final decree of divorce entered after the charging orders were granted. The Court determined that as of the effective date of the MSA, the wife's interests were her separate property and not subject to her husband's debts and judgments. Therefore, the charging orders were dismissed as to her LLC and partnership interests.		

State	Cases	Remedy	Jurisdiction	State Law Applied
	Phillips, Spallas & Angstadt, LLP v. Fotouhi, 197 Cal. App. 4th 1132, 128 Cal. Rptr. 3d 320 Cal. App. (2011).	**LLP/PC/Charging order.** Defendant left the plaintiff law firm to form a new partnership (LLP) as the managing partner with three associates from the old law firm and taking two major clients. Plaintiff law firm obtained a judgment against defendant that he had violated the partnership agreement and obtained a $2.4 million judgment. Defendant filed bankruptcy but was unable to discharge the debt because of false statement in his petition. In less than a month, defendant formed a PC with no change in location or other appearances and transferred all LLP assets to the PC. Plaintiff LLP moved for a charging order against the defendant's partnership interest and obtained an order requiring the partnership to pay all 15% of its gross revenue to a receiver until the judgment is satisfied. Plaintiff LLP also sought to "extend" the charging order to the PC "as a continuation of the LLP." Finally, both the LLP and the PC were added as judgment debtors as the "alter ego" of defendant. The lower court denied extending the judgments against the entities as alter egos but granted the charging order against defendant's partnership interest in the LLP and the "successor" PC. Defendant appealed arguing a charging order remedy was not available against a PC interest. Held, under principles of successor liability, the PC was deemed a continuation of the LLP and therefore the charging order against the PC interest was affirmed by effectively disregarding the PC and thus arguing the charging interest only applied to a partnership interest.		

State	Cases	Remedy	Jurisdiction	State Law Applied
	Global Money Management v. McDonnold, No. 06cv34 BTM (WMc), slip copy, 2009 WL 3352574 (S.D. Cal. Oct. 15 2009)		**Personal jurisdiction/LP:** California court had personal jurisdiction over a nonresident individual also the general partner of a Delaware limited partnership. The court did not have personal jurisdiction over the Delaware limited partnership. Because of the personal jurisdiction over the individual general partner, the court ordered an assignment of any rights to payments the GP might receive from services to the LP as well as entered a charging order on that GP interest. The court agreed that it could not compel the Delaware LP to make the payments without personal jurisdiction but noted the California judgment could be registered in a state that did have jurisdiction if that was necessary. The court refused to order production of books and records as beyond the scope of a charging order. Finally, even the though the LP was formed in Delaware, the partnership agreement provided that it should be "interpreted" under California law. Since the LP was not actually formed under California law the court refused further orders otherwise permitted against a California partnership.	**CA even though a DE limited partnership**

State	Cases	Remedy	Jurisdiction	State Law Applied
	Postal Instant Press Inc. v. Kaswa Corp., 162 Cal. App. 4th 1510, 77 Cal. Rptr. 3d 96 (Cal. Ct. App. 2008)	**Reverse Pierce/corporation:** Rejects outside reverse piercing, which seeks to protect the judgment creditor from the shareholder's fraudulent transfer of assets to the corporation. Conversion and fraudulent conveyance already afford judgment creditors protection in that situation. Outside reverse piercing, accomplished by the expedient means of a post judgment motion, is an unacceptable shortcut to pursue those remedies under California law.		
	United States Fidelity and Guaranty Co. v. Scott Companies, Inc., No. C-03-5376 SBA (EMC), 2008 WL 728874 (N.D. Cal. March 17, 2008) Hellman v. Anderson, 233 Cal. App. 3d 840, 284 Cal. Rptr. 830 (1991)	**Charging order/LLCs & LPs/receiver:** Uncontested charging order awarded; plaintiffs also sought appointment of receiver; despite prior constructive fraud by defendants in undervaluing assets, court did not find circumstances warranted receiver. However, to address plaintiffs' concern that partnerships and memberships will have no incentive to make distributions because of outstanding judgments against defendants, court ordered production of K-1s and also required parties to agree on an ongoing auditing system until judgment is met. **Charging order/partnership/foreclosure:** In discussing whether a charged partnership interest is subject to foreclosure and sale, Court looked to Cal. UPA, statutory construction, and public policy, and discussed Crocker decision (see below). Found that partner's interest in partnership (share of profits and surplus, which is personal property) is subject to		

State	Cases	Remedy	Jurisdiction	State Law Applied
		charging order, and court-ordered foreclosure and sale of the charged partnership interest is statutorily authorized. Distinguished between an execution sale and a court-ordered sale to foreclose lien created by charging order, which involves judicial supervision. Disagreed with Crocker Court's requirement that other partners must invariably consent to foreclosure sale. However, since one policy underlying UPA is to avoid undue interference with partnership business, court must evaluate effect of foreclosure on partnership on a case-by-case basis, in connection with its equitable power to order a foreclosure. Burden of proving undue interference as a result of foreclosure on judgment debtor.		
	Crocker National Bank v. Perroton, 208 Cal. App.3d 1, 255 Cal.Rptr. 794 (Cal. Ct. App. 1989); see also Evans v. Galardi, 16 Cal.3d 300, 546 P.2d 313 (Cal. 1976)	**Charging order/LP/foreclosure:** Court may authorize sale of debtor partner's limited partnership interest even in the absence of fraud, where three conditions are met: the creditor has previously obtained a charging order; the judgment nevertheless remains unsatisfied; and all partners have consented to sale of the interest. Absent consent by general partner, purchaser of limited partner's interest would have rights to profits and losses but would not become a substituted limited partner.		
	Baum v. Baum, 51 Cal. 2d 610, 335 P. 2d 481 (1959)	**Charging order/partnership:** Where former wife sought charging order against former's husband's interest in partnership for payment of owed alimony		

State	Cases	Remedy	Jurisdiction	State Law Applied
		and child support, plus the appointment of a receiver, and trial court denied relief sought, former husband moved to dismiss wife's appeal on grounds that denial of appointment of receiver is not an appealable order. Court denied motion to dismiss, finding that an order made after final judgment that affects enforcement of the judgment (such as a charging order) is appealable.		
Colorado **CAT I* Not Exclusive**	JP Morgan Chase Bank, N.A. v. McClure, 393 P.3d 955 (CO S. Ct. 2017).	JP Morgan obtained an Arizona judgment and Arizona charging orders against an Arizona debtor who held membership interest in several Colorado LLCs. JP Morgan domesticated its Arizona "judgment" in Colorado (but not did not obtain a Colorado charging order) and served its Arizona charging orders on the Colorado LLCs. Later, McClure also obtained an Arizona judgment, domesticated the judgment in Colorado and obtained a Colorado charging order (which JP Morgan had not). The debtor paid funds into the court for a determination of priority between JP Morgan and McClure. The Colorado trial court determined that McClure had priority because JP Morgan's Arizona judgment could only be enforced in Colorado according to Colorado law (a Colorado charging order) and not simply by Colorado enforcing an Arizona charging order. JP Morgan then domesticated its Arizona charging order in Colorado and argued the new Colorado charging order should relate back to the date the Arizona charging orders were issued (a timing issue).		

State	Cases	Remedy	Jurisdiction	State Law Applied
		The trial court once again ruled the Colorado charging order is effective when issued thereby granting priority to McClure (first Colorado charging order issued in time). The court of appeals affirmed and JP Morgan appealed to the Colorado Supreme Court. The Court first determined, after a review of split authorities, that the location of an LLC membership interest is in state where the LLC was formed (Colorado) and not where the member resides (Arizona). Therefore the applicable and controlling law is that of Colorado. The Court next determined that under Colorado law a charging order is not effective until issuance that in turn creates a lien. Because McClure was the first to obtain a Colorado charging order, its lien had priority.		
	McClure v. JP Morgan Chase NA, 2015 WL 4760275 (Col. App. August 13, 2015).	**Charging Order/LLC:** Chase obtained an Arizona charging order against a member of a Colorado LLC and McClure obtained a later charging order against the LLC member issued by a Colorado court. Chase served its charging order on the Colorado LLC prior to McClure serving its notice. The Colorado Court of Appeals determined that a foreign charging order (Arizona) is not enforceable against a domestic LLC until that judgment is first domesticated. The court specifically determined that a "charging order is a judgment subject to the Enforcement Act" but every charging order statute indicates a judgment creditor of an LLC member may seek a charging order to create a lien against the member's interest.		

State	Cases	Remedy	Jurisdiction	State Law Applied
		The only logical issue is whether Colorado should recognize a prior lien created in Arizona when the Colorado LLC had prior notice of the Arizona lien. To be safe, the holder of a foreign judgment should first domesticate the judgment in the jurisdiction where the LLC is formed before serving on the LLC, at least to assure compliance with preference for domestic over foreign judgments. Compare with Earthgrains (Utah) and Prodigy (Georgia).		
	In re Albright, 291 B.R. 538 (Bankr. D. Colo. April 4, 2003)	**Charging order/LLC/bankruptcy:** Charging order under Colorado's LLCA exists to protect other members of an LLC; in a single-member entity, there are no other members to protect; therefore, when sole member and manager of LLC filed for bankruptcy, it effectively assigned her entire membership interest in the LLC to Chapter 7 estate, and trustee became "substituted member" with all of her rights including right to control management of LLC and right to sell real estate and distribute proceeds to estate. In contrast, where a single member of a multi-member LLC files bankruptcy, the bankruptcy estate is only entitled to receive the share of profits or other compensation by way of income and the return of contributions to which that member would be entitled.		

State	Cases	Remedy	Jurisdiction	State Law Applied
	Raccoon Recovery LLC v. Navoi Mining and Metallurgical Kombinat, 244 F. Supp. 2d 1130 (D. Colo. 2002)	**Charging order/LLC/jurisdiction**: Assignee (as successor in interest to default judgment entered against creditor in bankruptcy avoidance proceeding) sought charging order against debtor; court denied, because charging order sought to attach assets outside United States in violation of Foreign Sovereign Immunities Act.	Under FSIA a federal court lacks subject-matter jurisdiction over a claim against a foreign state, unless a specific statutory exception applies; creditor met its burden of showing it is a foreign state subject to immunity; FSIA limits attachment to property of a foreign state or instrumentality located in the United States, so under facts charging order is inappropriate.	Mining operation is an LLC organized/registered under the laws of Uzebekistan, and all mining operations are confined to Uzebekistan.
	First National Bank of Denver v. District Court, 652 P. 2d 613 (Colo. 1982)	**Charging order/partnership/foreclosure:** Order of court entered on ex parte motion for execution and sale of partnership interests subject to a charging order was invalid; court should have first required notice to debtors and an opportunity for hearing.		
Connecticut **CAT IV* Not Exclusive**	City Line Distributors, Inc. v. Savin Rock Roasting Company III, Inc., 2014 WL 7272260 (CT. Nov. 18, 2014).	**Transfer of member's financial assets.** City Line obtained a judgment against Anthony Villano on December 14, 2011 and sought (i) a charging order against his interest in three LLCs and (ii) an injunction against a transfer of any interest in the LLCs. Defendant argued on September 29, 2011 he transferred his financial interests (but retained the voting rights) to a trust he settled and the Court may not charge an interest he no		

State	Cases	Remedy	Jurisdiction	State Law Applied
		longer owns. The operating agreements established transfer procedures including a right of first refusal. Plaintiff attempted to argue these provisions were not complied with but the court noted the creditor was neither a member nor a third party beneficiary of the operating agreements and could not enforce their provisions. Moreover, the remaining members waived their rights to enforce those provisions. The court determined the creditor has not sustained its burden of proof to show that the defendant owned the financial interests allegedly transferred to the trust even though the defendant conceded he owned the voting rights and was therefore a "member" under state law.		
	Voll v. Dunn, unpublished opinion, 2014 WL 7461644 (November 10, 2014).	**LLC/Incorrect Execution Order.** Court determined that judgment creditor was entitled to an execution order requiring the judgment debtor to turn over his entire interests in various LLCs (both economic and management rights) because the Connecticut LLC Act, unlike the Revised Uniform Act, did not "expressly" provide the LLC Act charging order remedy was exclusive. Not only did the Court improperly conclude the charging order remedy was not exclusive, it further determined the judgment creditor was entitled the debtor's entire interest (including voting interest) in a multi-member LLC. This case could not be more wrong.		

State	Cases	Remedy	Jurisdiction	State Law Applied
	Mack Film Development, LLC v. Benevolent Partners, LP, Not Reported in A.3d, 2014 WL 6462116 (October 10, 2014).	**No foreclosure permitted.** Neither party briefed whether the law of Delaware applied (jurisdiction of entity) or Connecticut (jurisdiction of member) applied with respect to a proper Connecticut charging order. Delaware precludes foreclosure while Connecticut does not. The court determined the plaintiff had adequate remedies other than foreclosure and thus foreclosure was not permissible.		
	Shanghai Real Estate Ltd. v. Greenberg, Not Reported in A.3d, 2014 WL 660624 (Conn. Super., Jan. 28, 2014) (NO. LLICV104011273S).	**Charging orders/foreign LLCs.** The judgment creditor registered Canadian judgments in Connecticut and sought charging orders against the debtor's interests in LLCs organized inside and outside Connecticut. Debtor challenged the motion against the foreign LLCs because it lacked jurisdiction over the foreign LLCs. The Court rejected the argument. The order with respect to the foreign LLCs was different than the order with regard to the domestic LLCs in that the foreign LLCs were not ordered to do anything. Rather, the foreign motion only orders the debtor members to: (1) provide the plaintiff's attorney with the name and address of each of the managers and managing members of each of the foreign companies; (2) charge the defendants' interests in the foreign companies to pay all present and future distributions, credits, drawings, or payments due to the defendants to be paid to the plaintiffs until the judgment is satisfied in full, including, interest and costs; (3) take no loans, directly or indirectly, from the foreign companies until the judgment is satisfied in full, including interest and costs; (4) not undertake, enter		

State	Cases	Remedy	Jurisdiction	State Law Applied
		into or consummate any sale, encumbrance, hypothecation or modification of the defendants' membership interest in any of the foreign companies except in the context of a bona fide sale to an unrelated third party and the defendants shall provide ten business days' notice of any such sale to the plaintiff's attorney. Thus, the language of the order being sought by the plaintiff is unobjectionable. It is directed to the judgment debtor members only. The case is instructive of how judgment creditors may avoid serving the foreign entity – specifically tailor the motion request as stated above.		
	Rockstone Capital v. Marketing Horizons, LTD, 2013 WL 4046597 (Conn. Super. July 17, 2013)	**Charging orders/foreign LLCs.** Judgment creditor sought charging orders in Connecticut against two foreign LLCs after a judgment debtor member failed to make payments on a Connecticut judgment. The two foreign LLCs were not named parties. The debtor argued the two foreign LLCs were necessary parties and the court lacked jurisdiction over them. The court first determined the debtor lacked standing to challenge lack of jurisdiction. Further, the court determined that the LLCs were not necessary parties because the entry of a charging order only grants the judgment creditor the "distribution rights" of a member and does not permit management participation. Finally, the debtor argued Connecticut law did not apply to a foreign LLC. Rather Connecticut was required to apply the foreign law where the LLC was organized.		

State	Cases	Remedy	Jurisdiction	State Law Applied
		The court dismissed two cited cases as inapplicable but in essence determined the entry of a charging order was not in the nature of an internal affair.		
	Peterson v. Woldeyohannes, 2013 WL 3119729 56 Conn. L. Rptr. 202 (Conn. Super., June 03, 2013).	**Charging order/economic rights.** A charging order cannot force the defendant, the sole member of an LLC, to assign the LLC interest to the plaintiff. Therefore, a turnover order is not appropriate. Rather, upon foreclosure, the LLC interest must be sold by a Marshall in a public sale.		
	Connecticut Fair Plan v. Wonder Package, LLC, Not Reported in A.3d, 2013 WL 1223895 (Conn. Super., March 08, 2013).	**Charging order/Insurance proceeds.** Insurance company filed action to determine who was entitled to insurance proceeds from a fire that destroyed part of property. The insurance company is entitled to attorney fees to determine who is entitled to these funds. The holder of a charging order is not entitled to any proceeds payable to the LLC because its interest is only in distributed proceeds.		
	Metcoff v. NCT Group, Inc., 2012 WL 6901181 (Unreported) (Conn. Super. 2012).	**Distributions defined.** Judgment creditors sought charging orders to collect on a final judgment in the amount of $2,127,967. The defendant objected to the terms of the order since it applied to all distributions of "property" (including contract and intellectual property rights) other than simply "money." The Court noted the charging order applicability to "distributions" but also noted that term was not defined. **Held**, the term "distributions" includes any distribution of an LLC's assets, in addition to and including money.		

State	Cases	Remedy	Jurisdiction	State Law Applied
	Commissioner of Environmental Protection v. State Five Indus. Park, Inc., 304 Conn. 128, 37 A.3d 724 Conn. (2012).	**Reverse Piercing.** Affirmed reverse piercing viability against corporations in Connecticut under Litchfield Asset Management Corp v. Howell, 70 Conn. App. 133, 799 A.2d 298 (2002) theory. However, doctrine factually inapplicable because of prejudice to third party creditors. Strong concurring opinion urged rejection of Litchfield.		
	Buckeye Retirement C., LLC, L. v. B, 2011 WL 3439022 (D.Conn.)	**LLC/Assets:** Buffa, the judgment debtor, owned 99% of the LLC and his spouse owned 1%. He was paid $19,000 annual salary for over full time employment whereas she was paid $120,000 for part time work. The salaries were discovered through a discovery motion to the LLC under a state discovery statute providing "[a] judgment creditor may obtain discovery from the judgment debtor, "or from any third person" the judgment creditor reasonably believes, in good faith, may have assets of the judgment debtor." The LLC was the third person. A deposition was scheduled to determine what portion, if any, of the spouse's compensation was unreasonable so to re- characterize 99% of that amount as a distribution properly due the creditor.		
	Litchfield Asset Management Corp. v. Howell, 70 Conn. App. 133, 799 A.2d 298 (2002)	**Reverse pierce/LLC:** Where judgment debtor established limited liability companies in patent attempt to frustrate the judgment creditor, Court approved outsider reverse piercing, in which an outside third party pursuing claim against a corporate insider seeks to have the corporate entity disregarded. Court examined both instrumentality	Judgment creditor entitled to a charging order even though LLC not a party (statute does not require LLC to be a party), because a charging order merely gives creditor rights of an assignee of the member's interest; similarly, even though Internal Revenue Service may	

State	Cases	Remedy	Jurisdiction	State Law Applied
		rule and identity rule and found both applied to defendant's actions (defendant never drew salary but used LLC funds to pay personal expenses and provide substantial, interest-free loans to family members).	have a lien on member's interest, no requirement that IRS be made a party.	
	Cadle Co. v. Ginsburg, 2002 WL 725500 (Conn. Super March 28, 2002)	**Charging order/LLC:** Since charging order merely gives judgment creditor the rights of an assignee of member's interests, but does not entitle creditor to participate in the management or affairs of the LLC, plaintiff is entitled to charging order in LLC that operated jai alai business, despite Conn. statutory requirement that no interest in a jai alai business may be held by an unlicensed individual. However, no showing at this time that court should appoint receiver or require disclosure of books and records of LLC.		
	PB Real Estate, Inc. v. DEM II Properties, 20 Conn. L. Rptr. 418, 1997 WL 625465 (Conn. Super. Sep. 25, 1997), aff'd. 50. Conn. App. 741, 719 A. 2d 73 (1998)	**Charging order/LLC/foreclosure:** Conn. LLC charging order section is construed in accordance with Conn. UPA and ULPA, which permit a charging creditor to foreclose on a partner's interest in the partnership. Since an LLCA charging order can be enforced through strict foreclosure, and the term "distribution" is broadly interpreted, plaintiff's motion for a turnover order is granted. Rejected defendants' claim that the payments at issue were merely compensation for their services to their law firm, which was organized as an LLC; since defendants' characterization was at odds with the firm's business records and tax returns, payments received by defendants were distributions subject to the charging order.		

State	Cases	Remedy	Jurisdiction	State Law Applied
	Madison Hills LTD Partnership II v. Madison Hills, 35 Conn. App. 81, 644 A.2d 363 (1994)	**Charging order/partnerships/foreclosure:** Extensive discussion of charging orders under both UPA and ULPA; foreclosure against partnership interests is an available remedy; in statutes, term "foreclosure" includes both "strict foreclosure" where property is appraised at fair market value, and a foreclosure sale ordered by court.		
Delaware **CAT II*** **Exclusive**	Delaware Acceptance Corp. v. Estate of Metzner, 2017 WL 2226668 (DE Ch, Ct. 2017). Peninsula Advisors, LLC v. Fairstar Resources Ltd., Not Reported in F.Supp.2d, 2014 WL 491671 (D. Del., Feb. 05, 2014) (NO. CV 10-489-LPS).	Delaware Acceptance Corp. v. Estate of Metzner, 2017 WL 2226668 (DE Ch, Ct. 2017). A judgment creditor held a judgment against the decedent and a charging order against his 49% interest in an LLC, the only asset of the estate. The executor rejected the creditor claim that upon death the LLC dissolved without the consent of the remaining members. The executor claimed the consent to continue was obtained but the court determined otherwise and removed the executor. **Foreign foreclosure/procedural dismissal.** Plaintiffs filed suit in the Delaware Court of Chancery on May 14, 2010, seeking a declaratory judgment that Defendant's foreclosures upon Plaintiffs' membership interests in eight Delaware limited liability companies ("LLCs") - which took place in Utah pursuant to a Utah court's charging orders - were invalid under Delaware law, as well as a declaration of the identity of the members and managers of the eight LLCs. After filing, plaintiffs informed the Court that the Utah State Court set aside its earlier order because it was obtained		

State	Cases	Remedy	Jurisdiction	State Law Applied
		at a time when defendants were not represented by counsel. Consequently, the judgment creditor's purchase of the LLC interests at foreclosure was declared null and void and the Delaware challenge to those cases was dismissed. Since the Utah foreclosure was cancelled on procedural grounds, there is no definitive declaration by a Delaware court that Delaware law applies when a foreign state forecloses on a charging order within the foreign state.		
	Picard v. Wood, 2012 WL 2865993 (Del. Ch. 2012).		**Long-Arm Statute**. Plaintiff suit based exclusively on amounts received by a Massachusetts resident limited partner in a Delaware limited partnership. The plaintiff argued his ownership of such an interest and connection to the partnership satisfied the requisite minimum contacts under the Delaware long-arm statute. In the alternative, plaintiff sought a limited discovery order based on those contacts. The plaintiff relied on the language of the long-arm statute that provides personal jurisdiction where the person transacts any business or performs any character of work or service in Delaware. Specifically, plaintiff argued purchasing an interest in a Delaware limited partnership and signed the partnership agreement. The Court noted that if these contacts satisfied the minimum contact requirement, every nonresident limited partner in every Delaware	

State	Cases	Remedy	Jurisdiction	State Law Applied
			limited partnership would be subject to personal jurisdiction in Delaware. Unless there is evidence that the limited partner controlled, managed, directed, or operated the affairs of the limited partnership, personal jurisdiction does not exist. Finally, limited discovery cannot be ordered to determine if personal jurisdiction exists absent adequate pleading of facts leading to personal jurisdiction.	
	American Institutional Partners v. Fairstar Resources, F. 3d , 2011 WL 1230074 (D.Del. March 31, 2011)	**Charging order/foreclosure:** Corporate creditors obtained a substantial judgment in a Utah action against several Delaware LLCs and the individual who owned 100% of the upper tier entity (SMLLC). Because Utah statutory law expressly permits foreclosure and also expressly permits a purchaser at foreclosure of the interest in a SMLLC to acquire all the rights of an owner, not merely the rights of a transferee (a statutory Florida Olmstead judicial result). In the Utah proceedings, judgment debtors contended that Delaware, not Utah, law controlled the charging order and foreclosure procedures since the entities were Delaware LLCs. The Utah court determined that (i) Delaware, law applied to the charging order and foreclosure proceedings, (ii) denied an objection to the sale of the LLC interests in a foreclosure action, and (iii) denied a request to stay pending the outcome of a Delaware action to determine applicable law.	Utah action against Delaware LLCs. Utah Court applied Delaware law; Delaware Court upheld Utah decision because both Utah (principal place of business) and Delaware (state of organization) courts have valid contacts.	

State	Cases	Remedy	Jurisdiction	State Law Applied
		The debtors filed a declaratory judgment action in the Delaware Chancery Court arguing that Delaware, not Utah, law controlled and sought an injunction. In response, the judgment creditors removed the case to Delaware federal court and the creditors sought to transfer back to Utah. The Delaware court refused to transfer back to Utah determining that both Utah (principal place of business) and Delaware (state of organization) courts have valid contacts. Therefore, the Utah court decision remains.		
	New Times Media LLC v. Bay Guardian Co., Inc. 2010 WL 2573957 (D. Del. June 28, 2010), adopting New Times Media LLC v. Bay Guardian Co., Inc., 2010 WL 1909558 (D. Del. May 11, 2010)		Bay Guardian obtained a multi-million dollar California judgment against against New Times Media, a Delaware LLC. New Times Media appealed in California but Bay Guardian obtained a charging order against its interests in various operating subsidiaries. Before Bay Guardian filed a motion for foreclosure of the charging order in California, New Times Media filed a motion in the Delaware Chancery Court seeking a declaratory judgment that Delaware and not California law applied to determine whether the charging order could be foreclosed. Delaware law precludes foreclosure while California law does not. Bay Guardian obtained a removal of the case to Delaware federal court. The federal court refused to decide the case under the Federal Anti-Injunction	

State	Cases	Remedy	Jurisdiction	State Law Applied
			Act. As a result, and because the California court has not ruled on the choice of law issue, New Times Media will be forced to argue that Delaware law controls in a California court.	
	B.A.S.S. Group LLC v. Coastal Supply Co., Civil Action No. 3743-VCP, 2009 WL 1743730 (Del. Ch. June 19, 2009)	**Charging order/LLC/constructive trust:** Charging order an insufficient remedy where judgment debtor was unjustly enriched and engaged in protracted litigation with judgment creditor; instead, court imposed a constructive trust.		
	Abbett v. Oya, LLC, 2016 WL 4071514 (June 28, 2016).	Charging orders are appropriate even if the LLC is in process of dissolution and winding up as long as all assets have not been distributed.		
District of Columbia **CAT I* Exclusive**				
Florida **CAT II* Exclusive** (excluding single-member LLCs)	Branch Banking and Trust Company v. Crystal Centre, LLC, ___ F.3d ___, 2017 WL 57345 (D. Ct. F 2014).	A charging order may not be entered against a debtor's membership interest in an LLC if the LLC interest is owned by spouses as tenants by entirety and only one spouse is obligated for the debt.		Florida law applied.

State	Cases	Remedy	Jurisdiction	State Law Applied
CAT I* Not Exclusive (single-member LLCs)	SE Property Holdings, LLC v. McElheney, ___ F.3d ___, 2016 WL 7494300 (ND FL 2016).	As a judgment creditor, SE sought charging orders and foreclosure on several LLCs owned by the debtor and his spouse. Debtor defended that the LLC interests were held in tenants by the entireties and Florida law shields such holdings from the creditors of just one spouse. The court determined that the charging order exclusivity prohibits alternative remedies such as a writ of garnishment to reach distributions but does not preclude garnishment of unpaid wages due for past work. Further, Florida fraudulent transfer law precludes a spouse from transferring a separate LLC interest into a joint interest with a spouse. However, a charging order may not be issued against a tenancy by entirety of spouse for the debts of only one of the spouses.		
	McClandon v. Dakem & Associates, LLC, 219 So.3d 269, 2017 WL 2298443 (FL Ct App 2017).	The court determined that after a charging order was issued, the judgment creditor was not entitled to a receiver to take management control of the LLCs to regulate distributions.	**SMLCC/Jurisdiction.** The debtor argued the Florida court could not foreclose on her interest in an LLC formed in Nevis, a foreign jurisdiction, because Nevis law applied. The Court determined that the situs of an LLC interest, as intangible personal property, was with the debtor's residence and in this case Florida. Secondly, the Court analyzed the conflict between Nevis (no foreclosure) and Florida (foreclosure permitted and in a SMLLC the creditor could acquire the management as well as economic interest. The Court determined that Florida law applied (albeit in a weakly argued case).	

State	Cases	Remedy	Jurisdiction	State Law Applied
	Wells Fargo Bank, NA v. Barber, 2015 WL 470589 (February 4, 2015).	Creditor domesticated a Nevada judgment against debtor in Florida and then sought a charging order against his membership interest in 12 LLCs. The order was granted and in addition the court appointed a receiver to take control of the financial management of four LLCs in order to facilitate payments on the charging order. The court of appeals affirmed the appointment of a receiver but reversed the power of the receiver to exercise any management control over the four LLCs.		
	Lefkowitz v. Quality Labor Management, LLC, 159 So.3d 147, 2014 WL 5877850 (November 14, 2014).	**LLC/Security Interest.** Holder of a charging order and also a perfected lien against property of the defendant sought to intervene post-judgment. Motion to intervene denied but reversed. Because it was simply seeking to protect its security interest in collateral.		
	Young v. Levy, 140 So.3d 1109, 2014 WL 2741060 (Fla. 4th Distr. App. June 18, 2014).	**LLC/charging order exclusive.** In a dispute between the majority and minority owner, the majority owner obtained a judgment for attorney fees against the minority owner. The Court entered a writ of garnishment to collect the amount from the LLC relating to amounts the LLC owed the minority owner. The Court of Appeals quashed the writ of garnishment since the charging order is listed as the exclusive remedy.		

State	Cases	Remedy	Jurisdiction	State Law Applied
	In re Cutuli, Slip Copy, 2013 WL 5236711 (Bkrtcy., S. D. Fla., Sept. 16, 2013) (NO. 11-35256-BKC-AJC).	**Bankruptcy/waiver of privilege.** The Bankruptcy Court granted a documents seizure request. That seizure determined that emails between debtor and her attorney and law firm disclosed discussions about asset protection, including the limitations on charging orders. The trustee contended the law firm held itself out as an asset protection law firm. The trustee seeks discovery from the law firm to determine whether assets were fraudulently transferred. The law firm claimed all communications were privileged. The Court determined that since the debtor and her husband both used the same firm, the privilege asserted by the debtor's wife is not available because of waiver. Moreover, any privilege held by the debtor or her spouse was waived by the crime-fraud exception.		
	Findling v. Bisaria, 2012 WL 3835079 (S.D.Fla., Sept. 4, 2012)	**LLC/receiver.** A Michigan receiver sought enforcement in Florida of a Michigan personal judgment against defendants. Specifically, the receiver sought a charging order against defendants' interests in Florida and Delaware LLCs as well as a judicial dissolution of a Florida LLC that owned the Michigan property subject to a debt personally guaranteed by the defendants. The defendants moved to dismiss the complaint because the receiver was not authorized to practice law in Florida. The court denied the motion because the receiver had associated with Florida counsel and was then admitted *Pro Hac Vice*.		

State	Cases	Remedy	Jurisdiction	State Law Applied
	Hage v. Salkin, 2012 WL 718644 (S.D. Fla., March 6, 2012).	**SMLLC/Statutory amendment.** Court interpreted new Florida LLC amendments as clarifying and retroactive and as a result determined that a court order involving the sale of an interest in a SMLLC transferred the entire interest of the judgment debtor under new Fla. Stat. Ann. § 608.433(6).		
	In re Inman, 2012 WL 2374419 (Bkrtcy. S.D. Fla. June 22, 2012).	**Marriage dissolution/Colorado judgment.** Florida bankruptcy court determined that amounts owed under a marriage dissolution agreement were not dischargeable in bankruptcy because they constituted alimony and not a dischargeable property settlement. Further, the Court refused to vacate Colorado charging orders entered upon domestication of a Florida judgment in Colorado. The charging orders were to enforce failed payments of the alimony agreement. The LLC owned real estate in Colorado.		
	Note: Florida cases below were issued prior to statutory amendment (eff. May 31, 2011) distinguishing between single-member and other LLCs (expressly precluding foreclosure for other LLCs but permitting foreclosure for single-member LLCs).			

State	Cases	Remedy	Jurisdiction	State Law Applied
	Olmstead v. Federal Trade Commission, 44 So. 3d 76 (Fla. 2010)	**Charging Order/LLC:** In a 5-2 decision, the Florida Supreme Court determined that since the Florida LLC Act charging order statute did not expressly state that it was "exclusive," the judgment creditor of the only member of a SMLLC was entitled to use other Florida collection remedies including execution and levy to obtain all the assets of the SMLLC. In part, the majority justified this interpretation because the comparable charging order provisions of the Florida general partnership and limited partnership acts do provide the remedy is exclusive.		
	Federal Trade Commission v. Olmstead, 528 F.3d 1310 (11th Cir. 2008)	**Charging order/LLC:** After discussing applicability of charging order remedy to single-member Florida limited liability companies, and whether that remedy is exclusive, Court of Appeals certified the following question to the Florida Supreme Court seeking guidance on the issues: "Whether, pursuant to Fla. Stat. § 608.433(4), a court may order a judgment-debtor to surrender all 'right, title, and interest' in the debtor's single-member limited liability company to satisfy an outstanding judgment."		
	Givens v. National Loan Investors L.P., 724 So. 2d 610 (Fla. 1999)	**Charging order/LP/foreclosure:** Florida's RULPA confers upon a judgment creditor the right to charge the limited partner's interest with payment of the unsatisfied amount of the judgment. However, in contrast to creditor's rights against a debtor partner's interest in a general partnership, a judgment creditor does not have the right to foreclose against the debtor partner's interest in a limited partnership.		

State	Cases	Remedy	Jurisdiction	State Law Applied
	Abukasis v. MTM Finest, Ltd., --- So.3d ---- 2016 WL 4446010 (2016)	MTM held a judgment, but not a charging order, against Abukasis who owned an interest in A&E Two Associates, LLC. MTM sought and obtained a state court order "judicially transferring" his entire full LLC interest. The appellate court reversed for lack of any procedure under Florida LLC statutes authorizing such a transfer.		
Georgia **CAT II*** **Not Exclusive**	Gaslowitz v. Stabilis Fund I, LP, 770 S.E.2d 245, 2015 WL 1059575 (Ga. App. 2015).	**Charging Order/Amount of Unpaid Judgment.** After obtaining a judgment against Gaslowitz, the sole member of an LLC, Stabilis sought and obtained a charging order against Gaslowitz and an accounting against the LLC. On appeal the accounting order was reversed but Gaslowitz also argued the charging order should be invalidated because the judgment alleged had been partially satisfied and therefore was incorrect. The Court determined the accurate amount of the unpaid judgment need not be stated in the charging order: "But the amount of distributions subject to the charging order will not necessarily correspond to the specific amount of the judgment that remains unpaid on the date that the charging order is issued. The unsatisfied amount of the judgment could be reduced or even eliminated by funds received from other sources, especially where, as here, there are co-debtors on the judgment." Contra, see Noble (Missouri).		

State	Cases	Remedy	Jurisdiction	State Law Applied
	Mahalo Investments III, LLC v. First Citizens Bank & Trust Co., Inc., 769 S.E.2d 154, 2015 2015 WL 687922 (Ga. App. Feb 19, 2015).	**LLC Not Necessary Party.** The LLC is not a necessary party to a charging order action against one of its members in a state different from the state of the LLC formation. First Citizens Bank & Trust Company, Inc. (FCB) obtained a Judgment against Mark Epstein, Andrew Kelly, and their LLC, Mahalo Investments III, LLC, in Georgia. During the post-judgment discovery of the debtors' assets, FCB learned that Epstein and Kelly owned interests in several other LLCs in other states not including Mahalo. So FCB applied and was granted a charging order against these LLCs. The debtors appealed arguing FCB SHOULD have brought actions against the LLCs in their state of formation. Since under Georgia law a charging order creditor could not obtain management rights in the foreign LLC, the LLC was not a necessary party to the proceeding.		
	Note: Georgia cases below were issued prior to statutory amendment prohibiting foreclosure, effective July 1, 2009. For full text, see LLC Charging Order Statute Table.*			
	Hopson v. Bank of North Georgia, 258 Ga. App. 360, 574 S.E. 2d 411 (2002)	**Assignment/LLC/foreclosure:** Bank made loan to LLC and required member to personally guarantee loan and sign a security agreement whereby he assigned all of his "right title and interest as a member" in and to the LLC. Despite language in Operating Agreement that an interest in the LLC		

State	Cases	Remedy	Jurisdiction	State Law Applied
		may not be transferred without the prior written consent of all members, court found that Operating Agreement specifically allows such a transfer so long as it is limited to a non-management, purely economic role. Under Georgia's LLCA, bank may foreclose on such economic interest.		
	Prodigy Centers/Atlanta No. 1 L.P. v. T-C Associates LTD, 147 F.3d 1324 (1998)	**Charging order/LLC/priority:** After certifying the question to the Georgia Supreme Court, the 11th Circuit determined that a partnership or LLC membership interest is a chose in action, and accordingly a judgment lien does not attach until the date of the entry of a charging order. Therefore, the prior recorded government lien was superior even though the government lien was recorded after the judgment.		
	Nigri v. Lotz, 216 Ga.App. 204, 453 S.E.2d 780 (1995)	**Charging order/LP/foreclosure:** Since charging order remedy is not exclusive, financial interests of limited partner could be reached by garnishment as well as through charging order. Where charging order was granted, court could order limited partner's charged interest be foreclosed by judicial sale at which partnership interest could be purchased by judgment creditor or third party. Prohibition against foreclosure in Georgia's version of UPA not applicable where its ULPA does not specifically prohibit sale of charged interest, even though that ULPA does not specifically provide for foreclosure and sale.		

State	Cases	Remedy	Jurisdiction	State Law Applied
Hawaii **CAT I*** **Exclusive**				
Idaho **CAT I *** **Exclusive**	International Real Estate Solutions, Inc. v. Arave, P.3d _, 2014 WL 7384199 (December 31, 2014). **Note:** Since the language of Idaho's LLC charging order statute is similar to § 503 of the Revised Uniform Limited Liability Company Act, the Idaho Code sets forth the Uniform Law Comments to § 503 after the Idaho statute. The comment to subsection (g) states that "This subsection is not intended to prevent a court from effecting a 'reverse pierce' where appropriate. In a reverse pierce, the court conflates the entity and its owner to hold the entity liable for a debt of the owner."	**Charging Order/Partial Satisfaction.** Creditor obtained default judgment in Utah against several defendants and domesticated the judgment in Idaho to seek a charging order in Idaho. In Utah foreclosure sales, International received partial satisfaction on property not owned by Arave and noted that in Idaho. The Idaho charging order was not dismissed.		

State	Cases	Remedy	Jurisdiction	State Law Applied
	Wheaton Equipment Co. v. Franmar, Inc., 2009 WL 464337 (D. Idaho Feb. 24, 2009)	**Reverse pierce/LLC:** Court noted that Idaho law allows for reverse piercing, citing Vanderford Co., Inc. v. Knudson, 144 Idaho 547, 165 P. 3d 261 (Idaho 2007) (remanding case for new trial because trial judge did not give a jury instruction allowing the jury to find an LLC to be the alter ego of the defendant). In this case, LLC was an alter ego of judgment debtors, who commingled their individual assets and funds with those of the LLC, used funds and assets of the LLC for noncompany purposes and for their own personal gain, and used the LLC to hide assets from the judgment creditor.	**Reverse pierce/Jurisdiction:** Nothing in record suggested that Texas LLC transacted business in Idaho, owned property in Idaho, or participated directly as transferor or transferee of any of the alleged fraudulent transfers forming the basis of present action. It did not have any contacts with Idaho, let alone minimum contacts necessary for *in personam* jurisdiction. Nevertheless, where the facts sufficiently supported allegation that LLC was alter ego of debtors, over whom court had personal jurisdiction, the alter ego status provided a basis for Idaho Court Idaho Court to exercise personal jurisdiction over LLC.	
	In re A-Z Electronics, LLC, 350 B.R. 886 (Bankr. D. Idaho Feb. 23, 2006)	**LLC/bankruptcy.** Upon debtor's filing for Chapter 7 relief, all of debtor's interests in single-member LLC became property of Chapter 7 estate and, as such, were subject to sole and exclusive authority of Ch. 7 trustee. Therefore, trustee was only one entitled to manage LLC and decide, inter alia, whether LLC would or would not file for bankruptcy protection.		

State	Cases	Remedy	Jurisdiction	State Law Applied
Illinois **CAT I*** **Exclusive**	FirstMerit Bank, NA v. McEnery, 2014 IL App (3d) 130231-U (October 29, 2014).	**Spouse's marital interests.** Bank obtained judgment against husband and then a 2011 charging order against his interests in several LLCs owning restaurants. In 2012, his spouse filed for divorce and the trial court determined she held a 50% marital interest in the LLCs charged. On a subsequent hearing the trial court determined her marital interest lien was subordinate to the Bank's prior charging order lien and ordered her to turnover any distributions received. Upon a subsequent involuntary bankruptcy petition against the husband, the court lifted the automatic stay to permit the distributions to be paid under the charging order. On appeal the Court affirmed that a spouse's marital interest in her husbands LLC interests was subordinate to the prior charging order judgment lien.		
	In re James, 490 Bankr. 795 (N.D. Illinois 2013).	***Barton* Doctrine/attorney's fees.** The Court followed the *Barton* doctrine precluding an outside party from suing a court appointed receiver or trustee without first obtaining court approval. The debtor's chapter 13 case was dismissed after the Court refused to confirm the plan. The debtor sought to reopen the case to pay attorney's fees as part of the administrative expense of the case while it was pending. The Court approved the payment.		
	In re Weitzman, 381 B.R. 874 (2008).	***Barton* Doctrine.** The *Barton* doctrine requires court permission to sue a bankruptcy trustee or receiver.		

State	Cases	Remedy	Jurisdiction	State Law Applied
	U.S. v. Zabka, 900 F.Supp.2d 864 (C.D. Ill., 2012)	**Charging order/LP/analogy.** Considered rights of a receiver over property of limited partnerships controlled by married taxpayers but arguably has further LLC implications. The government obtained judgments against the married limited partners for tax deficiencies and then secured appointment of a receiver to enforce against taxpayers property. Taxpayers argued that with respect to the property owned by the limited partnerships, the government was limited to a charging order under Illinois limited partnership law (same as LLC law). But the Court noted the lien attaches to "all" the taxpayer property, including all the limited partnership interests. The Court then argued, similar to the government's argument in the Florida case (Olmstead v. FTC, 44 So. 3d 76 (Fl 2010)) that the charging order purpose was to protect unrelated third party owners and here all the owners were subject to the same judgment. As such, the Illinois Federal Court essentially adopted the Florida Supreme Court analysis expressed in the cited case.		
	Bank of America, N.A. v. Freed, 2012 IL App (1st) 110749, --- N.E.2d ----, 2012 WL 6725894 (Ill. App. 1 Dist. 2012).	**LLC not necessary party.** Lender brought foreclosure action against borrower and sought judgment against guarantors in the amount of a guaranty. The trial court entered judgments, imposed charging orders, ordered foreclosure orders on 72 LLC distributional interests in which defendants had interests, and appointed a receiver for all of those interests.		

State	Cases	Remedy	Jurisdiction	State Law Applied
		Defendants appealed arguing in part that the LLCs were "necessary parties" that must be joined in the litigation prior to the entry of the charging orders. As a consequence, defendants argued the court entering the judgment must obtain jurisdiction over the LLCs because the orders affect the LLC property interests. **Held**, the charging orders grant the holder very limited rights similar to a transferee to simply receive distributions and without the ability to affect the LLC. Further, it would be impractical and unnecessarily costly to require a judgment creditor to serve all the LLCs, especially a large number as in this case.		
	In re Weiss, 376 B.R. 867 (Ill. 2007)	**Restrictions in agreements preclude transfers under statute.** Determines whether a security agreement in an LLC membership interest is effective to create a valid security interest in the LLC interest so as to make the creditor a secured creditor. The case focused on whether LLC statutory and operating agreement transfer restrictions preclude a security agreement attachment to the described LLC membership interest. If so, the creditor motion to lift the bankruptcy stay would be granted. Otherwise, the secured status would be negated and the trustee strong arm lien created under BRC § 544(a) would be superior to their unperfected lien. Weiss had previously executed a pledge agreement to the LLC membership interests to secure payment of promissory notes. The security agreement granted the creditors a "first priority security interest in and to all of [Weiss'] assigned		

State	Cases	Remedy	Jurisdiction	State Law Applied
		right, title and interest in, and to the Assigned Interests" as defined therein. Each of the relevant operating and partnership agreements contained a separate provision restricting any transfer of all or any part of any interest without consent of the other owners or managers. The Court determined that the net effect of these agreed transfer restrictions went further than the statutory transfer restrictions on management and governance rights by precluding a transfer of any part of the economic interests as well. Since the agreements required written consent prior to any transfer, Weiss lacked the power to execute a security agreement to transfer even his otherwise freely transferable economic rights. The creditor filed a financing statement to perfect its security interests in the instruments. Citing UCC § 9-213(b), the Court noted that the creation of a security interest requires that the debtor have "rights or power to transfer rights in collateral." In this case the statute and operating agreement precluded without the consent of the other members.		
	In re Lahood, ---B.R.---, 2010 WL 3842429 (C.D. Ill. Sept. 30, 2010)	**LLC/charging order/bankruptcy:** Court determined that "exclusive" charging order language meant that charging order was only method to obtain a lien against an LLC interest. Therefore a prior service of citation was ineffective to create a lien on the LLC interest (even though it was effective as a lien on other nonexempt personal property). The Court also determined that a member bankruptcy was not "wrongful" and		

State	Cases	Remedy	Jurisdiction	State Law Applied
		therefore the trustee was entitled to step into the shoes of the debtor to wind up the LLC when the remaining member caused dissolution. The Court did not analyze the application of the executor contract limitation.		
	First Mid-Illinois Bank & Trust v. Parker, 2010 WL 3179734 (Ill. App. 5 Dist.)	**Charging order/LLC/priority:** On January 8, 2008, a bank (creditor A) filed a motion for a prejudgment attachment (to preclude fraudulent dispersion) against all "property interests" owned by the two members of the Four S, LLC which the Court granted the next day on January 9, 2008. Creditor A was granted summary judgment on April 18, 2008 on the liability issue and was granted a monetary judgment on May 2, 2008. On June 6, 2008, the Court granted Creditor A a charging order to the Four S, LLC. The Court made the charging order lien effective as of the earlier **January 9, 2008**, date of attachment. The Court further ordered foreclosure by judicial sale if the liens were not satisfied in thirty days on July 7, 2008. On July 9, 2008, Creditor A filed a motion (i) to enforce the charging order by sale and (ii) direct the two LLC members to identify third parties which might claim a lien on the LLC interests and for those creditors to appear. The LLC identified two other creditors (B and C) with claiming a lien on the two members' LLC interests. Creditor B obtained a confession of judgment on December 7, 2006 pursuant to which a discovery of assets was served on the LLC on **March 29,2007**. Creditor C obtained a judgment on February 25, 2008 and		

State	Cases	Remedy	Jurisdiction	State Law Applied
		a charging order on **May 23, 2008**. The Court determined that since Creditor B did not obtain a charging order it had no lien as the charging order was the exclusive remedy. Since both Creditor A and C had obtained a charging order (A on June 6, 2008 and C May 23, 2008), the issue was the priority of two liens and granted Creditor C priority based solely on the date of the entry of the charging order. On appeal, Creditor A argued priority because its charging order "related back" to an earlier pre-judgment attachment order dated January 9, 2008 a date preceding the date of Creditor C's charging order on May 23, 2008. The Court determined on appeal that the exclusive charging order did not preclude other remedies to establish priority among competing charging order creditors. Specifically, the Court determined that the "relation back" doctrine merges a judgment with an earlier attachment date. Since an attachment lien does not attempt to "satisfy" a judgment but merely establishes a lien it is not a collection activity precluded by the exclusive charging order language. it merely secures and holds property to satisfy a debt the creditor hopes to establish by judgment. So while an attachment lien cannot be used to satisfy a forthcoming judgment, it does establish lien priority because it informs the LLC garnishee that any funds in its possession may become payable to someone other than the owner of the LLC interest. As a result of the attachment, Creditor A had charging order lien priority.		

State	Cases	Remedy	Jurisdiction	State Law Applied
	In re Lahood, Bankruptcy No. 07-81727, slip copy, 2009 WL 2169879 (Bankr. C. D. Ill. July 16, 2009) (Charging order exclusive remedy to satisfy judgment out of a member's distributional (economic) interest)	**Charging order/LLC/foreclosure:** Under express statutory provisions, charging order constitutes lien on judgment debtor's distributional interest; court may order foreclosure on that lien at any time; courts in other states with similar statutes have interpreted this provision to allow a court to order the distributional interest charged with the payment of a judgment (cites Herring v. Keasler, 150 N.C. App. 598, 563 S.E. 2d 614 (2002), for the holding that forced sale of judgment debtor's membership interest was prohibited).		
	In re Lahood, Bankruptcy No. 07-81727, slip copy, 2009 WL 803558 (Bankr. C.D. Ill. March 19, 2009)	**Charging order/LLC:** While finding that charging order is the judgment creditor's exclusive remedy against a debtor's distributional interest in an LLC, specifically did not address question whether a citation lien could go against a debtor's member's interest.		
	See also Bobak Sausage Co. v. Bobak Orland Park, Inc., No. 06 C 4747, 2008 WL 4814693 (N.D. Ill. Nov. 3, 2008) **Note:** Official Comments to the Illinois statute state that it is similar to section 504 of the ULLCA (1996)			

State	Cases	Remedy	Jurisdiction	State Law Applied
Indiana **CAT IV* Not Exclusive**	Boone County Utilities, LLC v. The Branham Corporation, 518 Bankr. 511 (SD Ind. 2014).	**Charging order/Rights limited to distributions.** Branham obtained a judgment and a charging order against Boone's sole member, Newland Resources, LLC. Branham initiated supplemental proceedings to discover assets and to set aside fraudulent conveyances both to satisfy the judgment. The Court determined that under Indiana LLC law, Branham had no right to participate in management, inspect books or records, or force a distribution or a sale of the membership interest. Thus, Branham's only ability to collect is to receive any distributions Newland was entitled to receive from Boone. Further, Branham may not engage in discovery of the Boone's officers to examine management decision to make or not make distributions to Newland.		
	In re Lee, 524 Bankr. 798 (S.D. IN 2014).	**Bankruptcy/Voting Rights.** Debtor filed a Chapter 7 petition when he was the managing member of the Lee Group, LLC. At that time he held no economic membership interest in the LLC as related parties held all economic ownership rights. However, he held 51% voting control but those voting rights terminated under the operating agreement upon his withdrawal or demise. After the filing, counsel for the trustee wrote a letter to the other members stating that the debtor's voting rights became part of the estate under BRC § 541. Thereafter, the remaining members adopted a resolution terminating the debtor's voting rights		

State	Cases	Remedy	Jurisdiction	State Law Applied
		and named a new manager. The trustee argued the attempt to terminate voting rights violated the stay because the voting rights were part of the estate. The Court deemed irrelevant that the debtor owned no economic interest. The debtor did own various rights including options to purchase other interests.		
	Brant v. Krilich, 835 N.E. 2d 582 (Ind. App. 2005)	**Charging order/LLC:** Member's interest in an LLC is personal property that is subject to execution under Indiana law; however, property that is subject to execution is only the economic interest; thus, execution against interest indistinguishable from charging order such that charging order is essentially creditor's exclusive remedy.	Judgment debtor a member in several LLCs and LLPs; in actions for garnishment of checking accounts and the acquisition of debtor member's ownership interests, they are indispensable parties requiring notice; charging order remedy applies solely to LLCs organized under the laws of the State of Indiana.	Facts uncertain as to whether limited liability partnerships were organized under Indiana law; judgment creditor domesticated Florida judgment.
Iowa **CAT I* Exclusive**	Dutrac Community Credit Union v. Hefel, 893 N.W. 2d 282 (Iowa 2017).	Dutrac moved for a charging order against Hefel's interest in Westgate, an Iowa LLC. Westgate moved to intervene and the court permitted the LLC intervention determining the LLC had standing. Also, Hefel and the LLC argued the LLC operating agreement precluded assignment of a membership interest and thus the entry of a charging order. The court simply determined that the entry of a charging order is not an assignment and so the operating agreement provision is irrelevant.		

State	Cases	Remedy	Jurisdiction	State Law Applied
	Note: Comments state that the Iowa statute is similar to § 503 of the Revised Uniform Limited Liability Company Act (2006). Wells Fargo Bank National Ass'n. v. Continuous Control Solutions, Inc., 2012 WL 3195759 (Iowa Ct. App., August 8, 2012).	 **Charging order/Limited access to information.** Following entry of a charging order, the LLC filed a "limited resistance" to the portion of the lower court order that required the LLC to "to provide to the judgment creditors, or the court, periodic cash flow statements." Those statements were ordered under the statutory provisions that provided the lower court could (i) "make all other orders necessary to give effect to the charging order" and (ii) appoint a receiver of the distributions subject to the charging order, with the power to make all inquiries the judgment debtor might have made. The appellate court concluded the expanded right to information ("power to make all inquiries the judgment debtor may have") is limited to a receiver appointed by the court. The court further supported its conclusion by the fact that even actual transferees were not entitled to access to records or other information concerning the company's activities. A judgment creditor is not entitled to more information than an actual purchaser of the economic rights.		
Kansas **CAT IV*** **Exclusive**	Meyer v. Christie, 2011 WL 4857905 (D. Kan. Oct. 13, 2011	**LLC/Assignments/Charging orders:** Plaintiff with Kansas judgment sought a charging order against Kansas LLC in Kansas federal court. Defendant objected that the charging order motion might conflict with the LLC operating agreement provisions prohibiting assignment.		

State	Cases	Remedy	Jurisdiction	State Law Applied
		The court recognized that the operating could prohibit transfer or assignments but that such a prohibition was subject to other law. In Kansas, the LLC assignment provisions expressly provide that where "the sole member of the LLC at the time of the assignment under the charging order, the assignee/creditor shall have the right to participate in the management of the business and affairs of the LLC as a member." The court viewed the operating agreement prohibition as inconsistent with this transfer provision and invalidated the operating agreement transfer restriction as well as the statutory transfer restriction. There was no foreclosure so the entry of a charging order usually does not trigger an assignment. As a result, this was unusual determination allowing the mere holder of a charging order to take over management of a SMLLC. The error is as a result of the court's treatment of a person with the "rights of an assignee" as an actual "assignee." This result assumes that the mere entry of a charging order is an assignment.		
	Beech Acceptance Corp. v. Connell, 771 F. Supp. 1154 (D. Kansas 1991)		**Charging Order/Foreign Partnership:** Judgment creditor sought charging order against debtor's partnership interest in a Texas partnership that had not transacted business in Kansas and was not involved in litigation against debtor. Since a charging order is intended to secure the rights of the judgment creditor without unduly interfering with the rights of the other	

State	Cases	Remedy	Jurisdiction	State Law Applied
	City of Arkansas City v. Anderson, 242 Kan. 875, 752 P. 2d 673 (1988)	**Charging order/partnership:** Charging order creates lien on partner's distributive share of profits as of time of service upon partnership, which is superior to prior unperfected security interest (assignment). Court recognizes that statute permits foreclosure but case does not require court to determine the proper procedure to actually sell a partnership interest.	partners, a charging order is issued after an adversary hearing with the non-debtor partners. Here, court has no jurisdiction over Texas partnership or its non-debtor partners and can not issue requested charging order, although court can order debtor to pay creditor all distributions, profits or income received by him from partnership. Court also noted that creditor could resort to other forums for additional relief against partnership interests.	
Kentucky **CAT I*** **Exclusive**	Limbright v. Hofmeister, 2012 WL 5605437 (E.D. Ky. 2012).	**Exclusive charging order remedy precludes receiver.** The case involved a request for appointment of a receiver over an LLC membership interest and an injunction to preclude further asset transfers upon an allegation that the defendant had fraudulently transferred assets to avoid creditor obligations. The defendant argued a receiver could not be appointed for an LLC when the debtor was merely a member. **Held**, the exclusive charging order remedy precluded a creditor		

State	Cases	Remedy	Jurisdiction	State Law Applied
		of a member obtaining the appointment of a receiver.		
Louisiana **CAT IV*** **Not Exclusive**	Seven Arts Filmed Entertainment Ltd. v. Jonesfilm, 538 Fed. Appx. 444, 2013 WL 4018659 (C.A.5, La., Aug. 08, 2013) (NO. 12-31176).	**Charging orders/contempt.** The district court determined that Hoffman, the other judgment debtors, and Leeway disobeyed specific information orders attached to the charging orders. In November 2011 and November 2012, it held them in contempt and ordered them to deliver the garnished funds and pay Jonesfilm more than $21,000 in attorneys' fees. The debtors challenged the contempt orders on appeal. Under a de novo review, the orders were affirmed.		
	Seven Arts Pictures, Inc. v. Jonesfilm, 512 Fed. Appx. 419, 2013 WL 599661 (5th Cir. Feb. 18, 2013).	**Jurisdiction/failure to object**. When a party violates a court order (charging order) without objection, asking the court to modify or vacate it, or even informing the court why it cannot or will not obey it, the court may hold the party in contempt without first deciding whether the disobedience was justified. Even if justified, the party must object before disobedience. In part, the objection is to Louisiana's personal jurisdiction over Hoffman under its long-arm statute. It was fair to subject Hoffman to suit in Louisiana. He has held himself out as a resident of the state, and the burden on him is minimal seeing as much of his business is done in the state and he owns residences there. Jonesfilm seeks to satisfy its outstanding judgments against Hoffman using his Louisiana property, which gives Louisiana an interest in the outcome of this litigation.		

State	Cases	Remedy	Jurisdiction	State Law Applied
	Seven Arts Pictures, Inc. v. Jonesfilm, 2012 WL 5398439 (E. D. La. 2012).	**Charging order/Louisiana LLC/California judgment.** Jonesfilm obtained a California judgment in 2004 against Hoffman and several of his affiliated entities. Receiving no payments, Jonesfilm registered the California judgments in Louisiana and commenced action to collect on the debts. Specifically, Jonesfilm sought and the court granted charging orders against defendant's interests in five Louisiana LLCs. Finally, the court ordered judgment debtors to deliver financial statements, tax returns, and K–1 documentation of the judgment debtors and the Louisiana limited liability companies. Upon later failure to do so the court ordered the defendants in contempt.		
	Channelside Services, LLC v. Chrysochoos Group, Inc., 194 So.3d 751 (2016).	Channelside, a judgment creditor of Chrysochoos with a charging order against its 50% interest in JTMC Enterprises, LLC, filed a motion to compel JTMC to produce records relating to any indebtedness to Chrysochoos. The appellate court denied the motion because Louisiana LLC statutes granted Channelside only the rights of an assignee, not the rights of a member, and only a member had the right to inspect LLC records.		
	Abbett v. Oya, LLC, ___ A.3d. __, 2016 WL 4071514 (2016).	A charging order may be issued against a member's interest in a dissolved LLC until it is proven that winding up has concluded and no further distributions may be made.		

State	Cases	Remedy	Jurisdiction	State Law Applied
Maine **CAT II* Exclusive**				
Maryland **CAT I* Exclusive**	Hanna v. Baier, No. 20-C-12-007903 (Md. Cir. Ct. Jan. 30, 2013).	**Foreign LLC/foreclosure precluded.** Judgment creditor sought to foreclose on a Maryland resident's interest in a Delaware LLC when a charging order was not effective in satisfying the judgment. Maryland law permits foreclosure but Delaware precludes foreclosure. Unlike the similar Fannie Mae case in Minnesota, the foreign LLC had registered to transact business in Maryland and therefore had consented to the application of its laws. Nonetheless, the court determined that since Maryland law applied to domestic LLCs by virtue of the definitions of domestic and foreign LLCs, that Maryland charging order law did not apply. Even if it did, the expansive language with regard to internal affairs of a foreign LLC (liability of a member) means that Delaware law must apply since this case implicates the liability of a member. The first prong of the opinion is in line with the Fannie Mae case in Minnesota. The second prong is clearly wrong. Internal affairs statutes referring to "liability of a member" refer to the member's liability for debts of the LLC, not to third party creditors.		

State	Cases	Remedy	Jurisdiction	State Law Applied
	Keeler v. Academy of American Franciscan History, Inc., 178 Md. App. 648, 943 A. 2d 630 (2008); see also In re Keeler, 257 B.R. 442 (Bankr. D. Md. Jan. 16, 2001) (charging order is a pre-petition lien that passes through bankruptcy unscathed)	**Charging order/partnership:** Under the circumstances and language of Maryland statute, charging order was a final judgment that settled the rights of the parties at time it was issued. Therefore, charging order remains enforceable even though the underlying judgment has expired. Does not discuss foreclosure, but quotes statutory language that foreclosure is permitted.		
	In re Modalno, 412 B.R. 715 (Bankr. D. Md. May 19, 2006), aff'd 266 Fed. Appx. 272 (4th Cir. Md. Feb 21, 2008)	**LLC/bankruptcy**: Where debtor's single member Delaware LLC was dissolved upon debtor's filing of bankruptcy, trustee in bankruptcy (who is the successor to property of debtor's estate and the legal representative of the state) may revive LLC and, by stepping into shoes of debtor, may exercise management and governance rights in LLC; court distinguished single member LLC's from multi-member LLC's. Cited In Re Albright as persuasive.		
	Lauer Construction, Inc. v. Schrift, 123 Md. App. 112, 716 A.2d 1096 (1996)	**Charging order/limited partnership/foreclosure:** Judgment creditor could force sale of debtor general partner's interest in limited partnership. Court noted that effective July 1, 1998, Maryland has repealed UPA and adopted RUPA, in which the pertinent provisions of the Act remain substantively the same, with the exception that the charging order provision now expressly provides that a charging order is the creditor's exclusive remedy against a partnership interest.		

State	Cases	Remedy	Jurisdiction	State Law Applied
Massachusetts **CAT IV*** **Not Exclusive**	First National Bank of Louisville v. Young, 1995 WL 549128 (D. Mass. July 21, 1995)	**Charging Order/Partnership:** Judgment debtor sought to modify charging order against his partnership interest, in order to pay to the IRS any federal income tax which might become due upon sale of such interest. The Court denied his motion, noting that the charging order created an equitable lien in favor of the judgment creditor, which is superior to subsequent liens, claims of the IRS, and the rights of a bankruptcy trustee as a "hypothetical lien creditor". The charging order is a final order of the Court and its integrity should not be disturbed.		
Michigan **CAT II*** **Exclusive**	Florence Cement Company v. Vittraino, 292 Mich. App. 461, 807 N.W.2d 917 Mich. App. 2011).	**LLC loan as distribution.** A creditor obtained a judgment against the LLC and both its members but neglected to obtain a charging order against the members. Subsequently, the LLC made payments to the members in the form of payments on a "loan" from the members to the LLC. The Court determined that the payments were "distributions" made with knowledge, consent and approval of the members at a time when the LLC was insolvent and thus the members were personally liable to repay the loan payments.		
Minnesota **CAT IV*** **Exclusive**	George E. Antrim, III, PLLC v. Samar Sabri, 2014 WL 4798922 (Mn. App. September 29, 2014.	LLC: Antrim, an attorney, represented Azzam and Samar Sabri, husband and wife, in a lawsuit regarding Samar's 38% interest in a Minnesota LLC. Azzam transferred his interest in the LLC to his spouse Samar prior to his death. The lawsuit asserted the other two LLC control members, one of which was Azzam's brother, were freezing Samar		

State	Cases	Remedy	Jurisdiction	State Law Applied
		out of the LLC. Azzam retained Antrim and the lawsuit was filed on Samar's behalf against the LLC and the other two members. Samar did not sign the retainer agreement. Following an appraisal of the LLC property, Samar offered to sell her interest to the defendants for $1,500,000 and they countered at $1,000,000 but no agreement was reached. While Azzam was quite ill the trial court dismissed Samar's claims and Azzam instructed Antrim to appeal. However, at that time Samar instructed Antrim to contact the defendants to negotiate a settlement but his calls were never returned. Later, with the assistance of other counsel and without notice to Antrim, Samar executed a settlement with Azzmi, Azzam's brother and member of the LLC, to buy her out for $1,300,000. Her husband passed away shortly thereafter. When Samar refused to pay Antrim's $350,000 legal bills, he sued and sought foreclosure of his statutory attorney lien (Minn. Stat. § 481.13, subd. 1(a) (2012)). The trial court denied his claims for attorney fees asserting that his contract was with her husband and not her. On appeal, the court determined she was also liable under an implied in fact contract. Antrim then sought to "foreclose" his resulting statutory attorney lien (now a judgment lien) that attached to the subject of the lawsuit, the LLC membership interests Samar had transferred to her deceased husband's brother. The brother had notice of the lien since he was a defendant in the lawsuit. Antrim's lawsuit established the judgment that he will now be able to collect through a foreclosure sale of the LLC		

State	Cases	Remedy	Jurisdiction	State Law Applied
		interests transferred. Presumably, Samar and her brother-in-law will be required to determine inter se responsibility for the unpaid fees.		
	Fannie Mae v. Heather Apartments Ltd. Partnership, Not Reported in N.W.2d, 2013 WL 6223564 (Minn. App., Dec. 02, 2013) (NO. A13-0562).	**Foreign LLC/remedies not exclusive.** Judgment debtor appealed civil contempt order that a transfer of his interest in a Swiss bank account to an offshore LLC, in which he had sole or nearly all the interests, violated an order entered in favor of the judgment creditor. Court affirmed and indicated in dicta that the exclusive remedy provisions of the Minnesota LLC law did not limit the judgment creditor because the offshore was not a Minnesota LLC. The opinion refers to the definition of domestic and foreign LLCs to determine that Minnesota LLC law did not apply but other Minnesota collection law did apply. The LLC itself was not registered to business in Minnesota nor had otherwise consented to the application of its laws. The Minnesota Supreme Court declined certiorari on the case. See related Hanna v. Baier, a Maryland case, where an appeals court used these definitions to determine Delaware law applied in a Maryland charging order case.		
	General Elec. Capital Corp. v. JLT Aircraft Holding Co. LLC, 2010 WL 3023316 (D. Minn. July 28, 2010)	**Charging order/LLC:** General Elec. Capital Corp. obtained a multimillion dollar judgment against Gerald Trooian and two LLCs in which he had an interest. Trooian also had interests in 28 additional Delaware and Minnesota LLCs and LPs. Applying Minnesota law, the federal court granted a charging order against Trooian's interests in the non-debtor		

State	Cases	Remedy	Jurisdiction	State Law Applied
		LLCs and LPs, and ordered them to produce various organizational and financial documents. The court also gave the non-debtor entities the opportunity to appear at a hearing to object to the production of certain documents, and show cause why an order requiring each entity to pay amounts distributable or payable to Trooian to the creditors until the judgment is satisfied should not be entered.		
	In re Hecker, 414 B.R. 499 (D. Minn. Sept. 25, 2009) See also In re Schwab, 378 B.R. 854 (D. Minn. Dec. 4, 2007) (accounts receivable of debtor's wholly-owned LLC, which LLC had billed as charges for debtor's labor, would as a matter of fact be treated as personal earnings of debtor on reverse-veil-piercing theory)	**Reverse pierce/LLC:** Trustee objected to chapter7's debtor's claim of a Minnesota homestead exemption in real property which he occupied , but which was owned by an LLC (part of an interconnected web of businesses primarily but not exclusively owned by debtor). Lengthy discussion by court of equitable remedy of reverse piercing under Minnesota law, noting that Minnesota courts allow a debtor, whose residence is owned by a corporate entity of which the debtor is the principal, to pierce the corporate veil under carefully controlled circumstances to claim a homestead exemption. This approach ("insider" reverse piercing in which a debtor exempts assets held by a corporate entity) "appears to be unique to Minnesota." In this case, debtor did not demonstrate a sufficient closeness of identity and a lack of prejudice to shareholders and creditors, nor did he demonstrate that it would be unfair and unjust not to pierce the corporate veil.		

State	Cases	Remedy	Jurisdiction	State Law Applied
	Chrysler Credit Corp. v. Peterson, 342 N.W. 2d 170 (Minn. App. 1984) **Note:** Comments to the charging order statute state that, consonant with partnership law, judgment creditor status does not give a nonmember creditor any right to become a member of a limited liability company or to exercise governance rights. A creditor who seeks such a right must become an assignee of governance rights under section 322B.313 (Assignment of a Complete Membership Interest and of Governance Rights Coupled with an Assignment of Financial Rights). **Note:** Charging order statute, M.S.A. § 322B.32 (Rights of judgment creditor), refers to assignees's rights under § 322B.31, which states in part: "Notwithstanding any provision of law, articles of organization, member control agreement, bylaws, other agreement, resolution, or action to the contrary, a security interest in a member's financial rights may be foreclosed and otherwise enforced…"	**Charging order/limited partnership**: Charge order is exclusive remedy for a judgment creditor of a limited partner. Where judgment creditor alleges fraudulent conveyance of limited partnership assets, he may be awarded charging order before determination of fraudulent conveyance; charging order attaches to whatever limited partnership interest, if any, debtor is later determined to have in property conveyed.		

State	Cases	Remedy	Jurisdiction	State Law Applied
Mississippi **CAT IV* Exclusive**	In re Madison Fish House, LLC, 2007 WL 5708962 (Bkrtcy. S.D. Miss. Sept. 20, 2007)	**Charging order/LLC/bankruptcy:** Where Madison Fish House filed under Ch. 11, court lifted automatic stay to allow judgment creditor to proceed with its application for a charging order against judgment debtor/100% owner of Madison Fish House, and to receive any and all distributions debtor would be allowed to receive up to full amount of judgment owed. The court also ordered that creditor should not proceed to execute, repossess, foreclose or in any other manner seek possession of the assets of Madison Fish House, and that debtor should make all payments under charging order to which creditor was entitled.		
	Benson v. City Finance Co., No. 1:02CV242-D-D, 2003 WL 21517998 (N.D. Miss. May 16, 2003)	**Veil piercing/LLC/jurisdiction:** Washington Mutual, Inc. moved to dismiss claims against it for lack of personal jurisdiction. Plaintiffs attempted to establish jurisdiction by piercing the corporate veil of Washington Mutual Finance Group, LLC. Since the liability of an LLC's members or owners is to be governed by the laws of the state under which the LLC is organized, Delaware law controls as to whether plaintiffs can pierce the LLCs corporate veil and exercise personal jurisdiction over Washington Mutual, Inc. based upon the LLCs contacts with the state of Mississippi. The plaintiffs did not meet the elements required under Delaware law, nor did they allege that the LLC was undercapitalized. Therefore the motion to dismiss was granted.	Defendant Washington Mutual, Inc. is a corporation organized and existing under the laws of the state of Washington, where it has its principal place of business. Defendant Washington Mutual Finance Group, LLC is a limited liability company organized under the laws of the state of Delaware.	**Delaware**

State	Cases	Remedy	Jurisdiction	State Law Applied
Missouri **CAT IV* Not Exclusive**	St. Louis Bank, LLC v. Kohn, 517 S.W.3d 666 (MO Ct App 2017).	The court reversed a charging order because the trial court granted the order solely on the basis of the facts pleased in the motion without adequate evidence the facts were true.		
	Disalvo Properties, LLC v. Bluff View Commercial, LLC, 464 S.W.3d 243 (Mo. App. E.D. 2015).	**Charging Order/LLC:** The trial court granted the judgment creditor a charging order against debtor's two Missouri LLC interests but denied foreclosure. In a case of first impression, the Court of Appeals affirmed that foreclosure of an LLC charging order is precluded. Like the limited partnership statute, the nearly identical Missouri LLC charging statute is silent regarding foreclosure and neither states it is an exclusive remedy. However, the Missouri general partnership statute in the LLC context because it used the identical limited partnership language but did not include any linkage language to general partnership law. As a result, the court determined that when the legislature so used the limited partnership language (that permitted foreclosure through linkage to general partnership law) it intended to "change" the limited partnership foreclosure result and silently and obliquely preclude foreclosure. The case was not appealed and so will remain controversial. Many state LLC charging order statutes use similar limited partnership language. In those states the issue will remain whether the legislature intended to allow or preclude foreclosure in an LLC context when using limited partnership language that permitted		

State	Cases	Remedy	Jurisdiction	State Law Applied
		foreclosure. Basing presumed legislative intent on the failure to include a linkage statute may be more tenuous than presuming the legislature intended the "same result" in the LLC context as in the limited partnership context – foreclosure permitted. Otherwise, as is now the case in Missouri, foreclosure is permitted in a general and limited partnership but not in an LLC and without clear language justifying the disparate impact.		
	Noble v. Noble, 456 S.W.3d 120, 2015 WL 1120058 (Mo. App. March 10, 2015).	**Charging order/indefinite judgment.** The wife's motions to quash charging order against her husband's LLC was granted because the marriage dissolution judgment was uncertain as to amount. Contra, see Gaslowitz (Georgia).		
	Regions Bank v. Alverne Associates, LLC, 456 S.W.3d 52, 2014 WL 6913237 (Mo. App. Dec. 9, 2014).	**Charging order/indefinite judgment.** Charging order denied because judgment inadequately definite.		
	Deutsch v. Wolff, 7 S.W.3d 460 (Mo. App. 1999)	**Charging Order/LP:** Where court found trustee and general partner misappropriated partnership assets and breached his fiduciary duty to abstain from self-dealing, court could enter a charging order on behalf of limited partner, and appoint a receiver to administer general partner's interest in partnership, authorize sale thereof, and temporarily assume any management duties with respect to partnership. A partner's individual interest is personal property, not partnership property, and may be sold to satisfy that partner's individual debts.		

State	Cases	Remedy	Jurisdiction	State Law Applied
	Wills v. Wills, 750 S.W. 2d 567 (Mo. App. 1988)	**Charging order/partnership:** Harmonizing the provisions of Missouri's Uniform Partnership Law with its Child Support Court Enforcement Act, Court found that charging order against former spouse/judgment debtor's partnership interest was appropriate process by which former spouse/judgment creditor could "seize" partner's share of the profits and surplus in the partnership up to the unsatisfied amount of judgment or arrearages for child support. Without discussion Court observed partner's interest in the partnership was subject to foreclosure.		
Montana **CAT I* Exclusive**	Jonas v. Jonas, 2010 WL 4527053 (Mont. Nov. 9, 2010) **Note:** The Official Comments state that charging order statute is modeled after ULLCA (1996): "A charging order is the only remedy by which a judgment creditor of a member or a member's transferee may reach the distributional interest of a member or member's transferee. Under Section 503(e) [35-8-707(6)], the distributional interest of a member or transferee is limited to the member's right to receive distributions from the company and to seek judicial liquidation of the company."		**Jurisdiction/charging order/ foreclosure.** Montana Court enforced a one million dollar New Jersey judgment by a spouse against her former husband pursuant to the Uniform Enforcement of Foreign Judgments Act. A few months later she filed a Motion for Charging Order, Appointment of Receiver, Foreclosure of Interest and Judicial Dissolution of his LLC. The motion was granted with proceeds applied to satisfy the judgment and any excess sales proceeds, if any, to the former spouse.	

State	Cases	Remedy	Jurisdiction	State Law Applied
	In re Neal, ___ B.R. ___, 2013 WL 12108275 (W.D. Ten. 2013)	Husband and wife owned 100% of a Montana SMLLC (not a debtor in bankruptcy) holding a motor home and a motorcycle when they filed a Chapter 7 petition in Tennessee. The trustee sought to sell the SMLLC assets directly but the debtors argued the trustee must first dissolve the SMLLC. The Tennessee bankruptcy court applied Montana state LLC law to resolve the question under the governing internal affairs law. The court determined the SMLLC dissolved upon filing a petition and the trustee had the authority to wind up its affairs, including the right to sell its assets.		
Nebraska **CAT I* Exclusive**	Janice M. Hinrichsen, Inc. v. Messersmith Ventures, LLC, 296 Neb. 712 (NE S. Ct. 2017). Lincoln Provision, Inc. v. Puretz, PMP, LLC, 2013 WL 595212 (D. Neb. February, 15, 2013).	The judgment creditor corporation (JMH) held a judgment against Risk Assessment and Management, Inc. (RAM) which later transferred assets to a controlled LLC (MV). The transfer was alleged a fraudulent transfer. The court determined that the LLC exclusive charging order remedy did not preclude assertion of a fraudulent transfer action against the LLC after the judgment. **Charging order/disassociation.** A corporate member (Lincoln - P) sued the other member (Puretz - D) of a two- member LLC (Hastings) in Federal Court seeking "fair value" of its interest due to a voluntary dissociation (7/2) under the Illinois Act. D asserted P dissociated under an earlier email (6/21) agreeing that if full operating agreement not reached by certain date (7/2), the nonperforming party could be bought out by the performing party for a return of "cash contributed," not fair value.		

State	Cases	Remedy	Jurisdiction	State Law Applied
		Agreement was not reached by 7/2. On that date P gave written notice to dissociate under the terms of the Illinois Act entitling it to a return of the fair value of its interest. Later, D adopted a specific operating agreement for the SMLLC (Hastings) providing that P dissociated on an earlier date and according to the later adoption was not entitled to receive a distribution and remained obligated to make the capital contribution. Held: The later amendment did not bind the transferee to the terms regarding the alleged earlier dissociation and factual dispute precluded summary judgment on date of P's dissociation.		
	American National Bank v. Medved, 801 N.W. 2d 230, 2011 WL 2586341 (Neb.)	**LLC/community property/conflict of laws:** Nebraska judgment domesticated in Arizona raising issue of applicable law. Court determined whether there was a true conflict since Nebraska law clearly permits a charging order. Assumed that Nebraska LLC interests were community property under Arizona law. Case determined that no difference between the law of the two states affected the result.		
Nevada **CAT III* Exclusive**	In re Tarkanian, 562 Bankr. R. 424 (D. Nev. 2014).	When the sole member of a Nevada LLC whose interest is subject to a valid charging order, the trustee takes control of both economic and management rights.		

State	Cases	Remedy	Jurisdiction	State Law Applied
	Transfirst Group, Inc. v. Magliarditi, ___ F. 3rd __, 2017 WL 2294288 (NV D Ct 2017).	The court determined that the charging order exclusive remedy against an LLC member does not preclude the creditor from pursuing the LLC directly under an alter ego theory.		
	Sand Creek Partners, Ltd. v. American Federal Savings and Loan, Slip Copy, 2015 WL 316750 (DC NV 2015).	**LLP/Charging order/jurisdiction.** Bortles sued American in a Colorado state court and prevailed because the Bank failed to completely fund a Colorado. The Bank removed the case to Colorado federal court and it prevailed on its counterclaims. The judgment was about to expire after nearly twenty years. The then current creditor assignee moved to renew and was granted. The Colorado judgment was registered in Nevada where Bortles then resided. In the debtor exam Bortles indicated he was a general partner in two limited partnerships but he owned a zero interest in both. Bortles argued the judgments were invalid because of faulty assignment but the Court refused to reconsider the validity of a judgment issued by another court in another state. Finally, the creditor requested that Bortles be required to surrender his partnership interests in two Hawaiian limited partnerships. However, the Nevada Court determined that the creditor's request for a charging order "is governed" by the Hawaiian charging order statutes, where the limited partnerships were formed. Bortles argued a charging order was improper because (i) Nevada law precluded a charging order and (ii) there was no property to charge. The Court disagreed and determined Hawaiian law applied and therefore granted a charging order applying Hawaii law (even though he testified he had a zero interest).		

State	Cases	Remedy	Jurisdiction	State Law Applied
	In re Cleveland, 519 Bankr. 304 (D. Ct. Nev. 2014).	**SMLLC/Trustee's rights.** Cleveland filed a Chapter 7 petition while owning 100% of two Nevada LLCs. The Bankruptcy Court ruled that the trustee had no right to sell or take ownership of the assets of the two SMLLCs. The LLC interests were property of the estate and not exempt however on appeal the debtor argued that the trustee was limited to a charging order against the financial interests in the two SMLLCs. Citing *Albright*, the court determined that the trustee succeeded to the debtor's rights, including the right to control the entity. The debtor however further argued that the trustee's rights to "manage" were limited when the LLC is run by or deals with matters such as professional practices or professional. So, a trustee could not manage a law or medical firm. The Bankruptcy Court agreed this limitation applied because the LLC required state examination and licensing. On appeal, the Court determined, even in such cases, the limitation applied to management, not liquidation and sale of all assets.		
	Renteria v. Canepa, 2013 WL 3155348 (D. Nev. June 19, 2013) (NO. 3:11-CV-00534-RCJ).	**Charging order/small corporation; priority**. In connection with operation of a bankrupt corporation, Canepa guaranteed unpaid notes to Renteria subsequently reduced to judgment. When unpaid, Renteria sought a charging order against Canepa's membership interest in a Nevada LLC as well as his "stock in two Nevada corporations." The motion was approved because Nevada statutes (Nev. Rev. Stat. § 78.746) specifically permit a charging		

State	Cases	Remedy	Jurisdiction	State Law Applied
		order against a small corporation with less than 100 shareholders that is not also a professional corporation). The professional corporation prohibition against a charging order is related to the ownership restriction in such entities stated in Nev. Rev. Stat. § 89.070(1)(a) (no professional entity may issue "any of its owner's interest" to anyone other than a natural person who is licensed to render the same specific professional services). Canepa also sought to resist a charging order on the basis that the IRS had filed a Notice of Federal Tax Liens before the judgment at issue. The Court granted the charging order on the basis that priority between the judgment creditor and the IRS did not preclude a subsequent charging order and that the IRS would have to assert its priority.		
	Rock Bay v. Maybourne, Inc., 298 P. 3d 441 (2013)	**LLC/records/discovery.** An appeal concerning an LLC motion to quash subpoenas for LLC records. Held: The relationship between the judgment debtor and the nonparty LLC raised reasonable suspicion as to the good faith of asset transfers between the two so the judgment creditor was entitled to conduct discovery of LLC's assets; there was nothing about the relationship between company and judgment debtor that raised suspicion sufficient to allow judgment creditors access to company's actual financial records; but the judgment creditors were entitled to subpoena bank records of the nonparty LLC.		

State	Cases	Remedy	Jurisdiction	State Law Applied
	In re Blixseth, B.R. _, 2012 WL 6562839 (9th Cir. BAP, Nev. 2012).	**Bankruptcy: Venue over LLC Assets.** In issue of apparent first impression, the Ninth Circuit Bankruptcy Appellate Panel determined that an involuntary Chapter 7 case filed by a petitioning creditor seeking execution on an individual bankrupt's interest in a Nevada LLC was properly filed in Nevada. Under BRC § 1408(1) a petition may be properly filed in the debtor's (1) domicile, (2) residence, (3) principal place of business in the United States, or (4) principal place of assets in the United States. The bankrupt failed the first three tests so the involuntary petitioner sought a declaration that the "principal place" of the debtor's assets was located in Nevada where the debtor's principal LLC equity interests were formed and held Nevada real property. The debtor did not contest that the LLCs were formed in Nevada, owned Nevada real estate and the LLCs constituted his principal assets. However, the debtor contended that the LLC interests were intangible personal property without a physical location other than the owner's domicile. Since the owner was not domiciled in Nevada, he contended the Nevada venue was improper. The Court "created" a special bankruptcy rule that determined venue over a debtor's intangible personal property (the LLC interests) based on the LLC ownership of assets (Nevada). The Court relied upon the Nevada charging order that permitted a judgment creditor to obtain a charging order over a Nevada LLC.		

State	Cases	Remedy	Jurisdiction	State Law Applied
	Weddell v. H2O, Inc., 271 P. 3d 743 (Nev. 2012).	**LLC operating agreement/charging order/ purchase option.** Complex case involving displacement of a manager of an LLC. A judgment creditor of the manager was not entitled to exercise the management rights of the judgment debtor but rather was merely entitled to exercise the rights of an assignee (but is not an assignee). Importantly, the operating agreement may expressly specify that the entry of a charging order triggers a purchase option in favor of the other members; payments made pursuant to that operating agreement option are not distributions from the LLC and hence not subject to payment to the creditor under the charging order.		
	LFC Marketing Group, Inc. v. Loomis, 116 Nev. 896, 8 P.3d 841 (2000). See Bighorn Development, Inc. v. Trumpower, No. 3:05-CV-00161-ECR (RAM), 2008 WL 873595 (D. Nev. March 27, 2008). (Here, the equities favor using reverse piercing, but the facts do not.)	**Reverse pierce/corporation:** Under Nevada law, reverse piercing is appropriate in those limited instances where the particular facts and equities show the existence of an alter ego relationship and require that the corporate fiction be ignored so that justice may be promoted.		
	Tupper V. Kroc, 88 Nev. 146, 494 P.2d 1275 (1972)	**Charging order/LP/foreclosure:** When sole limited partner obtained judgment against general partner, limited partner entitled to receive charging order against general partner's interest in partnership, and to foreclose on that interest		

State	Cases	Remedy	Jurisdiction	State Law Applied
		(i.e., receive proceeds from sale of general partner's share of the profits and surplus). Rejecting debtor partner's claim that assignment of his partnership interest was inconsistent with the terms of the partnership agreement, the Court stated: "[T]he partnership agreements could not divest the district court of its powers provided by statute to charge and sell an interest of a partner in a partnership."		
New Hampshire **CAT II Exclusive** (excluding single-member LLCs) **CAT I Not Exclusive** (single-member LLCs)	Baybank v. Catamount Construction, Inc., 141 N.H. 780, 693 A.2d 1163 (1997)	**Charging order/limited partnership/foreclosure:** Court looked to remedies under state UPA to supplement state ULPA, which allows for charging order against limited partner's interests, but does not explicitly provide a method for enforcing the charging order. Court concluded foreclosure on and sale of limited partner's economic interests in the partnership, as well as remedies such as appointment of a receiver, are appropriate, but that trial court erred in allowing judgment creditor with charging order to petition for dissolution of limited partnership.		
New Jersey CAT I EXCLUSIVE	Leonard v. Leonard, 52 A.3d 214, 2012 WL 4458390 (N.J.Super. 2012).	**Former spouse/higher lien priority.** Former spouse obtained charging order against former husband's 10% minority LLC interest. Notwithstanding that the applicable NJ statute provided that the charging order was the exclusive		

State	Cases	Remedy	Jurisdiction	State Law Applied
		remedy to a judgment creditor, the family court ordered a writ of execution ostensibly to create a higher lien priority against the husband's other lien creditors.		
	Zavodnick v. Leven, 340 N.J. Super. 94, 773 A.2d 1170 (2001).	**Charging order/partnership:** Judgment creditor received order charging debtor's partnership interest in a law firm. Since New Jersey UPA subjects judgment creditor's rights to exemption laws, the New Jersey "wage execution statute" applies to the charging order. In this case, money distributed to debtor from the law firm is income derived from net profits, analogous in the partner's economic life to an employee's wages, and within the terms of the statute. Even though statute caps liens on certain wages at ten percent, creditor here may seek an order directing partnership to pay him more than ten percent of debtor's distributive share of partnership profits. Court will strike an equitable balance between the interests of the creditor and debtor, taking into consideration the economic circumstances of debtor and his family, the size of the judgment, the length of time it has remained unpaid, the efforts debtor has made to satisfy his obligations, and other circumstances the court finds relevant.		

State	Cases	Remedy	Jurisdiction	State Law Applied
	Federal Deposit Insurance Corp. v. Birchwood Builders, Inc., 240 N.J. Super. 260, 573 A.2d 182 (1990).	**Statute of Limitations/Charging Order:** New York statute under which a lien on real estate expires after ten years is not applicable; the debtor's interest in the partnership is not real property but personal property. Thus New York statute under which civil judgments have a twenty- year life applies to underlying judgment, and action is not time barred. Under New Jersey UPL, a judgment creditor of an individual partner may levy on or charge that partner's interest in the partnership, and force a sale of it. Debtor partner has burden of proof that debt can be satisfied from the debtor's share of the profits in a reasonable period of time; in the absence of such proof, court has discretion to order sale.	**Personal jurisdiction:** In action by judgment creditor to "domesticate" New York judgment in New Jersey, Court denied debtor's contention that it lacked personal jurisdiction. Debtor was a New York resident, who owned a forty percent interest in a New Jersey partnership, which in turn owned a valuable tract of land in New Jersey. Debtor paid all taxes and expenses for the real property. As a co-owner of the land, debtor had requisite interest in New Jersey.	**New York** (to underlying judgment); **New Jersey** (to charging order)
New Mexico **CAT IV*** **Not Exclusive**	Galef v. Buena Vista Dairy, 117 N.M. 701, 875 P.2d 1132 (N.M. Ct. App. 1994)		**Foreign Judgment/Statute of Limitations:** Judgment creditor domesticated California judgment in New Mexico, and subsequently sought a charging order against debtor's interest in a New Mexico partnership. Debtor sought to dismiss as a violation of the statute of limitations. Court found: 1) action to domesticate California judgment was brought within the time period set forth in the California statute applicable to the underlying judgment; 2) the New Mexico court's judgment in that action converted the California judgment into a separate New Mexico judgment, with applicable New Mexico	**California** (to underlying judgment) **New Mexico** (to domesticated judgment & charging order)

State	Cases	Remedy	Jurisdiction	State Law Applied
			statutes of limitations to be measured from that date; and 3) creditor's proceeding for a charging order satisfied the limitation period of any of three alternative statutes of limitations, so the court did not need to decide which alternative is correct.	
	In re Lucas, 107 B.R. 332 (Bankr. D. N.M. Nov. 7, 1989)	**Charging order/partnership/bankruptcy:** Charging order against partner's interest in a partnership (i.e., his share of the profits and surplus, which is personal property) is an appropriate but not exclusive method of levy where state law also provides for garnishment.		
New York **CAT IV* Not Exclusive**	In re Vivaro Corporation, 524 B.R. 536 (2015).	**LLC Distribution/Statute of Limitation.** New York law normally extends a six-year statute of limitations to fraudulent transfers, whether actual or constructive fraud is alleged. However, the three-year specific LLC distributions recapture provision overrides the more general six- year statute of limitation.		
	Scher Law Firm, LLP v. DB Partners, LLC, 948 N.Y.S.2d 335 (2012).	**Charging order/Prior security agreement.** Court determined Bank had priority over deposited funds through a security agreement that defeated a later plaintiff's charging order lien. As a result, the charging order was a nullity to the extent of the Bank's prior lien.		

State	Cases	Remedy	Jurisdiction	State Law Applied
	Hotel 71 Mezz Lender LLC v. Falor, 2010 WL 519821 (N.Y. Feb. 16, 2010), 2010 N.Y. Slip Op. 01348	**Jurisdiction/intangible property:** Lender brought guaranty enforcement action against nondomiciliary guarantors of loan, seeking to attach defendant's ownership/membership interests in 22 out-of state LLCs and one privately held corporation. Guarantor's intangible and uncertificated ownership interests in these were "property" for purposes of attachment. Where court has personal jurisdiction over a nondomiciliary present in New York (as in this case), court has jurisdiction over that individual's tangible or intangible property, even if the situs of the property is outside New York. The Court reviewed previous law holding that where a creditor seeks to attach a debt (an intangible form of property) solely for security purposes (i.e., the debtor is subject to the court's personal jurisdiction), the situs of the debt is wherever the debtor is present. The Court then extended this analysis by noting that there is no real distinction between debt and intangible property under New York's attachment statute. Since the order of attachment was served on one defendant who is both subject to the personal jurisdiction of the court and is the proper garnishee of defendants' interests, "it follows that defendants' uncertificated ownership interests, which defendant Mitchell possesses or has custody over, travel with him, and were attachable in New York based on his presence in this state." In other words, the court concluded that the situs of defendants' property is in New York.	Nondomiciliary defendants signed guaranty of debt; guaranty was negotiated in New York, was to be governed by and construed in accordance with laws of New York State, and included defendants submission to the jurisdiction of any federal or state court in New York. Defendants had interests in 22 limited liability corporations formed in Delaware, Georgia and Florida, plus a privately held Florida corporation. Defendant Mitchell was served with the order of attachment in New York.	**New York**

State	Cases	Remedy	Jurisdiction	State Law Applied
		The relevant dividing line under New York's attachment statute is simply whether the interests are evidenced by written instruments, such as certificates, or not. Here, defendant's interests are not evidenced by "ownership" certificates or other written instruments.		
North Carolina **CAT IV* Exclusive**	McVicker v. McVicker, No. COA14-47, N.C.App., June 17, 2014)	**Charging order/Divorce agreement.** Husband and wife entered a divorce settlement agreement approved by the Court. In part, the agreement made the wife a 50% owner in her ex-husband's SMLLC, MVOC, LLC. The agreement required several other payment forms and also provided wife a remedy for the husband's default - "may file a Motion for a Charging Order" with respect to any distribution that becomes due the husband from MVOC, LLC. The husband defaulted and the wife sought and was granted a contempt order against the husband's willful failure to pay. On appeal, the husband argued the charging order remedy in the agreement was "exclusive" and so the contempt order was inappropriate. The wife prevailed and the contempt order was sustained.		
	First Bank v. S&R Grandview, L.L.C., 755 S.E.2d 393, 2014 WL 846671 (N. C. App., March 04, 2014) (NO. COA13-838).	**Charging order not an assignment.** Judgment sought and obtained a charging order against debtor's membership interest in LLC in which he was also the manager. The court granting the motion stated that the order "effectuated an assignment" of debtor's interest in the LLC and thus the creditor had the rights of an assignee and that the LLC and all its members must treat the creditor		

State	Cases	Remedy	Jurisdiction	State Law Applied
		as an assignee. Moreover, the debtor was enjoined from exercising his rights as a member until the debt was satisfied. Debtor appealed. The Court reversed on both points that a charging order is an assignment and that debtor could be enjoined by the order from exercising his management rights.		
	In re S & R Grandview, LLC, Slip Copy, 2013 WL 5525729, 70 Collier Bankr.Cas.2d 703, (Bkrtcy. E. D. N. C., Oct. 04, 2013) (NO. 13-03098-8-RDD).	**Charging order/bankruptcy.** Bankruptcy court dismissed a petition for an LLC on motion of a member that the manager did not have authority to file the petition. The lack of authority argument, relied upon by the Bankruptcy court, was that a state charging order motion against the manager's LLC interest also provided that the manager was not to exercise any of the rights of a member. That order is on appeal but seems overly broad and outside scope of the charging order.		
	Simms v. Ball Street Ventures, LLC, 2012 WL 4755233 (M.D. N.C. 2012).	**LLC/charging order/garnishment.** After registering a District of Columbia judgment in North Carolina, the North Carolina court issued a charging order against defendant's interests in nine North Carolina LLCs. Plaintiff also sought to require the LLCs to appear to answer a garnishment action on the belief that the LLCs held money owned by the defendant. North Carolina law could be used to require the LLCs to produce records regarding property of the judgment debtor and to submit to examination regarding the same. However, the plaintiff sought neither		

State	Cases	Remedy	Jurisdiction	State Law Applied
		form of garnishment relief and hence the writ of garnishment against the LLCs was denied.		
	Herring v. Keasler, 150 N.C. App. 598, 563 S.E. 2d 614 (2002)	**Charging order/LLC/foreclosure**: Judgment creditor not entitled to seize and sell membership interests in charging order setting, but could only receive distributions from LLC; forced sale of a membership interest to satisfy a debt would necessarily entail the transfer of a member's ownership to another, thus permitting the purchaser to become a member without required consent of other members.		
North Dakota **CAT I* Exclusive**	Moen v. Moen, 519 N.W. 2d 10 (N.D. 1994)	**Charging order/partnership/foreclosure:** Ex-wife was granted charging order in former husband's partnership interest; the order stated the lien shall remain in effect until the judgment is satisfied. When former husband did not pay first of five installment payments awarded to wife, she foreclosed on the partnership interest, which was sold to her former brother-in-law at a sheriff's sale; her continuing lien survived the sheriff's sale. Court's determination that brother-in-law bought partnership interest subject to the continuing lien did not entitle him to rescission based on mistake of fact and law.		

State	Cases	Remedy	Jurisdiction	State Law Applied
Ohio **CAT IV* Not Exclusive**	Kerr Bldgs., Inc. v. Bishop, 2014 WL 6871355 (December 8, 2014).	**Charging order/Receiver.** Kerr obtained judgment, charging order and an appointment of receiver. Appeal to quash appointment of receiver was not timely and dismissed.		
	FirstMerit Bank, N.A. v. Xyran, Ltd., 2013 WL 1183340, (Ohio App. 8 Dist. March 21, 2013).	**Charging order/lien.** The Bank sought a charging order against an LLC that employed a physician. The LLC signed a note guaranteed by its two physician employees. Later the Bank discovered one of the physicians owned an interest in a separate LLC and sought a charging order against the physician's interest in that LLC. The physician argued this violated statutory law and the operating agreement that prohibits assignment of an interest to a person other than a physician (violating unauthorized practice rules). The Court determined the mere entry of a charging order is not an assignment but rather a lien on the economics associated with that interest.		
	Hicks v. The Cadle Company, F.Supp. (N.D. Ohio 2011) (2011 WL 3652439)	**Charging order/LLC:** A Colorado judgment creditor was precluded by Ohio law in using the general execution statutes to levy on an LLC interest and was limited to a charging order. No discussion of foreclosure. The decision indicates Ohio law is a common law exclusive remedy jurisdiction.		

State	Cases	Remedy	Jurisdiction	State Law Applied
	In re Foos, 405 B.R. 604 (Bankr. N.D. Ohio April 24, 2009)	**Charging order/partnership/foreclosure:** Remedies affording by charging order constitute the exclusive remedy for a judgment-creditor, and by extension a trustee in bankruptcy, against a debtor's economic interest in a partnership. Foreclosure under charging order is possible, although partners, including the judgment-debtor, are afforded the right of redemption.		
	Firstmerit Bank v. Washington Square Enterprises, No. 88798, 2007 WL 2206545 (Ohio App. 8 Dist. Aug. 2, 2007)	**Charging order/LLC:** Lower court abused its discretion by placing LLC and the real property it owned in receivership, when judgment debtor is a member of the LLC.. Judgment-creditor's remedy was a charging order with right to receive distributions that would have been paid to debtor. No discussion of foreclosure; Court noted that it expressed no opinion as to whether a judgment creditor of a member of an LLC could seek judicial dissolution of the company.		
	Monroe v. Berger, 297 B.R. 97 (S.D. Ohio June 13, 2003)	**Charging order/LP:** Where a charging order against judgment debtor's interest in a partnership was obtained prior to judgment debtor's bankruptcy, creditors enjoined from action to revive judgment. Stating that "it is not established in Ohio statutory or case law that a charging order constitutes a lien or creates a lien," the Court concluded that Ohio law does not provide that a charging order passes through bankruptcy unscathed.		

State	Cases	Remedy	Jurisdiction	State Law Applied
	OHIO. Vista Communications Group LLC v. Highline Capital Corp, __ F. 3rd __ (SD OH 2017).	Highline obtained an Ohio judgment against Williams the sole member of Vista, LLC, an Ohio LLC. Williams was a resident of Florida. It then domesticated the Ohio judgment in Florida. It then sought to garnish a bank account in Florida over which Williams had authority. Vista sought to intervene arguing it had an interest in those funds. Highline then filed a foreclosure action in Florida to foreclose on Williams' sole interest in Vista, an Ohio SMLLC. Under Florida SMLLC law, Highline purchased the entire Vista interest with a credit bid. Williams disputed the action arguing that Highline improperly applied Florida SMLLC foreclosure law to an Ohio LLC that allows only a transfer of economic rights upon foreclosure. The case was removed from the Ohio federal court to a Florida federal court to determine the proper outcome as to whether Highline owns the entire Vita membership interest (as permitted by Florida law) or only the economic rights in Vista (as permitted by Ohio law).		
Oklahoma **CAT II* Exclusive**	In re Stewart, 2017 WL 1740365 (WD Ok 2017).	The bankruptcy court followed the majority view that 11 USC § 105 grants the bankruptcy court the equitable power to exercise "substantive consolidation" to add a related but nondebtor assets to the debtors assets. A creditor has standing to bring such an action as well as the trustee. Moreover, the charging order exclusive remedy does not preclude the exercise of this equitable power over the alter ego LLC.		

State	Cases	Remedy	Jurisdiction	State Law Applied
	Southlake Equipment Co., Inc. v. Henson Gravel & Sand, LLC, 313 P.3d 289, 2013 WL 5657702, 2013 OK CIV APP 87 (Okla. Civ. App. Div. 4, Sept. 06, 2013) (NO. 110347).	**Charging order/no assignment.** The trial court order that defendant assign, transfer and convey debtor's entire interest in LLCs was clear error as the judgment creditor is limited to a charging order.		
	Scottsdale Insurance Company v. Tolliver, 2012 WL 524414 (N. D. Okla., February 16, 2012).	**LLC/Charging order/Fraudulent transfer.** LLC was not served with notice of fraudulent transfer action against its two owners and plaintiff failed to establish the transferors were insolvent at the time of the transfers as defined under the Uniform Fraudulent Transfer Act. Held – remanded to prove insolvency at time of transfer to LLC. The judgment creditor argued it should be able to execute against the LLC's assets since the existing charging order was ineffective unless distributions were actually made. On remand, the Court determined that in fact the judgment debtors were not insolvent (in part because transfers to the LLCs resulted in an increased value of the LLCs). However, the Court determined the transfer was nonetheless fraudulent because the transfers to the LLCs were made to use the charging order remedy to hinder or delay collection. See Scottsdale Ins. Co. v. Tolliver, 2012 WL 1581109 (N.D. Okla., May 04, 201).		
	Baldwin v. Bill and Carolyn Ltd Partnership, 2006 WL 2034217 (B.A.P. 10th Cir. July 11, 2006)	**LP/Bankruptcy:** Debtor's interests in limited family partnership became property of her estate at the time of filing petition in bankruptcy. Trustee in bankruptcy steps into shoes of debtor with respect to partnership interests and may assert whatever		

State	Cases	Remedy	Jurisdiction	State Law Applied
		rights debtor had as a partner under partnership agreement and state law, including right to seek dissolution. However, where debtor has neither management power under partnership agreement, nor any present right to dissolve or liquidate partnership, then neither does trustee.		
Oregon **CAT IV* Not Exclusive**	Robert M. Law Profit Sharing Plan v. Zemp, 279 Or.App. 808, 2016 WL 4014078 (2016).	In addition to the charging order, the court issued other orders to effectuate the charging orders including: (1) the companies were prohibited from making any loans until the judgment was paid; (2) the companies and their members were prohibited from transferring, modifying, or encumbering any partnership or membership interest without approval from the court or from Law until the judgment was paid; (3) the companies were required to open their books and certain tax records for inspection by Law; and (4) the companies were required to provide future financial statements to Law. On a motion for reconsideration, the court agreed these other orders were inappropriate and modified the earlier order.		

State	Cases	Remedy	Jurisdiction	State Law Applied
Pennsylvania **None** – The PA LLC Law of 1994 does not contain a provision expressly relating to a member's creditor's rights.	Marcharg v. Marcharg, 151 A.3d 187 (Pa Ct App 2016).	Former wife domesticated a Vermont judgment against her former husband in Pennsylvania and sought a charging order and foreclosure of that order. The husband argued the Pennsylvania limited partnership law did not authorize foreclosure but the court determined that the same law linked to general partnership law that did permit foreclosure. Accordingly, foreclosure was ordered.		
	In re Hantman, 508 B.R. 339, (E.D. Pa April 2, 2014).	**Charging Order/LLC.** Debtor guaranteed a bank note to a separate entity. Upon default, the creditor obtained a judgment against the entity and the guarantor. The creditor then filed a writ of garnishment against an unrelated LLC in which the debtor held an interest. The debtor sought to quash the writ arguing the funds held in the LLC capital account were exempt "wages." The state court denied debtor's argument and the writ remained valid. Debtor later filed bankruptcy to discharge the judgment but the creditor argued it held a secured interest perfected by garnishment. The bankruptcy court agreed that its proof of claim was secured by the prior writ.		

State	Cases	Remedy	Jurisdiction	State Law Applied
	In re Zambrano Corp., Slip Copy, 2014 WL 585305 (Bkrtcy. W. D. Pa., Feb. 13, 2014) (NO. ADV 09-02045-JAD, BR 09-20453-JAD).	**Charging order/partnership and LLCs/Trustee settlement.** Trustee sued and obtained judgments against Mr. Zambrano. Thereafter, the Trustee sought and obtained charging orders against Zambrano's interests in a partnership and LLCs but the trustee received no distributions. Zambrano was in control of all the entities and therefore the timing of the distributions. The Trustee therefore entered a settlement agreement but an unsecured creditor objected. In part, the Trustee argues that the hurdles to collection (entity owns assets in which Zambrano owns a portion of the entity) seriously reduce the value of the judgments. For various reasons, the Court rejected the settlement.		
	Klein v. Weidner, Civil Action No. 08-3798, slip copy, 2010 WL 571800 (E.D. Pa. Feb. 17 2010)	**Reverse pierce/LLC**: Where former spouse/judgment debtor used LLC form to perpetrate an injustice, former spouse/judgment creditor may reverse-pierce the corporate veil and treat LLCs assets as debtor's assets for purpose of collecting her judgment.		
	Zokaites v. Pittsburgh Irish Pubs, LLC, 962 A. 2d 1220 (Pa. Super. 2008) (charging order provisions of the PA General Partnerships (15 PA C.S.A. § 8345) and Limited Partnerships (15 PA C. S. A. § 8563) statutes apply by analogy; membership interest is divided into economic rights	**Charging order/LLC:** In the absence of unanimous approval of other members of LLC, judgment debtor member's interest in LLCs may not be transferred to a purchaser of all member rights. Court did not address whether foreclosure is possible assuming the purchaser acquired only transferee and not member rights. Extensive discussion of charging order as appropriate remedy by analogy to partnership statutes.		

State	Cases	Remedy	Jurisdiction	State Law Applied
	and governance rights; unless otherwise agreed by other members, a member can freely transfer only membership rights)			
	In re Allen, 228 B.R. 115 (Bankr. W.D. Pa. Dec. 18, 1998)	**Charging order/partnerships:** Under PA UPA and ULPA, a charging order is not the sole remedy of a judgment creditor against a partnership or limited partnership interest in Pennsylvania; therefore, judgment creditor could garnish the debtor's interest in the limited partnership interest and receive a garnishment lien.		
	Auburn Steel Co. v. American Steel Engineering Co., 1993 WL 257379 (E.D. Pa. July 2, 1993)	**LP/Charging order/Foreclosure:** Judgment creditor obtained charging order against debtor's LP interest and subsequently moved for an order to sell such interest. Court found that right of judgment creditor to charge partner's interest and force a sale applied to LPs as well as to partnerships. Debtor argued that provisions of Partnership Agreement precluded sale. Citing Tupper v. Kroc, 495 P. 2d 1275 (Nev. 1972), court concluded that a partnership agreement could not divest the District Court of its powers provided by statute to charge and sell an interest of a partner in a limited partnership. Court also noted that consent of nondebtor partners was not required for the purpose of foreclosing on a charged partnership asset.		

State	Cases	Remedy	Jurisdiction	State Law Applied
Rhode Island **CAT IV* Not Exclusive**				
South Carolina **CAT I* Exclusive**	Levy v. Carolinian, LLC, 763 S.E.2d 594 (SC 2014).	**LLC/Transferees.** Levy obtained a judgment and then a charging order against Patel, who owned an interest in Carolinian, LLC, a South Carolina LLC. Subsequently, Levy foreclosed and was the successful bidder ($215,000) at the foreclosure sale outbidding the LLC ($195,000) for the interest. The LLC operating agreement provided that the interest could be "redeemed" any time up to the foreclosure sale and that the LLC had a right to purchase the interest if an attempt to transfer was made without prior approval. The operating agreement also provided that no member could voluntarily or involuntarily sell an interest without approval of 67% of the remaining members and any purported sale was void. Levy refused to sell the interest arguing he was not subject to the terms of the operating agreement and filed a declaratory judgment action seeking to determine his purchase right at the foreclosure sale. The lower court determined that Levy "became subject to the operating agreement" when he became a transferee and thus was forced to sell to the LLC. The court reversed because the operating agreement only applied to members and he only became a transferee after the foreclosure sale. The Court cited		

State	Cases	Remedy	Jurisdiction	State Law Applied
	Kriti Ripley v. Emerald Investments, 746 S.E.2d 26, 2013 WL 3200596 (S.C. 2013).	South Carolina law that the operating agreement could not bind "third parties." Further the LLC failed to redeem because it was unwilling to pay an adequate price. **Foreclosure.** Kriti contributed cash to a South Carolina real property development LLC in exchange for a 30% interest and Emerald contributed real property for development in exchange for a 70% interest. Kriti obtained an arbitration monetary award against Emerald and its sole owner for misappropriation of funds (and other violations including failure to disclose that Emerald controlled a bankrupt entity that was dealing with the developed property). The award also divested Emerald of its 70% right and sought foreclosure of Emerald's economic interest in the South Carolina LLC. Emerald argued foreclosure would involve "forfeiture" of a significant, if not all , its equity in the LLC. The court ordered foreclosure and determined that while foreclosure is a drastic equitable relief, it is not a penalty or a forfeiture. Foreclosure was appropriate because distributions would not satisfy the judgment over a reasonable period of time. to vote. A New York court later confirmed the award. Unable to collect, Kriti registered the judgments in South Carolina.		

State	Cases	Remedy	Jurisdiction	State Law Applied
	Note: The official Comment to the statute states that: "A charging order is the only remedy by which a judgment creditor of a member or a member's transferee may reach the distributional interest of a member or member's transferee. Under Section 33-44-503(e), the distributional interest of a member or transferee is limited to the member's right to receive distributions from the company and to seek judicial liquidation of the company."			
South Dakota **CAT II* Exclusive**	**Note:** The official Comment to this section states that this section is similar to § 504 of the Uniform Limited Liability Company Act (1996).			
Tennessee **CAT IV* Exclusive**	Peach REO, LLC v. Rice, ___ F. 3d ___, 2017 WL 2963511 (W.D. TN 2017).	The creditor had a Tennessee money judgment and sought a charging order against the debtor who held a membership interest in several Tennessee LLCs. Each LLC had a choice of law provision in its operating agreement: some Tennessee, some Mississippi, and some Delaware. The court determined that the entry of a charging order is a lien and not an assignment or transfer. Therefore, anti- assignment language in the operating agreement was not applicable (this addresses a problem of federal tax law that struggles with the		

State	Cases	Remedy	Jurisdiction	State Law Applied
		question of whether a creditor holding a charging order lien is taxable on distributions – no, because the member remains the owner of the interest). Moreover, the operating agreement should not have been relevant to a third party creditor's charging order motion because the third party creditor was not a party to the operating agreement and cannot be bound, even as a third party beneficiary. The court respects the operating agreement choice of law provision and applies Delaware and Mississippi law to the charging order question for those LLCs. Once again, since the operating agreement should only apply to the members, respecting the choice of law provision does violate Tennessee law. In Tennessee, the Delaware and Mississippi LLCs are foreign limited liability companies and thus a judgment creditor in Tennessee is not restricted to the charging order remedy (unless, as here, the foreign law is applied). This becomes quite important on the issue of foreclosure because some states, like Delaware, preclude foreclosure (although not an issue in this case presumably if Peach seeks to foreclose on the Tennessee member's Delaware LLC interest, the Tennessee court would approve).		
	Arvest Bank v. Byrd, 2014 WL -------- (WD Ten. 2014).	**Charging order/Exclusive remedy.** Bank obtained a Tennessee judgment for fraud against husband and wife and their three Tennessee LLCs. A money judgment for a Federal judgment is usually enforced by a writ of execution unless the Court directs otherwise. Fed. Rule Civ. Proc. § 69.		

State	Cases	Remedy	Jurisdiction	State Law Applied
		However, the judgment must accord with the collection procedure of the state where the court is located. Since Tennessee law provides that the exclusive remedy of a judgment creditor with respect to the judgment debtor's interest in an LLC is a charging order against that member's distributional interest, that law applies.		
Texas	Gillet v. Zupt, LLC, --- S.W.3d ---- 2017 WL 716633 (Tx Ct App 2017).	In a case of first impression, the court determined that the exclusive charging order remedy does not preclude a turnover order with regard to the member's entire interest when the judgment creditor is the LLC itself.		
	TEXAS. Imes v. Galasso, ___ F. 3d ___, 2011 WL 13196081 (WD Tx 2011).	Imes, a judgment creditor sought and received a charging order against a Professional Corporation that was a 1% general partner in a Texas limited partnership law firm. Galasso, the debtor owned 100% of the PC and 99% of the LP law firm. It was clear that the judgment was against Galasso personally but unclear whether his PC was also a judgment debtor. If not, the charging order was improper. The court also refused to appoint a receiver for the PC in part because it would interfere with Texas law on who may own an economic interest in a PC (also deemed unnecessary).		
	Pajooh v. Royal West Invetments LLC, Series E, 518 S.W.3d 557 (Tx Ct App 2017).	An LLC Series obtained a judgment against a limited partner of a limited partnership. Later the Series obtained a turnover order as well as an order for the appointment of a receiver over the individual and the assets of the limited partnership. The court		

State	Cases	Remedy	Jurisdiction	State Law Applied
		determined that the exclusivity aspect of a charging order remedy does not preclude a turnover order or the appointment of a receiver but does preclude that receiver from exercising authority over the assets of an entity in which the debtor owns an interest.		
CAT II* Exclusive	In re Wilson, BR _, 2104 WL 3700634 (ND Tex, July 24, 2014).	**Bankruptcy/passive members.** Citing Ehmann, an Arizona case, the court determined that passive members of an LLC that owed no duties to the LLC were not parties to an executory contract and thus their full rights were transferrable.		
	In re Prodigy Services, LLC, 2014 WL 2936928 (Texas 14th Ct App June 26, 2014).	**LLC/Turnover Order.** The exclusive remedy language of the Texas LLC statute does not preclude a turnover order after distributions have been improperly made.		
	Scheel v. Alfaro, 406 S.W.3d 216, 2013 WL 2015103, Tex. App.–San Antonio 2013).	**Receiver's sale.** A motion to set aside a receiver's sale of assets was affirmed on appeal. The case involved a receiver's sale of a judgment debtor ownership in and assets of an LLC. The judgment creditor purchased both at a grossly inadequate price at the receiver's sale.		

State	Cases	Remedy	Jurisdiction	State Law Applied
	Stanley v. Reef Securities, Inc., 2010 WL 2252633 (Tex. App.-Dallas)	**LP/LLC/Distributions.** A judgment creditor's writ of execution was returned unsatisfied. It then sought a turnover order issued directly against the judgment debtor who held a limited partner interest in a limited partnership as well as a controlling interest in the limited liability company general partner. The turnover order sought past and "future" distributions from both the limited partnership and the limited liability company. The debtor asserted but lost the argument that the "distributions" were actually exempt "wages." The Court rejected the argument because the debtor failed to prove that the services provided were extraordinary to escape the default rule that payments must be for services beyond those expected at formation to enter the realm of wages. The debtor also lost the argument that the charging order provision was the exclusive remedy because that rule only applied to distributions not yet made. After a distribution occurs, it is subject to execution as any other asset. The case establishes that a turnover order issued to the debtor can be as effective as a charging order issued to the entity.		
	Goodman v. Compass Bank, ___ S.W.3d , 2016 WL 4142243 (2016).	The court determined a charging order is appropriate to reach future distributions if and when the distribution is authorized. However, the LLC is not required to be a party to the charging order suit as "a judgment creditor seeking a charging order has no justiciable cause of action against the entity to be charged."		

State	Cases	Remedy	Jurisdiction	State Law Applied
	Devoll v. Demonbreum, 2016 WL 4538805 (Tx Ct App 2016).	Demonbreum held a judgment and charging order against a former partner Norris Devoll who allegedly fraudulently transferred that partnership interest to his brother Gene Devoll who thereafter attempted to sell partnership assets. Demonbreum sought an injunction to prevent the partnership asset sale but Gene Devoll argued an injunction against a partnership could not arise from an action against a partner. The court determined otherwise to preclude fraud.		
	Fritts v. McDowell,, 2017 WL 3821889 (Tx Ct App 2017).	Affirmed dismissal of suit to foreclose a judgment lien. In 2012 Fritts obtained a charging order against McDowell and CMP, a related partnership. In 2013, Fritts filed a suit against other related parties and entered into a settlement agreement with a bankruptcy after the defendant filed. The agreement released McDowell and CMP and so the court determined that release dispositive. So, the judgment and lien no longer existed to foreclose.		
	Note: Texas cases below were issued prior to statutory amendment prohibiting foreclosure, effective September 1, 2009. For full text, see LLC Charging Order Statute Table.*			

State	Cases	Remedy	Jurisdiction	State Law Applied
	Moore v. Brunswick Homes, LLC, 379 B.R. 284 (Bankr. N.D. Tex. Nov. 15, 2007). See also Bramante v. McClain, 2007 WL 4555943 (W.D. Tex. Dec. 18, 2007)	**Reverse pierce/LLC:** Court noted that, while notion of reverse piercing has "rather thin roots in Texas jurisprudence," the theory has nevertheless been recognized as viable under Texas law by the Fifth Circuit. Further, while the case law deals with "alter ego" and veil piercing in the context of corporations, whether a business enterprise is an LLC or a corporation is a distinction without a difference in this context. Also, while the Texas legislature has significantly narrowed the alter ego doctrine in traditional veil piercing, it has not addressed reverse piercing. The court concluded reverse veil piercing should only be applied when it is clear that it will not prejudice non-culpable shareholders or other stakeholders (such as creditors) of a corporation.		
	World Fuel Services Corp. v. Moorehead, 229 F. Supp. 584 (N.D. Texas 2002)	**LLC/LP/Turnover/Charging Order:** Where requirement of Texas Turnover Statute was satisfied, and circumstances warranted Court to appoint receiver to collect, sell and liquidate all of defendant's non-exempt assets in satisfaction of judgment, including his interest in any limited partnerships and limited liability companies, a charging order was not necessary and was therefore denied.		
	Dispensa v. University State Bank, 951 S.W. 2d 797 (Tex. App. 1997)	**Partnership/charging order:** Trial Court order issuing charging order was not appealable by judgment debtor because (1) order did not resolve		

State	Cases	Remedy	Jurisdiction	State Law Applied
		all issues (*i.e.*, it did not address judgment creditor's request for an accounting); and (2)order did not fully determine rights of the parties involved (*e.g.*, it does not provide a method to determine extent of debtor's partnership interest).		
Utah **CAT I*** **Exclusive**	White v. White, 2017 WL 3326790 (UT Ct App 2017).	Wife sued former husband and obtained a judgment. She then sought and obtained a charging order against his SMLLC that owned his personal residence and she sought to foreclose the charging order. Before the foreclosure, the former husband sold the LLC residence and claimed a state homestead exemption made the proceeds largely exempt from execution. The court determined that even though the home was the former husband's personal residence, the homestead exemption must be claimed by the owner of the property – here the SMLLC. As a result, he was ordered to turn over the entire sales proceeds.		
	Baking Companies, Inc. v. Sycamore Family Bakery, Inc., F.3d. , 2015 WL 5009376 (D.C. August 21, 2015	**Charging Order/LLC:** Plaintiff sought civil contempt sanctions in Utah against a Nevada LLC for violating a Utah charging order against one of its two members, a Utah resident. The LLC argued the charging order was ineffective because it was not issued in Nevada. The court rejected the argument because the charging order did not implicate the internal affairs of the LLC and so the LLC was bound by a valid Utah judgment. Also, the LLC manager (judgment debtor's spouse) was		

State	Cases	Remedy	Jurisdiction	State Law Applied
		served with notice of the charging order and failed to object. Plaintiff argued that notwithstanding the order the LLC made non-proportional distributions (against the terms of the operating agreement) to the judgment debtor's spouse (the managing member). The LLC defended that the family LLC owned by the husband and wife made separate payments to the wife as compensation for her services.		
Vermont **CAT I*** **Exclusive**				
Virginia **CAT III*** **Exclusive**	Wooten v. Lightburn, Civil Action No. 1:08cv00049, slip copy, 2009 WL 2424686 (W.D. Va. Aug. 4, 2009) (court granted summary judgment allowing plaintiff to enforce earlier judgment through a charging order)	**Charging order/LLC:** Charging order is exclusive remedy by which judgment creditor may create a lien on defendant's transferable interest in two VA LLCs, under both VA LLC and limited partnership statutes; foreclosure not discussed.	Jurisdiction under 28 U.S.C. § 1332 based on diversity of citizenship: Plaintiff is Texas resident, Defendant is Virginia resident **Note:** Defendant is member of two VA LLCs; neither is a party to the case.	Virginia law applied under Fed. R. Civ. Pro. 69(a)(1)—when party seeks to enforce a money judgment, it must "accord with the procedure of the state where the court is located."

State	Cases	Remedy	Jurisdiction	State Law Applied
	C.F. Trust, Inc. v. First Flight LTD Partnership, 306 F. 3d 126 (4th C i r. 2 002) , a ff 'd 33 8 F. 3d 316 (2003). See also C.F. Trust, Inc. v. First Flight LTD Partnership, 266 (Although Va. Rev. ULPA prescribes certain remedies for creditors, such as § 50-73.46 which permits a court to charge the partnership interest of a limited partner against whom a judgment has been entered, nothing in the Act prohibits a court from piercing, or reverse piercing, the veil of a limited partnership.)	**Reverse pierce/LP:** After protracted litigation over a number of years, which included the issuance of various charging orders, court found factual grounds to "reverse pierce" limited partnership and declare that limited partnership was alter ego of limited partner, whose assets were therefore subject to judgments entered against limited partner.	Diversity jurisdiction asserted by two plaintiffs, a Florida corporation and a Nevada corporation, against a Virginia limited partnership, whose limited partners lived in Virginia, and various other entities; not challenged by defendants.	**Virginia**
	In the Matter of Pischke, 11 R.R. 913 (Bankr. E.D. Va. June 18, 1981)	**Charging order/partnerships.** Construing VA's UPA and ULPA, Court held that Virginia charging order statute supersedes other legislation in the area concerning satisfaction of a judgment creditor's claim against a partner's interest in a partnership; therefore, defendant judgment lien holders obtain priority, if at all, in the sequence in which they were granted charging orders by a court of competent jurisdiction.		

State	Cases	Remedy	Jurisdiction	State Law Applied
	Sky Cable, LLC v. Coley, 2016 WL 3926492 (July 18, 2016)	With an unsatisfied judgment, Sky Cable requested the Virginia court determine Randy Coley was the alter ego of his three Delaware LLCs such that the assets of each LLC was subject to the judgment (reverse pierce). The court applied Delaware law under the internal affairs doctrine. The court noted that while Delaware law had not applied the reverse pierce doctrine, it also had not rejected it (although one case hinted it might be applicable if properly presented). Given the serious abuse of formalities and other misdeeds (commingling assets, payments of personal expenses, etc.), the court granted the reverse pierce.		
Washington **CAT I*** **Not Exclusive**	Soundbuilt Northwest v. Price, 2011 WL 4929137 (Wash. App. October 18, 2011)	**Charging order/subsequent release.** The plaintiff secured a judgment and charging order against Price and Um personally for breaches related to a prior sale agreement of an LLC where both parties were members. Soundbuilt also received a judgment and charging order regarding breach of a sale to Price and Um of its interest in the LLC. Later, Sunbelt purchased the property that was the subject of the LLC agreement from the lender who received it in lieu of foreclosure. The lenders agreement of sale required Soundbuilt to sign a release for all claims arising out of any connection to the real		

State	Cases	Remedy	Jurisdiction	State Law Applied
		estate. Price and Um thereafter sought dismissal of Soundbuilt judgment and charging order because of the later release. The court vacated the prior judgment and charging order.		
	TCAP Corp. v. Gervin, 163 Wash. 2d 645, 185 P. 3d 589 (2008)		**Expiration of Foreign Judgment:** Where judgment creditor registered a Texas judgment in Washington and was granted a charging order against debtor's interest in a Washington LP, but only sought a writ of execution on such partnership interest after nineteen years of litigation, Washington court quashed writ of execution. Under the express language of Washington's Foreign Judgment Act, the lifetime of a registered foreign judgment does not extend beyond the lifetime of its underlying judgment. Here, since the underlyng Texas judgment expired 12 years after it was originally entered and there was no record of any attempt by the creditor to revive the Texas judgment, the writ of execution was invalid.	**Texas** (to underlying judgment)

State	Cases	Remedy	Jurisdiction	State Law Applied
	Ivy v. Brown, 2007 WL 1739696 (Wash. App. June 18, 2007)	**Charging order/LLC:** Where trial court erroneously denied judgment creditor's motion for charging orders on the basis that he failed to conduct supplementary proceedings to ascertain debtor's interests, court remanded. Court examined provisions of Washington LLC statute, as well as statutory alternatives for a judgment creditor to enforce a judgment against his debtor.		
	Delta Development and Investment Co. v. Hsiyuan, 114 Wash. App. 1057, 2002 WL 31748937 (Wash. App. Div. 1 Dec. 9, 2002)	**Charging order/LLC/constructive trust:** Charging order statute does not rule out possibility that LLC member's interest can be reached by a constructive trust; term "judgment creditor" in statute does not include beneficiary of constructive trust because the judgment is not monetary; since beneficiary is not a judgment creditor it is not limited to non-managerial rights of an assignee.		
	Koh v. INNO-Pacific Holdings, LTD, 114 Wash. App. 268, 54 P. 3d 1270 (2002)	**Charging order/LLC:** Judgment creditor received a valid money judgment against debtor in California. Under Full Faith and Credit Clause and Washington State Foreign Judgments Act, Washington Court had jurisdiction over LLC, such that judgment creditor could enforce its judgment through a charging order against debtor's interest in LLC. Since a member's interest in an LLC is personal and intangible, location of that interest is properly in state whose LLC act created the entity.	Court found that judgment creditor may seek a charging order in LLC's state of organization, regardless of whether that state would have jurisdiction over the claim that resulted in the judgment.	LLC formed and registered under Washington laws, maintained office and registered agent in Washington, and owned parcel of

State	Cases	Remedy	Jurisdiction	State Law Applied
				property in Washington; debtor is a Singapore public corporation and partial owner of LLC; judgment against debtor issued in California.
West Virginia **CAT I* Exclusive**	Official Comments note that this section is based upon § 504 of the Uniform Limited Liability Company Act (1996).			
Wisconsin **CAT IV* Not Exclusive**				
Wyoming **CAT II* Exclusive**	**Note:** Wyoming case below was issued before statutory amendment prohibiting foreclosure, eff. July 1, 2010.			

State	Cases	Remedy	Jurisdiction	State Law Applied
	Christensen v. Oedekoven, 888 P. 2d 228 (Wyo. 1995)	**Charging order/partnership:** Judgment creditor of partner impermissibly redeemed property held in the partnership's name at a foreclosure sale; only a judgment creditor of the partnership could have redeemed such property. Appropriate remedy for partner's judgment creditor was a charging order against partner's interest in the partnership. Charging order procedure protects the interests of the non-debtor partners by giving the judge wide latitude to control creditor's actions against the partnership.		

Appendix D: Ehmann and Its Progeny

- *Movitz v. Fiesta Investments, LLC (In re Ehmann)*, 319 B.R. 200 (D. Ariz. 2005)—Debtor-member's nonmanaging interest in "Family LLC" arrangement did not require any further significant action on the part of the debtor to receive distributions, and thus were nonexecutory in nature, and section 365 would not apply. Future potential obligations, such as to respond to cash calls, did not render the contract executory. The interest thus comes into the debtor's bankruptcy estate under section 541, and restrictions in the operating agreement that would prohibit transfer are rendered inapplicable under section 541(c)(1).
- *In re Capital Acquisitions & Management Corp.*, 341 B.R. 632 (N.D. Ill. 2006)—Future and remote contingencies do not render an operating agreement to be an executory contract under section 365.
- *Miller v. Bill & Carolyn Limited Partnership (In re Baldwin)*, 463 B.R. 142 (10th Cir. BAP 2006)—The debtor-member's limited partnership interest comes into her bankruptcy estate under section 541; thus, the bankruptcy trustee is not limited to pursuing a charging order against the debtor-member's interest. However, the bankruptcy trustee takes the interest subject to restrictions under the operating agreement, and thus would be prohibited from dissolving the limited partnership even if such were otherwise allowed under applicable Oklahoma law.
- *Meiburger v. Endeka Enterprises, LLC (In re Tsiaoushis)*, 383 B.R. 616 (Bk. E.D. Va. 2007)—The debtor-member's nonmanaging interest comes into his bankruptcy estate under section 541, but was not an executory contract under section 365 where the debtor-member had no unperformed duties, but only "remote or speculative future duties" under the operating agreement, commenting, "There is no per se rule. Each operating agreement is separately analyzed." The bankruptcy trustee was then able to enforce the provisions of the operating agreement that required the LLC to be dissolved upon a member's filing for bankruptcy, overcoming objections that such clauses amounted to impermissible *ipso facto* clauses.
- *Fursman v. Ulrich (In re First Protection, Inc.)*, 440 B.R. 821 (9th Cir. BAP 2010)—Post-petition, the husband and wife debtors diluted their 100-percent interest in an LLC by issuing interests to Thompson (wife's mother), who agreed to provide financing to finishing a constructive project. The bankruptcy trustee commenced an adversary action to set aside the transfer because it

was post-petition. The court held that the LLC's issuance of new interests to Thompson was in a way of a transfer, and the transfer was void because the debtors did not own any interests post-petition, but rather those interests were owned by their bankruptcy estate. The court held that the trustee was not limited to a charging order against the LLC interests, but rather took possession of the totality of the debtors' rights under section 541 per *In re Albright* (because the LLC was essentially a single-member LLC owned by codebtor husband and wife), and that because section 365 was designed in part "to protect non-debtor third parties whose rights may be prejudiced by having a contract performed by an entity other than the one with which they originally contracted," and there were no nondebtor members here, that section 365 would not apply to restrict the trustee's ability to essentially take over *in toto* the LLC.

- *Bensusan v. Prebul* (*In re Prebul*), 2011 WL 2947045 (Bk. E.D. Tenn. 2011)—Operating agreement was not an executory contract under section 365 merely because of a potential future obligation to contribute additional capital, where the debtor-member was nonmanaging member and had no other substantial duties.
- *Matter of H&W Food Mart, LLC*, 461 B.R. 904 (Bk. N.D. Ga. 2011)—Debtor, who was the managing member of a two-member LLC, filed for personal bankruptcy whereupon other member took the position that the debtor had forfeited his management rights under the operating agreement. Other member then admitted a new member (Howell) and appointed him the manager to file a petition to place the LLC into bankruptcy. The court held that when the individual debtor filed for bankruptcy, the entirety of his interest came into his bankruptcy estate under section 541. Given that the trustee did not agree to admit Howell as a new member, he never became a member and never acquired management rights; therefore, he was without authorization to place the LLC into bankruptcy. Given that the individual debtor owed no obligations to the LLC at the time of his individual bankruptcy filing, section 365 would not apply.
- *Norberg v. Hawks Prairie Casino, LLC* (*In re McSwain*), 2011 WL 4706982 (Bk. W.D. Wa. 2011)—Nondebtor member sought declaratory judgment that the debtor had lost his management rights upon filing for bankruptcy, and that the trustee was bound by Washington law relating to charging orders and restrictions in the LLC's operating agreement. Given that the debtor had numerous duties under the operating agreement, the court indicated that it was probably in the nature of an executory contract under section 365, but the court did not reach the issue because debtor's interest became part of his bankruptcy estate under section 541, and the trustee could assume the operating agreement, including all management rights. Further, the nondebtor member was deemed to have waived her rights to enforce the

operating agreement's dissociation provisions against the debtor because the nondebtor member had continued to treat the debtor as a full member even after the debtor's bankruptcy filing.

- *Caymus Ventures LLC v. Jundanian* (*In re Jundanian*), 2012 WL 1098544 (Bk. D. Md. 2012)—A nondebtor member and the LLC sought a declaratory judgment that the debtor lost his management rights in the LLC when he reacquired his membership interest in an auction held pursuant to the debtor's reorganization plan, arguing that the LLC's operating agreement prohibited the transfer of management rights. The court held that the debtor's interest, including voting and management rights, became property of the bankruptcy estate under section 541, and that "Section 541(c)(1) overrides both the ipso facto provisions in the [Maryland] Act and the restriction on transfer provision in the Operating Agreement." Given that the debtor's interests were part of his bankruptcy estate under section 541, it was proper for those interests to be auctioned; however, the provisions of the operating agreement, which prohibited the transfer of management rights, would be respected as it related to the debtor's reacquisition of his interest through the auction.
- *In re Strata Title, LLC*, 2013 WL 1773619 (D. Ariz. 2013)—The debtor-member (and trustee-in-possession in a Chapter 11 reorganization) was one of three members of the LLC, which was managed by a third-party nonmember. The nondebtor members advised the debtor that its filing of a bankruptcy petition constituted an "event of withdrawal" under the operating agreement, and that the nondebtor members would be exercising their option to purchase the debtor's interest. The court held that because there were significant outstanding decisions to be made by the debtor, including the sale and refinancing of properties, and because the debtor's failure to make these decisions would constitute a breach of the operating agreement, that it was an executory contract under section 365. The court also held that the debtor's interest was property of its bankruptcy estate under section 541, and that the purchase option which was triggered by the debtor's bankruptcy constituted an impermissible *ipso facto* clause, stating "once the membership interest became property of the estate under § 541(c), § 363(l) invalidates any provision that limits the debtor-in-possession's continued use or sale of the property based on the filing of bankruptcy." Indeed, exercising the purchase option would amount to a violation of the automatic stay; however, the court set a time limit on the debtor to assume or reject the operating agreement.
- *In re Alameda Investments, LLC*, 2013 WL 3216129 (Bk. C.D. Cal. 2013)—Debtor-member and other member of a two-member LLC argued that the trustee was limited to an economic interest in the LLC. The court held the operating agreement was not an executory contract under section 365

because the debtor had no outstanding performance due, no management rights, and "no obligation to provide any personal expertise or service to the company." However, the entirety of the debtor's interest came into the debtor's bankruptcy estate under section 541; thus, the trustee held all of the debtor's rights in the LLC, including liquidation rights.

- *In re Denman*, 513 B.R. 720 (Bk. W.D. Tenn. 2014)—In a Chapter 13 consumer reorganization case, the court held that an LLC operating agreement is not a "contract" for purposes of section 365, but rather was in the nature of company formation documents. Therefore, no section-365 analysis was required, and the husband and wife debtors' interest in the LLC came into their bankruptcy estate. The attempt by the nondebtor member to purchase the debtor's interest by way of a purchase option amounted to an impermissible *ipso facto* clause; thus, the court would not lift the automatic stay to allow the nondebtor member to attempt to exercise that option.
- *Northwest Wholesale, Inc. v. Pac Organic Fruit, LLC*, 183 Wash. App. 459 (Wash. App. 2014)—Husband and wife debtor members of LLC filed a breach of contract case against the LLC and other of its members, alleging various malfeasances and breaches of fiduciary duty. The other members responded that the debtors had been dissassociated from the LLC as of the date of their bankruptcy filing, under both Washington law and provisions of the operating agreement, and thus they had no standing to sue. The court held that the debtors' interest became part of their bankruptcy estate under section 541. It didn't matter if the operating agreement was executory or nonexecutory because section 365(e) "excuses further performance under the agreement." Thus, the debtors lacked standing to bring their derivative action.
- *Sullivan v. Mathew*, 2015 WL 1509794 (N.D. Ill. Mar. 30, 2015)—Trustee filed an adversary action against the nondebtor members of a general partnership in which the debtor was a partner, seeking to dissolve the partnership as allowed by the partnership agreement. The court held that the partnership agreement was an executory contract because each partner had liability for cash call, affirmative duties that they were required to perform, and negative duties that they were prohibited from performing. The court rejected the *Denman* reasoning that the partnership agreement was in the way of formation documents. Further, the court held that the trustee had rejected the partnership agreement by not adopting it timely; thus, the trustee had no power to enforce the dissolution provisions, and the Trustee's suit was dismissed.